Actuarial Aspects of Individual Life Insurance and Annuity Contracts

Albert E. Easton, FSA, MAAA
Timothy F. Harris, FSA, MAAA

ACTEX Publications
Winsted, CT

Requests for permission should be addressed to:
    Actex Publications, Inc.
    P.O. Box 974
    Winsted, CT 06098

Manufactured in the United States of America

10 9 8 7 6 5 4 3 2 1

Cover design by Kathleen H. Borkowski

Library of Congress Cataloging-in-Publication Data

Easton, Albert.
    Actuarial aspects of individual life insurance and annuity
contracts/Albert Easton, Timothy Harris
        p.   cm.
    Includes bibliographical references.
    ISBN 1-56998-346-0 (hardcover)
I. Harris, Timothy, 1948-   . II. Title
HG8861.E37   1999   99-12561
368.31'01--dc21   CIP

ISBN 1-56698-346-0

PREFACE

Individual Life Insurance and annuity contracts have become increasingly complex in recent years. Throughout this period, however, the basic risks insured by these contracts have not changed. Policyholders pay premiums in return for the contract benefits and services provided by the insurer. Insurers continually adapt their product offerings in order to satisfy the demands of consumers within the requirements that the regulators establish while maintaining a level of profitability that will enable them both to grow and to satisfy their obligations to their clients and stockholders.

This book focuses on the relationships among the various types of values that are associated with Individual Life and Annuity contracts. For the student, we illustrate the dependencies that exist between premiums, cash values, reserves, dividends and other non-guaranteed elements when designing individual products. For the experienced actuary, this text provides a comprehensive summary of current actuarial practice in the design, pricing and daily maintenance of individual products.

The authors acknowledge the assistance of Stephen Batza, FSA, and Mark Milton, FSA, who headed up the teams that reviewed the early drafts. Steve Batza also played an important part in the original development of the text, including the initial outline of the work. The authors also acknowledge Steven Schreiber, FSA, for his contribution to term insurance reserve requirements.

Albert E. Easton   March, 1999
Timothy F. Harris

TABLE OF CONTENTS

SECTION I: INTRODUCTION

SECTION IV: PROFIT TEST CALCULATIONS

Chapter 10: Profit Testing   157

Chapter 11: Profit Testing Examples   163

SECTION IV: OTHER TOPICS

SECTION I

INTRODUCTION

CHAPTER 1
TYPES OF CONTRACTS

In its simplest form, an insurance policy is a contract between two parties. The first party, the insured, agrees to make one or more payments (**premiums**) to the second party, the **insurer**. The insurer, agrees in return to make a payment (the **amount of insurance**) to the insured, if and when the **event insured against** occurs.

In the case of **life insurance**, there may be two other parties involved. Since the event insured against is the death of the insured, it will not be possible to pay the amount of insurance to the insured. The third party to whom the insurance is payable is called the **beneficiary.** Also, it is not necessary that the insured pay the premiums. If they are paid by a fourth party, this party is called the **policyholder** or **owner**. In return for payment of premiums, the policyholder is a party to the contract and has certain rights, including the important right to name the beneficiary.

An **annuity** contract differs fundamentally from life insurance in that the survival of the annuitant is the event that is being insured against. In the case of an annuity, premiums are paid by the **annuitant** or some other individual (who becomes the **contract holder** or **owner**) to the **annuity payor**. The annuity payor begins annuity payments to the annuitant or some other beneficiary at a time specified in the contract. The contract may provide flexibility as to the date when annuity payments can begin, and the terms under which they will be made. Most annuity contracts have some payments that are only made as long as the annuitant survives. Many contracts have features that guarantee some minimum payout regardless of the survival of the annuitant.

Life insurance policies exist in many forms, many of them providing considerable flexibility as to the amount, duration, and frequency of premiums, and also more or less flexibility in the amount of the death benefit and the circumstances under which it will be paid. Many life insurance policies and annuity contracts also provide **cash values** and other

nonforfeiture benefits, payable if the policyholder discontinues premium payments earlier than originally agreed upon, or wishes to terminate the insurance earlier than the policy provides. In some cases, if the insurer finds that experience is favorable, it pays dividends or reduces charges to the policyholder as a partial return of the premiums. Many policies also include additional benefits of various kinds, for example, an agreement to waive premiums if the policyholder becomes disabled.

Insurers have always taken the responsibility for the pricing and selling of life insurance and annuities. Since the insurer always receives premiums *before* making any payments in return, the insurer has the opportunity to invest the funds and earn an investment return. An important part of insurance administration consists of determining the **reserve** each year, i.e., that part of the premiums received which will need to be held to provide future benefits. In addition, the insurer hopes to recover the expenses of selling, issuing and administering the policy or contract. The insurer has accepted risks, then, not only of having adequate funds to pay benefits as they come due, but also the risk of paying expenses, receiving adequate investment cash flows, paying surrender values if they are called for, etc. Balancing the risks, and determining appropriate benefits, reserves, dividends and nonforfeiture values to pay in return for a given series of premiums is an important function of the actuary in a life insurance company. This text describes the techniques actuaries use in fulfilling this function. While many of the techniques do not vary by type of insurance or annuity, a different combination of them may be called into play for different products. Therefore, the text begins with a description of the common product types available. Some of the products described are available as **riders**, that is, they may be offered as an additional benefit with some other product.

1.1   TERM INSURANCE

Term insurance, by definition, is insurance that does not extend for the entire life span, but ends (**expires**) after a specified time, if the insured is then still alive. Term insurance often includes provisions guaranteeing the rights to:

1.   **renewal**: to buy a new term policy or extend the existing one for a period of time after the expiry of the initial term period without providing any additional evidence of insurability.

2. **conversion**: to buy a new policy which is not term insurance at some specified time at or before expiry of the term (again, without evidence of insurability).

Since the renewal and conversion rights often involve extension of insurance to an individual whose health is impaired (an individual with impaired health will be most likely to exercise the rights) they have cost associated with them which must be taken into account in pricing the term insurance. Term insurance (as the term is used here) is a type of **traditional** life insurance. Generally there is no internal accumulation of value.

Because term insurance generally does not extend into the later years of life when mortality is highest, premiums and reserves can be lower for term insurance. In part, because the reserve is low, the nonforfeiture laws do not require the provision of cash values or other nonforfeiture benefits for most term insurance. Term insurance can include provision for the payment of dividends when experience is favorable. Instead of paying dividends, some term insurance provides that premiums less than the guaranteed premiums can be paid to keep the policy in force when experience is favorable. This is equivalent to allowing a dividend only as a reduction in the next year's premium. Term insurance can also be sold at premium levels which are not guaranteed with the guaranteed premium acting only as a maximum premium should experience under the plan deteriorate.

Features and characteristics of term insurance offered by the major writers tend to vary by plan. Very often, term insurance is offered as a rider to some other plan of insurance. Plans of term insurance commonly encountered in the U. S. and Canada, either as stand-alone policies or riders are described on the following four pages.

1.1.1 ONE-YEAR RENEWABLE TERM

One-year renewable term, sometimes called **annually renewable term (ART)** provides term insurance for a period of one year which is renewable each year at higher rates. This renewability is guaranteed for a specified period, often to age 70 or 80, or sometimes for life. When ART is renewable for life, the policy is in some respects not a term policy but a whole life. Some insurers even call such a policy "increasing premium whole life." It is unlikely that such a policy would actually be renewed up to the end of the mortality table, since premiums at the extreme ages could be very close to the face amount. As a practical matter, however, most insureds die at ages before the extremes of the mortality table, and very little life insurance of any kind is maintained to such ages, even with level premiums .

ART always has terminal reserves[1] of zero on a net level basis. If renewal is guaranteed at premiums that are less than those specified in state valuation statutes (as is often the case, since valuation statutes usually specify a conservative mortality basis), insurers are usually required to establish an extra reserve (a **deficiency reserve**) to cover these guarantees. Insurers often deal with this issue by incorporating a set of guaranteed premiums in the contract which do not produce any deficiency reserves but then charge a lower "current premium" which is not guaranteed for more than the current policy year. Nonforfeiture benefits are not required for ART. Conversion is usually included as a benefit, at least to age 65 or 70, and sometimes to whatever is the highest age at which the term issuer sells whole life.

1.1.2   RE-ENTRY TERM

ART is sometimes offered with a renewal feature that guarantees renewal only at fairly high premiums. However, insureds who meet insurability criteria are allowed to "re-enter," i.e., to renew at a lower premium. Often the evidence of insurability is only required at intervals, such as three years or five years. The required evidence may be a short questionnaire, with a physical examination or other additional evidence required if the questions are not answered satisfactorily. Since the guaranteed renewal premiums are fairly high, re-entry term usually does not produce deficiency reserves beyond the three to five years for which premiums are guaranteed to be lower. Other features of re-entry term (such as convertibility) are similar to ART.

1.1.3   LEVEL TERM

Level Term provides level death benefits for level premiums. The term of coverage is often 5, 7, 10, 15 or 20 years. Terms longer than 15 years generally require nonforfeiture benefits. Term to age 65 is also occasionally seen and includes nonforfeiture features. Renewal of level

---

1   The discussion of reserves and nonforfeiture benefits in this chapter refers to U.S. statutory requirements.

term, if offered, is sometimes only for one additional term. Reserves are low, but non-zero, and as with ART, additional reserves may be required if the premiums are below those required by the valuation statutes. Conversion features usually cover the entire term period. Level term may be either a rider or a stand-alone policy. Level Term for short periods (e.g., five years) is sometimes offered on the re-entry basis.

Spouse Term is a rider providing level term insurance on the life of the spouse of the insured, often to the insured's age 65, but sometimes to the spouse's age 65. **Child Term** is a similar level term rider providing term insurance on the lives of the insured's children to their age 21 (or, sometimes, 25). A conversion feature is available at expiry, sometimes for a multiple of the face amount. Since the insurance must be priced to cover any number of children, some of whom may not even have been born at the time the policy is issued, usually only small amounts ($5,000 or $10,000) are available. Both spouse and child riders usually require no additional payment of premiums if the primary insured dies. Very often spouse and child term are combined and the package sold as a **Family Rider**.

1.1.4   DECREASING TERM

Decreasing term provides decreasing benefits for level premiums. Terms are usually 10, 15, 20, or 30 years. Three common patterns of decrease are:

1. **Uniform**: Benefits decrease uniformly throughout the term, e.g., at the rate of 10% of the initial amount each year over a ten-year term.
2. **Family Income**: Benefits are in the amount required to purchase an annuity-certain for the number of years remaining in the specified term. (E.g., if the insured dies in the twelfth year of a twenty-year family income policy, the benefit will buy an eight- year annuity certain: the insurer guarantees the availability of the annuity certain at the specified price.)
3. **Loan Amortization**: Benefits each year are at the level of the unamortized portion of a loan that began at the initial amount and was amortized by level payments over the term at some specified interest rate. Table 1.1, on the following page, shows a comparison of the common pattern of decreases.

Table 1.1
Decreasing Term Patterns

Beginning of Year	Uniform Decrease	Family Income*	Loan Amortization**
1	$1,000.00	$1,000.00	$1,000.00
2	$950.00	$966.68	$981.27
3	$900.00	$931.99	$960.79
4	$850.00	$895.90	$938.38
5	$800.00	$858.33	$913.88
6	$750.00	$819.24	$887.07
7	$700.00	$778.55	$857.75
8	$650.00	$736.20	$825.68
9	$600.00	$692.13	$790.60
10	$550.00	$646.26	$752.23
11	$500.00	$598.53	$710.26
12	$450.00	$548.85	$664.35
13	$400.00	$497.14	$614.14
14	$350.00	$443.33	$559.22
15	$300.00	$387.33	$499.14
16	$250.00	$329.04	$433.43
17	$200.00	$268.38	$361.55
18	$150.00	$205.25	$282.94
19	$100.00	$139.55	$196.94
20	$50.00	$71.17	$102.88
21	$0.00	$0.00	$0.00

*   These lump sums would provide a monthly annuity certain for the remainder of the period equal to $6.06 based on a 4% interest guarantee.

**   These lump sums represent the unamortized balance, at the beginning of the year, of a $1,000, 9% mortgage with monthly payments.

Under any of the three patterns of decrease described, the benefit is likely to be much less than the level premium would purchase as ART in the last year or two of coverage. The product may also generate negative reserves at this point. There is also a greater probability that a prudent policyholder, especially a healthy one, will discontinue premium payments under these conditions. Therefore, premiums for decreasing term benefits are often calculated for some period shorter than the entire term period (e.g. the premium paying period would be eight years for a ten-year decreasing term). Decreasing term of the Family Income type is almost always a rider, and the other two patterns are frequently also offered as riders. Spouse Term is sometimes offered in the Family Income rider form. These products are generally designed so that nonforfeiture benefits are not required. Convertibility is for the entire term period, but only for the amount in force when the conversion is elected.

1.1.5 AUTOMATICALLY CONVERTIBLE TERM

Automatically convertible term is a special type of level term, usually with a term of 1, 2, 5, or 10 years. Conversion is automatic at the end of the term period to some whole life plan. There is no renewal and sometimes no conversion available before the automatic one. A special policy form is used that includes the whole life plan so no new policy needs to be issued at the time of the automatic conversion. Automatically convertible term can also be considered as a whole life plan with low initial premiums. **Deposit Term** is a special case of automatically convertible term in which a high first premium is followed by nine or ten low premiums and then the automatic conversion to a level premium whole life takes place. Premiums for the whole life tend to be at about the level of the (high) first premium. There are no nonforfeiture values until the automatic conversion takes place, but at that point the cash value for the first year after conversion (i.e. the tenth year of the policy) is set to equal the "deposit" (i.e. the high first-year premium). The chief advantage of deposit term is often to the selling agent, who receives a first-year commission on the higher first-year premium.

1.2 WHOLE LIFE INSURANCE

Whole life insurance guarantees coverage for the entire life span of the insured, thus ensuring that a death benefit will be paid if the policy is kept in force by payment of premiums. Except for "increasing premium whole life" (another name for some forms of ART), whole life insurance almost always generates reserves and cash and other nonforfeiture values. There are forms of whole life without cash value in other countries including Canada. The creation of a reserve is a natural result of the fact that death benefits become very costly at the extreme ages, and the build-up of a reserve from the accumulation of excess premiums in the early years allows for the collection of premiums at the later ages that are less than the full cost of death benefits.

Whole life is sometimes considered to consist of two pieces, the reserve and the **net amount at risk**; the difference between the reserve and the amount of the death benefit. When considering whole life in this way, the policy is described as consisting of two benefits: a savings account and a decreasing term insurance. It is important to recognize that such a view is artificial with respect to traditional whole life. The policy does not provide for such a separation, and a decreasing term insurance of this type is not generally available on a stand-alone basis. However, it is possible to create such a combination and, in fact, some companies sold these combinations in the past. Such a separation does have some applicability to Universal Life Insurance, as will be described further on.

While it is still possible to buy whole life insurance on a fully guaranteed basis, the very high interest rates of the early 1980's made fully guaranteed whole life very non-competitive in price, and almost all whole life now available includes dividends or some other non-guaranteed element such as **indeterminate premiums** (i.e., premiums that may be lower than the guaranteed maximum premiums if the experience in the policy is favorable) and/or excess interest. The existence of the non-guaranteed elements has made policy illustrations an important aspect of the sale of whole life.

The ledger page of a policy illustration usually shows the premium, the dividend (on the current dividend scale), the cash value, and the death benefit each year for twenty years or more. The intention is to provide the prospective policyholder with an idea of the expected operation of the policy. The guaranteed values are also shown with equal premiums. An example of the numerical detail part of a simple policy illustration showing non-guaranteed values for a level premium whole life is shown in Table 1.2 on the following page.

1.2.1   LEVEL PREMIUM WHOLE LIFE

Level premium whole life is the most common form of whole life. Level premium whole life is sometimes called **Ordinary Life**, although this term is also sometimes used to refer to individual life insurance in general. Premiums are level and payable for the entire life of the insured. Reserves, eventually becoming substantial, are required, and nonforfeiture values are normally required, usually beginning in the second year (but in the first year at very high ages, and at some younger ages, not until the third or fourth year.) Many insurers offer whole life of two distinct forms. Although both types may provide whole life insurance with level premiums for life, one form is high premium and provides high dividends, if participating, and generally higher cash values. The intention is to allow the policyholder as much advantage as possible from the savings element

Table 1.2
Sample Life Insurance Illustration, $100,000 Whole Life, Male, Age 35
Dividends Reduce Premium, Excess Paid in Cash

End of Year	Attained Age	Premium for Next Year	Non-Guaranteed Dividend	Premium Net of Non-Guaranteed Dividend	Guaranteed Cash Value	Total Death Benefit *
0	35	$1,350	$0	$1,350	$0	$100,000
1	36	$1,350	$0	$1,350	$0	$100,000
2	37	$1,350	$144	$1,206	$0	$100,144
3	38	$1,350	$152	$1,198	$0	$100,152
4	39	$1,350	$170	$1,180	$778	$100,170
5	40	$1,350	$193	$1,157	$1,936	$100,193
6	41	$1,350	$219	$1,131	$3,128	$100,219
7	42	$1,350	$247	$1,103	$4,355	$100,247
8	43	$1,350	$276	$1,074	$5,615	$100,276
9	44	$1,350	$305	$1,045	$6,909	$100,305
10	45	$1,350	$336	$1,014	$8,238	$100,336
11	46	$1,350	$371	$979	$9,602	$100,371
12	47	$1,350	$403	$947	$11,001	$100,403
13	48	$1,350	$432	$918	$12,436	$100,432
14	49	$1,350	$462	$888	$13,907	$100,462
15	50	$1,350	$494	$856	$15,416	$100,494
16	51	$1,350	$581	$769	$16,962	$100,581
17	52	$1,350	$624	$726	$18,545	$100,624
18	53	$1,350	$669	$681	$20,162	$100,669
19	54	$1,350	$719	$631	$21,811	$100,719
Total for 20 years		$27,000	$6,797	$20,203	$23,488	$100,774

* Including non-guaranteed dividend payable at death
Dividends are not estimated or guaranteed but are based on the current scale

of the whole life insurance, including the right to fund some of the premiums through policy loans, or to allow the policy to become paid up through higher dividends or excess interest. The lower premium form is intended to offer the most competitive annual level outlay.

1.2.2   LIMITED PAYMENT LIFE

As the name implies, limited payment life policies provide whole life insurance at level premiums payable for a period less than the full lifetime of the insured. A variety of terms are offered. Under U.S. tax law [1] the advantage of not being taxed on withdrawals or loans is denied to the policyholder for policies with premiums higher than a seven-payment life defined by regulation, so policies with less than seven premiums are infrequently offered (except for the special case of single premium). 20-pay life is quite common, as is life paid up at age 65. Many companies offer a life paid up at age 85 or 90 as a high premium form of ordinary life. (See the discussion of high premium ordinary life in Section 1.2.1 above.)

Single premium life is quite often encountered, in spite of the fact that it is considered a "modified endowment" under U.S. tax law, and the gain on cash withdrawals of any kind is therefore taxable. Many companies allow single premium "pour-ins" as a rider to other traditional forms of life insurance as well as universal life. The "pour-in additions" purchased may later be used to make the base policy paid up. Considerable flexibility in premium payment can be achieved in a traditional policy with a well-designed pour-in option. Reserves and nonforfeiture values are, of course, required for single premium and all other forms of limited-pay life, and dividends are the most frequently encountered form of non-guaranteed elements.

1.2.3   GRADED PREMIUM LIFE

Another form of whole life is graded premium life. Graded premium life provides whole life coverage with non-level premiums that may be payable for the entire life span of the insured or some shorter period. Usually, the intention is to offer a whole life plan at a premium that is at least initially lower than ordinary life (but above ART). Therefore, the plan can be used for situations where coverage is desired throughout life, but the funds available for its purchase are limited at first and expected to grow over time. Cash values and other nonforfeiture benefits also tend to be less than for ordinary life.

1.2.4   JOINT LIFE

Joint life insurance offers a benefit that depends on the lives of two insureds. In the case of **First-to-die** joint life, the death benefit is payable and premiums cease at the death of the first of the insureds. Premiums are level, and nonforfeiture values are required. **Second-to-die** joint life (also sometimes called **Survivorship Life**) provides a benefit that is not payable until the last death. Usually, premiums are also payable until the last death of the two, although some insurers offer a policy that is paid-up at the first death. Early products had premiums and values that changed at the first death. Today, it is much more common for cash values and reserves on second-to-die to be "frasierized" if the insurance does not become paid-up at the first death. "Frasierized" premiums, reserves, and values do not change at the first death. Term insurance riders are sometimes offered on joint life policies, but they usually provide insurance on only one of the insureds. True joint term riders are rare, as are joint term policies. Single premium second-to-die is sometimes offered for estate planning purposes. Joint policies involving more than two lives are also occasionally encountered, especially in situations where a business wants to cover several owners.

1.2.5   ENDOWMENT

An endowment policy provides a death benefit for a term of years, and at the end of that period, the amount of the benefit is payable, even if the insured is then still alive. Technically, an endowment is not a whole life policy, since it does not extend for the insured's entire life span. Traditional whole life policies are a special form of endowment in that they technically endow at the end of the mortality table used for nonforfeiture values. However, an endowment has high premiums and nonforfeiture values in common with whole life and tends, therefore, to be included in the whole life category rather than term. Since endowments before age 95 have distinct tax disadvantages in the U.S., they are not often offered at the present time.

1.2.6   COMBINATION PLANS

There is no difficulty mathematically in calculating reserves and other values for plans that offer other combinations of variations in the premiums or face amount. Two common ones are:

1. **Juvenile Insurance**: The benefit and, sometimes, the premium increases when the insured reaches age 21 (or 25). The products are sometimes called "Jumping Juveniles".
2. **Double Protection**: The face amount is cut in half after the insured's age 65. However, the premium does not change at age 65, so double protection is not identical to ordinary life with a term to age 65 rider.

1.2.7   DIVIDEND ANTICIPATION PLANS

Many companies that offer participating insurance have one or more plans that offer a low premium in anticipation of the dividend scale. Sometimes these are called "Economatic" plans. Many such plans utilize some combination of one-year term and paid-up (i.e,. single premium) dividend additions to maintain a level face amount at a low level premium for as long as possible, ideally for the entire life of the insured. If experience is exceptionally unfavorable, of course, additional premiums will be required to maintain the level amount in later years. Even companies that do not have such a plan frequently offer as riders some combination of one-year term insurance and single premium whole life "pour-in" (which may later be surrendered) to enhance premium flexibility in a traditional insurance plan.

This same approach was used in the past with Excess Interest Whole Life plans (EIWL). These plans used the higher interest rates that were being experienced in the 80's to illustrate a plan of insurance where the premiums "vanished" after a short period of time, say five to ten years. With the ensuing drop in interest rates in the 90's the premiums did not vanish as projected, if at all. This disappointment led in part to current regulations on illustrations as well as a number of class action law suits.

1.3   UNIVERSAL LIFE

In a **universal life** policy, sometimes called **interest sensitive life insurance**, each premium is deposited into a fund, sometimes given a name like "savings element", as it is received. The fund is periodically (usually monthly) charged with mortality costs and expenses, and interest is credited to the fund. Universal Life Insurance may be offered with fixed premiums, or as "flexible premium life insurance," where the plan allows maximum

Table 1.3
Activity for Policy Year Ending October 10, 1997
Policy Number 18312467
Death Benefit $100,000

Date	Transaction Type	Gross Amount	Expense Charges	Insurance Charges	Interest Credited	Accumulated Fund
10/11/96	Previous Balance					$4,809.17
11/08/96	Payment	$644.00	$6.30	$12.73	$21.14	$5,455.29
11/11/96	Monthly Summary		$0.67	$1.35	$ 2.57	$5,455.83
12/11/96	Monthly Summary		$6.97	$14.00	$26.56	$5,461.41
01/11/97	Monthly Summary		$6.97	$14.00	$26.58	$5,467.03
02/11/97	Monthly Summary		$6.97	$14.00	$26.61	$5,472.67
03/11/97	Monthly Summary		$6.97	$14.00	$26.64	$5,478.34
04/11/97	Monthly Summary		$6.97	$14.00	$26.67	$5,484.04
05/11/97	Monthly Summary		$6.97	$14.00	$26.69	$5,489.77
06/11/97	Monthly Summary		$6.97	$14.00	$26.72	$5,495.52
07/11/97	Monthly Summary		$6.97	$13.99	$26.75	$5,501.31
08/11/97	Monthly Summary		$6.97	$13.99	$26.78	$5,507.12
09/11/97	Monthly Summary		$6.97	$13.99	$26.81	$5,512.97
10/11/97	Monthly Summary		$6.97	$13.99	$26.83	$5,518.84
Total		$644.00	$83.64	$168.05	$317.35	

flexibility in timing, frequency and amount of premiums. Once a year the policyholder receives a statement showing the operation of the fund for the year. An example of some of the information included in such a statement is shown in Table 1.3 on the previous page.

Universal Life was first offered in the 1970's. In the earliest forms of the plan, the entire fund was offered as a cash value, which required charging higher expense rates for the first year or two to cover the extra expense of policy issue. Universal Life on which high early expense rates are charged is called "**front-loaded**." Today most Universal Life is "**back-loaded**," that is, it has a surrender charge, which reduces the proportion of the fund available as a cash value in the early years. Usually the surrender charge reduces over the life of the policy, and becomes zero at about the tenth duration. Some Universal Life currently being sold is both front and back-loaded. That is, it has both higher early expense charges and a surrender charge.

Two patterns of death benefit are offered on Universal Life. "Option A" death benefits were originally level until the fund exceeded the face, and then were equal to the fund. To preserve the tax advantages of life insurance, however, in policies now issued in the U.S., the amount of insurance is never allowed to be less than a defined multiple of the cash value. The multiple declines at the older ages as determined by rules specified in the internal revenue code and regulations [2]. Thus, Option A provides a decreasing net amount at risk until the net amount at risk reaches the specified level, and then a corridor of net amount at risk.

"Option B" provides for a constant net amount at risk, since the amount of insurance under Option B is defined as the face amount plus the fund. However, since the fund might grow very large resulting in the total insurance being less than could be as required under tax laws, Option B also provides for an increase in net amount at risk should this happen. The policyholder elects one of the options at the time of issue. If Option A is elected, the policyholder can change to Option B after issue, but must present evidence that the insured is insurable at the time of the change if there is an increase in the net amount at risk.

Under either Option A or B, there can be considerable flexibility in premium payment. After premiums have been paid for two or three years, it may be possible for the policyholder to reduce premiums for a few years or skip them entirely. Since unanticipated anti-selection could occur if unlimited premiums were allowed when the fund is large, insurers typically restrict the amount of premium they will accept when the fund is large enough to force increases in the net amount at risk.

To aid in the administration of a flexible premium plan, the policyholder is usually asked to designate a schedule of premiums at the time of issue, and the insurer sends periodic bills for the amounts so designated. Generally, insurers will allow changes to the schedule after issue; that is, if the policyholder requests, they will bill for different amounts than originally agreed on. Of course, the policyholder may always elect to pay other than as billed, within certain limits.

While one of the original intentions of issuers of universal life was to make clear the exact costs of life insurance by showing and charging exactly the interest, mortality and expenses incurred, most insurers do not observe this at the present time. Not only are high early expenses now covered by a surrender charge, but mortality charges may frequently include expense or income tax, and interest rates credited may even be reduced by expense costs other than investment expense.

1.4 VARIABLE LIFE

Variable life insurance provides the policyholder with the opportunity to invest the funds, usually in one or more separate accounts with specified investment goals. As the value of the separate account(s) varies, (usually it is recalculated on a daily basis) the death benefit may also vary, according to mechanisms described elsewhere in this text.

Since the policyholder is assuming investment risk, variable life insurance is regulated under the laws governing the securities industry [3]. Among other things, these require distribution of a prospectus to the prospective policyholder, and registration of the soliciting agent as a securities dealer. The requirements of the securities acts are considered a significant disadvantage, and these, together with significantly more complicated administrative requirements, have limited the number of insurers who offer variable life.

Variable Universal Life is Universal Life with the fund invested in one or more separate accounts, as selected by the policyholder. Generally, the mortality and expense charges are made on a daily basis, since the amount of insurance is subject to daily variation based on the value of the separate account(s).

1.5 RIDERS AND ADDITIONAL BENEFITS

A rider provides some additional benefits under an insurance policy which is not provided in the basic policy, usually at an extra premium. As mentioned above, it is not uncommon to combine two kinds of life insurance (especially term and whole life) by issuing one kind as a rider to the other. Riders are also used to add non-life insurance benefits to life insurance policies. Sometimes, also, non-life insurance benefits are routinely added to all policies or a large group of policies at issue, so that the benefit becomes part of the policy itself rather than a rider. This section will describe some of the benefits most commonly added to life insurance policies. Most riders involve benefits that do not require nonforfeiture values, and the benefits described here do not, except where noted.

1.5.1   ACCIDENT BENEFITS

The most common form of accident benefit provides an additional death benefit equal to the face amount if the insured's death is a result of accident. Usually, this benefit, sometimes called "double indemnity," ends when the insured reaches some age (70 is a common ending age). Many companies will issue some amount of accidental death benefit other than the face amount. Some companies include a dismemberment benefit with their accidental death benefit, paying the full amount of the additional death benefit in the event of an accidental dismemberment. Another common variation provides a multiple of the additional benefit (usually double) if the accidental death results from a common carrier accident.

1.5.2   DISABILITY BENEFITS

A very common disability benefit provides that the premiums will be waived if the insured is totally disabled, but the policy values will continue to build, dividends will be paid, etc. The disability waiver feature often provides that the disability must begin before the insured's age 60, and continue for at least six months before the premiums begin to be waived. In the case of flexible premium universal life, where fixed premiums are not required, the waiver feature usually provides an amount to offset the mortality (and sometimes expense) charges. Sometimes the insured for the waiver feature is not the insured for the death benefit. This feature can then be used on a policy covering the life of a child where a parent or grandparent has the responsibility for premium payment, and wants assurance that it will continue if the premium payor becomes disabled. Less commonly, a level monthly income disability benefit may be added to a life insurance policy. Level monthly income benefits are usually subject to limits on the relationship between the amount of life insurance and the amount of income (e.g., $10 of monthly income for each $1000 of death benefit).

1.5.3 LONG-TERM CARE BENEFITS

The high cost of the long-term care that many individuals require, especially at advanced ages, has led a few insurers to offer additional benefits under a life insurance policy if long-term care becomes medically necessary. When such riders are designed along the lines of disability income benefits (i.e., by paying a daily or monthly indemnity as long as long-term care continues to be medically necessary) they must continue to remain in force until very high ages and can result in required nonforfeiture benefits in some jurisdictions. For that reason they have not been widely offered. Long-term care benefits funded out of the death benefit are discussed in the following section.

1.5.4 ACCELERATED DEATH BENEFITS

Many life insurance policies now contain a provision, either by rider or as a part of the policy, that the death benefit or some part of it may be paid before the death of the insured if certain other conditions are met. The most common provision of this type pays some high percentage of the face amount if the insured has an illness in which death is expected to result within 12 or 24 months. If a very high percentage of the face is prepaid in this way, no additional benefit is paid at death. There is commonly no extra charge for this benefit, the extra cost being funded out of the reduction in death benefit. Another variation pays a percentage of the face if the insured has a specified disease. Diseases commonly specified in such a rider include cancer, heart disease and end-stage renal disease. Still a third rider offered by a few companies pays a percentage of the face on a monthly basis if long-term care is medically necessary for the insured. It is more difficult to design the last two riders in such a way that they can be funded out of the death benefit, and an extra premium is usually charged. Sometimes these riders use a lien approach, where the benefit at death is reduced by the prepayments with interest.

1.5.5 GUARANTEED INSURABILITY

Guaranteed insurability riders almost always require an extra premium. The most common form of rider, sold at the younger ages, offers 6 options, at each of the 25th, 28th, 31st, 34th, $37^{th,}$ and 40th birthdays for a specified amount of purchase (e.g., $25,000). The birthday options may be exercised early if the insured becomes married, has a child, or legally adopts. A few companies now offer options at later ages for specified purposes. Since the cost of a renewal right is a large part of the premium at younger ages for ART, it is difficult to price guaranteed insurability options for the later ages in such a way that they appear to a prospective policyholder to offer good value for the money.

1.5.6   AUTOMATIC INCREASE ("Cost of Living Adjustment")

Automatic increase riders provide additional insurance automatically, without evidence of insurability, at specified intervals. The premium charged for the increase depends on the insured's attained age. If an increase is rejected (by failure to pay the increased premium for the additional amount) the rider terminates. Such riders are also sometimes offered on flexible premium Universal Life. In that case, the increased death benefit is funded as an increased monthly cost.

1.6   DEFERRED ANNUITIES

It is important to keep in mind that there are two different products called "annuities" offered by the insurance industry, and they have very little in common. The first such product, the deferred annuity, is basically an investment vehicle. Deferred annuities, in common with life insurance, have settlement options which provide a periodic income, but the settlement options are most often not elected and almost never play an important part in the purchase or selection of a particular deferred annuity.

The key distinguishing element at the point of sale for deferred annuities is the investment return during the accumulation period. While deferred annuities following the "traditional" model (i.e., with fixed premiums and cash values, along the lines of traditional life insurance) were once common, they are fairly rare now, except for single premium. Virtually all deferred annuities sold in the 90's other than single premium are flexible premium, along the lines of universal life, with accumulation funds, surrender charges, and expense charges. There is no charge, however, corresponding to the mortality charge of universal life, since there is generally little or no mortality element during the accumulation period. Deferred annuities always include a time at which they will convert to payment status, usually based on an age of the annuitant, such as age 65 or 75. Rarely is the age less than 60 or more than 90.

Since the election of a periodic income affords the issuer of the annuity an opportunity for additional profits, most issuers waive surrender charges and some actually pay a higher rate of return retroactively if a periodic payment option (instead of a lump sum surrender) is elected. Annuities with higher rates of return for periodic payment are called "**two-tier annuities**." An occasional feature of deferred annuities is the "**bail-out**" provision. Annuities with a bail-out feature provide that if the interest rate credited falls below an agreed upon level (usually a percentage point or two below the rate being credited at issue), the contract holder may surrender without surrender charge. In the United States, however, the recipient of a lump sum from the surrender of an annuity before the recipient's age 59 ½ must generally pay a 10% penalty tax [4], in addition to the regular income tax on the amount that has built up in the contract.

Deferred annuities sometimes allow for the investment of the funds during the accumulation period in one or more separate investment accounts that may resemble mutual funds. Such annuities are called "**variable annuities**." Variable annuities may or may not include an option to make the periodic payments from the insurer to the annuitant or beneficiary vary according to the performance of the separate account. Variable annuities often include a mortality guarantee (Minimum Guaranteed Death Benefit) during the accumulation period which provides that the lump sum payable on surrender at the death of the annuitant will be not less than an accumulation at a specified interest rate (e.g., 5%) of the amounts paid in, regardless of the performance of the separate account. The mortality feature only has value when the performance of the separate account is less than the index rate. Typically, no separate charge is made for the mortality feature, but the issuer usually hopes to recover it out of the investment charges on the separate account.

Since variable annuities are, in many ways, similar to mutual funds, their issue and sale is subject to many of the same legal requirements that apply to mutual funds. Thus, prospective buyers must receive a prospectus, selling agents must have a securities license, and the issuing company must meet various requirements.

Recently, a popular variation on the deferred annuity has been the **equity index annuity**. Like deferred annuities, equity index annuities are mainly investment vehicles. In an equity index annuity, the rate of return above the minimum rate guaranteed in the contract is tied to some index of common stock values, most often the Standard and Poor's 500. The owner receives a rate of return tied to the performance of the equity markets. A key advantage of equity index annuities over variable annuities is that no securities license is required of the selling agent.

1.7   IMMEDIATE ANNUITIES

Immediate annuities provide a series of periodic payments, usually depending on the life of an individual, the annuitant. Immediate annuities are purchased with a single premium, and payments begin a short time (one year or less) after the premium is paid. They represent the other main branch of contracts called annuities. As mentioned earlier, both life insurance and deferred annuities include provisions for settlement options that convert the lump sum amount of the value in the contract (or the death benefit) to a series of payments. This exchange of lump sum value for a series of payments is essentially identical to an immediate annuity, except that the issuer of the settlement option already has the lump sum amount, and the internal insurance company accounting transactions are used to transfer this value.

The simplest form of immediate annuity is the life annuity, which provides level periodic payments during the life of the annuitant, ending with the last payment due before the annuitant's death. A few issuers provide a **complete annuity**, similar to a life annuity, except that a final pro-rata payment is made after the annuitants death proportional to the period of time the annuitant lived after the last payment, but before the next one was due. **Joint and survivor** life annuities are payable for as long as either of two lives is alive, and are quite common. Also common are joint and survivor annuities which reduce the (otherwise level) periodic payment at the first death, or at the death of a particular one of the two annuitants. Much rarer are "joint annuities," payable until the first death of two lives. Also rare are joint and survivor annuities depending on three or more lives. Since life annuities expire without value at the death of the annuitant(s), there could be severe anti-selection if any values other than the periodic payments were provided. Therefore, life annuities seldom provide a cash value except during any certain period.

Variations of life annuity providing a death benefit after the annuitant's death are quite common. Some frequently encountered ones are the "period-certain life annuity," sometimes called the certain and continuous annuity, which provides payment guaranteed for a period of years (e.g., 10 or 20) even if the annuitant is not then alive and provides payments continuing until the annuitant's death if it is after the period certain. The "installment refund" annuity is a period certain life annuity that provides payments guaranteed for a period that will refund the single premium. Usually, this results in a final payment that is less than the normal level periodic payment. Also common is the "cash refund" annuity, which provides a lump sum at the annuitant's death equal to the difference between the single premium and the amount which has been paid in periodic payments. Combinations of joint and survivor annuities with one of the death benefits described are frequently encountered. Annuities with death benefits sometimes provide a cash value at least equal to the minimum present value of the death benefit.

A few issuers make available a "cost of living" annuity which provides increasing payments, either with a guaranteed percentage increase, or indexed to consumer prices. These have not been popular, however, because the initial periodic payments are very low relative to the premium. Somewhat more common are "variable payout annuities," on which payments vary in relation to the performance of a separate account. As noted under deferred annuities, sale of variable annuities requires meeting some requirements similar to those for the sale of mutual funds or other securities. Variable payout and cost of living annuities may involve joint and survivor or death benefit features.

An important subset of immediate annuities is "structured settlements." Structured settlements arise as a way of satisfying the defendant's liability to the plaintiff in a tort case. They are purchased by a premium from the defendant and provide periodic payments to the plaintiff, usually with life contingencies and often not level. Pricing structured settlements is a challenge for the issuing company, since the very competitive market is characterized by sophisticated buyers (liability insurers) and allowance must frequently be made for the impaired health of the plaintiff-annuitant in determining the cost of life contingent benefits. Also, benefits often have unusual patterns such as large lump sums at stated intervals and benefits that increase by duration.

REFERENCES

[1]   IRC Section 7702.
[2]   Ibid.
[3]   Securities Act of 1933, Securities Exchange Act of 1934, and Securities Act of 1941 in the U.S.
[4]   IRC Section 72(q). Also, note that there are provisions under which the annuity may be exchanged for another annuity without the penalty tax (IRC Section 1035).

REVIEW QUESTIONS

1. Define and distinguish among: policyholder, insured, beneficiary, contract holder, annuitant.

2. What are the principal distinguishing features of term insurance? What features distinguish different types of term insurance? Name four different types of term insurance.

3. How does whole life insurance differ from term? What is permanent insurance? Name three types of permanent insurance.

4. What features does endowment insurance have in common with term insurance? How does it differ?

5. What charges and credits are usually made to the fund in a universal life insurance policy?

6. What is the distinguishing feature of variable life insurance?

7. Name six riders sometimes available for addition to life insurance policies.

8. An advertisement by a life insurance company offers "A 6% accumulation certificate". What type of annuity does this advertisement most likely refer to?

9. How does an immediate annuity differ from a deferred annuity?

CHAPTER 2
FINANCIAL ELEMENTS OF LIFE INSURANCE AND ANNUITY CONTRACTS

2.1   PREMIUMS

Payments by the policyholder to the insurer are called premiums. Generally, the premiums required to keep the policy or contract in force are stated in the contract, and they may be increasing, decreasing, or level. Such premiums are called guaranteed premiums. Actuarially, the guaranteed premiums are calculated on a fairly conservative set of assumptions, since the insurer must agree to continue the contract as long as they are paid. Many contracts also state a lower "current" or "non-guaranteed" set of premiums, which will keep the contract in force only if the current experience continues to be realized over the life of the policy. The current premium is based on less conservative assumptions than the guaranteed premium.

Many formulas have been proposed for determination of premiums, relating the premium to such variables as: mortality, interest, expected level of policy termination, and the insurer's expected level of future expenses. Using a formula approach, it is possible to offer an insurance policy that allows payment of premiums at intervals and in amounts that the policyholder may select (within limits). Policies that permit the policyholder to vary premiums in this way are called **flexible premium** policies, in contrast to **fixed premium** policies that require payment on a schedule that is fixed at the issue of the policy.

Even fixed premium policies can be constructed to allow some variation in premium payment, but this usually allows change only from one fixed schedule to another. Fixed premiums usually vary at least by issue age and sex, and almost always by smoking habits, since these variables clearly affect mortality. Premiums varying by age, sex, and smoking habits are usually published by the insurer in a **rate table**. Sometimes the insurer also includes rates for one or more risk classes that have mortality differing from those insureds accepted at the standard rate. The additional risk classes may have better mortality than standard (preferred) or worse than standard (substandard). The premiums from the rate table are multiplied by the number of units (units are typically $1,000 of face amount) to determine the premium for the policy.

Fixed premium policies also usually include some way of covering those expenses that do not vary by policy size, frequently in the form of a **policy fee**, which is an additional charge added to each policy, after the rate table premium has been multiplied by the face amount. Another way of dealing with variation of the expense element by policy size is premium banding, where different rate tables are published for different groups of policies, with the groups differentiated by policy size. For example, the highest premiums per thousand for policies less than $50,000, a slightly lower set for policies of $50,000 to $250,000, and the lowest premiums for policies of $250,000 or more. Some policies have both rate bands and policy fees.

The basic premium for traditional policies is annual, payable at the beginning of each year. Usually, **modal premiums** are also available, payable more frequently than annually. Modal premiums are usually greater than a pro-rata share of the annual premium. For example, a semi-annual modal premium might be 51% of annual. The extra charge compensates the insurer for lost interest, additional premium collection costs, and a higher risk that the policy will lapse.

Premiums actually charged for the policy are called **gross premiums**. Actuaries also make use of the concept of **net premiums** in determining reserves. Net premiums follow the benefit and premium payment pattern of the policy, but are based only on interest and mortality assumptions, that is, they include no provision for expenses, and no assumption as to policy termination experience. The difference between net and gross premiums is sometimes referred to as **loading**. Early formulas for gross premium determination sometimes were based on a simple addition to the net premium, but such an approach would be very unusual today.

2.2   RESERVES

In its most general sense, the word "reserve" in a life insurance policy refers to a liability that the insurer has established for payment of obligations that are not yet due. Reserve is such an important concept in life insurance that a number of different kinds of reserves are used for different purposes. Also, confusingly, the word "reserve" is occasionally used to describe an asset as in "reserves are invested in long-term bonds." "Reserve" in this text will always refer to the insurer's liability.

In level premium life insurance, fairly large reserves usually arise, a result of the fact that the incidence of human mortality generally increases with age, and a substantial part of early premiums must be set aside to cover the cost of claims at the older ages. The classical actuarial model establishes a **net level premium reserve** based on a mortality table usually one with rates of mortality that increase monotonically with age and a single interest rate. In the classical model, a net level premium is established as the amount at policy issue that, if paid according to the policy provisions for the term of the insurance, will exactly equal in present value the present value of the benefits. In this model, reserves may be calculated either **prospectively** (i.e., by subtracting the present value of future premiums from the present value of future benefits) or **retrospectively** (i.e., by subtracting the accumulated cost of past benefits from the accumulation of past premiums at interest.) Under the very simplified assumptions in the classical model, (a single mortality table and interest rate) the prospective and retrospective reserves are equal. The equality of prospective and retrospective reserves is also true of most of the more complex kinds of reserves that have been developed to fill various needs in the financial analysis of life insurance.

For net level premium reserves, the net premium calculated is level by duration, or if gross premiums vary by duration, the net premium is a level percentage of the gross premium. Contrasted with net level premium reserve, **modified reserves** are based on net premiums that are not level by duration (or not a level percentage of the gross premium.) Since almost all modified reserve methods are intended to accumulate less reserve in the early years than the net level premium method provides, (to allow the insurer extra margins to pay higher expenses at the early durations) modified reserves usually involve a lower net premium in the first year or two than net level. Therefore, premiums in later years are higher than net level, since the total present value of net premiums must still equal the present value of benefits. Like net level, modified reserves may be calculated either prospectively or retrospectively.

2.2.1   STATUTORY RESERVES

Among the earliest laws regulating life insurance in the United States were the laws establishing minimum reserves. At first, and for many years, it was common for state laws regulating insurers to specify a mortality table and interest rate on which the insurer was required to establish net level premium reserves, which would either be calculated or audited periodically by the insurance commissioner of the state in which the company was domiciled. The commissioner of the domiciliary state would certify the reserves to other states in which the company operated.

As the expense of life insurance selling grew, companies found it more difficult to establish net level premium reserves from the beginning of each new policy, and state laws began to allow calculation of modified reserves to meet the statutory reserve requirement. In the 1940's, all states passed more-or-less uniform **standard valuation laws** establishing a modified reserve basis called the **Commissioner's Reserve Valuation Method (CRVM)**.   Much later, states adopted a standard for annuity reserves called the **Commissioner's Annuity Reserve Valuation Method (CARVM)**. The standard valuation law also establishes mortality tables and interest rates for the calculation of reserves. Standard valuation laws provide minimum reserves, so it is possible for insurers to hold reserves that are higher than the minimum provided in the law, and many do so. At one time, many insurers held net level premium reserves, since they are always at least as high as the statutory minimum, but few insurers do so today because to do so reduces surplus substantially at the early durations, and high visible surplus has come to be an important competitive attribute. (The competitive marketplace gives less importance to the "hidden surplus" inherent in net level premium reserves.)

The simplest methods of calculating reserves assume that premiums are to be paid annually on policy anniversaries. Reserves calculated at policy anniversaries in this way, just before the premium is paid, are called "terminal reserves." After the premium is paid, the reserve includes an additional year's premium, and is called an "initial reserve." State laws recognized early that not all policies would be at an anniversary on the annual valuation date (December 31), so they required that the calculation method assume that all policies are midway between anniversaries called **"mean reserves."** Mathematically, mean reserves are equal to one-half the initial reserve on the anniversary just before the valuation date plus one-half the terminal reserve on the anniversary just after the valuation date.

Mean reserves are still based on the simplifying assumption that premiums are paid annually, so they overstate the reserve when premiums for the full year are not paid by the valuation date. To offset this overstatement of liabilities, state valuation laws permit holding the amount of any unpaid or deferred premiums for the policy year as a "due and deferred premiums" asset. It is common in health insurance (though rare in life insurance) to establish a **"mid-terminal reserve,"** equal to the average of the last and next terminal reserves. The mid-terminal reserve does not require the establishment of a deferred premium asset, since it differs from the mean reserve by an amount exactly equal to one-half a net premium. A company holding mid-terminal reserves also needs to hold an **unearned premium reserve** equal to that part of any premiums paid before the valuation date which are for an insurance period after the valuation date. It is now quite common to hold reserves based on the actual portion of the policy year before the valuation date, rather than artificially assuming that all policies are halfway through the year.

2.2.2   TAX RESERVES

Although most insurers are anxious to have earnings as high as possible, since high earnings contribute to an increase in surplus, they are not equally anxious to show high earnings for the purpose of computing income tax, since taxes reduce surplus. For that reason, most companies desire to have reserves as high as possible in the income tax computation. At one time, reserves even higher than those held for statutory purposes were possible. Since this reduces taxes, however, the taxing authorities have generally specified bases for calculating reserves that produce reserves at or below those held for statutory purposes, especially for companies whose statutory reserves are higher (as is permitted) than the minimum prescribed by the standard valuation law. Generally, statutory reserves equal or exceed tax reserves, which equal or exceed cash values.

2.2.3   GAAP RESERVES

It often costs more than the first year's gross premium to put a policy on the books, and when it does, any reserve that is non-negative will cause the insurer to show a loss at the end of the first year. If the insurer has properly priced the business, this loss represents an investment in the business that will be recovered, with interest, from future profits. This leads to the illogical result, however, of publishing a profit and loss statement showing a loss on business that will ultimately be profitable. Moreover, it causes a distortion that may hide the ultimate profitability of an insurer from an interested party reviewing the insurer's accounts, especially if sales of insurance are substantial and growing.

The accounting profession has required that all financial statements which receive the review and unqualified approval of a qualified accountant use reserves that are calculated according to **Generally Accepted Accounting Principles (GAAP)**. GAAP reserves differ from statutory reserves in that expenses which vary by policy duration must be spread over the life of the policy. GAAP reserves are generally calculated on a slightly less conservative mortality and interest basis than statutory reserves, and they are also reduced by the unamortized portion of the extra expenses associated with policy sale and issue often called "**Deferred Acquisition Cost (DAC)**."

2.3   CASH VALUES

Beginning in the mid-nineteenth century, laws were passed in North America requiring a cash value on level premium whole life insurance. The intent of the cash value requirement was to provide a return to the policyholder of the excess of the level premiums paid for the insurance over the actual cost of insurance. The cost of insurance was understood to be lower in the early years because of the continuing increase by age of the mortality curve. Early cash values often consisted of the net level premium reserve less a surrender charge that varied little by age or duration.

Gradually, more sophisticated techniques for calculating cash values were developed. The first Standard NonForfeiture law (c.1940) prescribed cash values that were essentially a kind of modified reserve, with the modified premiums in the prospective reserve formula equal to net level premiums plus an "expense allowance." Current nonforfeiture laws also follow this general pattern.

Almost universally, the policyholder is permitted to borrow funds from the insurer secured by the cash value under terms spelled out in the policy. Such borrowing is called a **policy loan**. The death benefit is always reduced by the amount of any unpaid policy loan. If a policy loan has not been repaid by the time a policy terminates for some reason other than death, the unpaid amount of the loan is deducted from the amount available for other nonforfeiture benefits.

2.4   OTHER NONFORFEITURE VALUES

Modern nonforfeiture laws generally require the insurer to provide, in addition to the cash value, two other equivalent benefits. The first, **reduced paid-up insurance**, provides a level benefit for the same term of years as the original policy (i.e., for life, if the policy is a whole life policy) for as much as the cash value will buy. The interest rate and mortality table used in determining the equivalence are the same as those used to determine the cash value.

The other required nonforfeiture benefit is **extended term insurance**. Extended term insurance provides a death benefit equal to that in the original policy, but for a shorter term, based on what the cash value will buy as a single premium. The number of years and days for which the extended term is provided is calculated using the same interest rate as is used in calculating the cash value, but insurers are permitted to use a special mortality table which has somewhat higher levels of mortality than the tables usually required for cash values. This is intended to reflect the fact that extended term is more likely to be elected by the policyholder if the insured is in impaired health at the time of nonforfeiture. Except for policies that carry an extra premium reflecting that the insured's health is substandard, (laws do not require extended term for such policies, and it is seldom provided) extended term is usually the automatic option put in effect when a premium is unpaid at the end of the **grace period**. The grace period is a time specified in the policy, usually 30 days, during which the nonpayment of a premium, even though after its due date, will not cause the policy to lapse.

Not strictly a nonforfeiture benefit, but operating like one in some ways is the **automatic premium loan**. The automatic premium loan provides that if the premium is unpaid at the end of the grace period, it will be paid by a policy loan, together with any accrued loan interest. This prevents the policy from lapsing until the available loan value becomes less than one premium. Because the premiums paid are gross, the automatic premium loan provision usually keeps the policy in force for less time than would be provided by extended term insurance. For this reason, one or two states do not allow automatic premium loan provisions. The automatic premium loan provision is not required by the nonforfeiture law, so many companies allow the payment of only one or two years premiums by automatic loan, with the policy reverting to extended term insurance at the end of that period if there is still sufficient value left.

2.5   DIVIDENDS AND NON-GUARANTEED ELEMENTS

When reserves and premiums are calculated on a conservative basis, as they should be for participating policies, the insurer must have in place a mechanism for distributing the excess earnings that result from actual experience that is better than the conservative assumptions used to establish reserves and premiums. Usually, this mechanism (in the case of participating fixed premium policies) provides annual dividends that the policyholder may either receive in cash, use to pay part of the premiums, leave on deposit at interest, or use to purchase additional insurance. Some fixed premium policies, especially term policies, have no dividends, but allow payment of a lower than guaranteed premium to reflect the favorable experience. For universal life policies and excess interest whole life, the extra earnings are reflected by allowing higher interest rates or lower mortality and expense charges than those that were guaranteed in the policy. Therefore, for universal life, favorable experience results in higher fund values than those that would result from the policy guarantees.

Since the non-guaranteed elements are usually illustrated in the course of selling the policy, they are usually calculated for all durations. In the case of dividends, the array of values for all durations, based on a single set of assumptions, is called the dividend scale. Usually, a participating policy has many changes in **dividend scale** over its lifetime, as the underlying experience changes.

An important distinction exists between *dividends*, which are determined based on the actual results of the recent period (retrospective), and *other non-guaranteed elements* for, indeterminate premium, excess interest whole life and universal life policies, which are based on the actuary's best estimate of the current and future experience (prospective).

2.6   ASSET SHARES

Reserves represent the insurer's liability for a policy. For many reasons, insurers have an interest in determining what share of their assets arose from the operations of a given policy. Usually, this **asset share** is compared to the reserve for the purpose of determining, at a given point in the life of a policy, how much the insurer has earned on the policy or, at durations where the reserve exceeds the asset share, how much surplus is invested in the policy.

By their nature, asset shares are retrospective, that is, they represent an accumulation of income less disbursements up to the time for which the asset share is calculated. Depending on the use to which they will be put, asset shares may be historical (that is, they may attempt to represent an actual accumulation), or they may be projected (that is, based on assumptions as to what the accumulation will be in the future). The most important uses of asset shares include pricing, by comparing proposed premiums or dividend scales with reserves at various durations, and valuation of the profit or profit potential of entire blocks of business for purchase or sale of the block.

Asset share formulas are often quite complex, since they must take into account (at a minimum) premiums, death benefits, surrender payments, investment income, dividends, taxes, and expenses of all kinds. Depending on the intended use, asset shares may also take into account other experience factors, such as policy loan usage. Arriving at appropriate assumptions, and formulas that reflect them, can be a challenge to the actuary who is responsible for their determination.

REVIEW QUESTIONS

1. Define premium. List five characteristics of premiums which may cause them to vary.

2. What factors affect the calculation of premiums?

3. Define: reserve, net level premium reserve, mean reserve, and mid-terminal reserve.

4. Why do insurers usually use modified reserves instead of net level premium reserves in their statutory statements?

5. Which is usually higher, statutory reserve or cash value? Tax reserve or statutory reserve? GAAP reserve or statutory reserve?

6.   If there is an unpaid policy loan at the time extended term insurance becomes effective, how is the length of the extended term period calculated? How would reduced paid-up insurance be calculated? How does an unpaid policy loan affect the operation of an automatic premium loan?

7.   Distinguish between dividends and other non-guaranteed elements, describing all differences.

8.   Define asset share.

SECTION II

PRODUCT DEVELOPMENT
AND
PRICING OF CONTRACT
BENEFITS

CHAPTER 3
THE PRODUCT DEVELOPMENT PROCESS

Like all insurance, life insurance is a very attractive buy to those who expect that they will benefit from it, i.e., those who expect to die soon, and less attractive to others. Since insurers want as broad as possible a spread of risk and do not, of course, want to make sales to those who expect to die soon, marketing is an essential part of the operation of a successful insurer. Designing products that will appeal to a broad enough segment of the marketplace is an essential part of marketing.

Actuaries play a key role in the product development process, because their training enables them to understand the financial consequences of product decisions, and to weigh the advantages of proposed product features. Actuaries cannot do successful product development in a vacuum, however. Product development requires knowledge and understanding of the market. Within every insurance company there is some organizational structure corresponding to what will be referred to here as **the marketing department**, which also plays a key role in product development.

The marketing department is that part of the company responsible for supervision of the sales process. In the very common case of a company which sells insurance through an agency force, the marketing department will be responsible for their recruitment and training. If a company employs more than one distribution method, there may be several departments playing the role of marketing department, but since products hardly ever cross distribution methods, only one marketing department is usually dealt with for any single product's development. Two characteristics are usually encountered in the marketing department: its officers know the market very well because of their intimate involvement with it, and their primary motive is to increase sales to the greatest possible extent.

There is also usually a **top management** within the insuring organization, at least one of whose primary motives is profit. Top management is responsible for seeing that both the product development actuaries and the marketing department follow a course dictated by the goals top management has chosen to pursue. Of course, both the actuaries and the marketing department must do their best to keep top management informed about what they view as the potential consequences of the various courses.

3.1   PRODUCT IDEAS

Most often, the source of product ideas will be the marketing department. Frequently, product ideas represent an adaptation of an existing product to changing features of the market. Since the marketing department is aware of competition in the market, product ideas may also be an adaptation of a competitor's product. Product development actuaries may also suggest product ideas based on their awareness of their own company's competitive strengths and their knowledge of competitor's products. Product ideas may also come directly from the field organization, or other sources inside or outside the company. They may also be suggested by environmental changes: tax changes, regulatory changes or demographic changes.

In practice, there are usually more product ideas than resources to develop them, so there needs to be some kind of formal process for considering product ideas and deciding which merit further consideration at a particular time. Some companies use a **product development committee** with periodic meeting dates and an agenda distributed in advance. The product development committee includes at least: the product development actuaries, the marketing department, and top management.   Product development affects many areas of the organization, however, and others may be present to contribute to the decision-making process.

Product ideas can vary considerably in size and complexity. At one extreme is a decision to enter an entirely new line of business, such as variable life insurance. As another example, most insurers revamp their entire portfolio of products from time to time, and the consideration of what changes to make as part of a portfolio revision constitutes a kind of "product idea." At the other end of the scale might be consideration of some minor change in an existing product, with implications for effects on the level of sales or profits. The usual product idea is somewhere between these two extremes.

3.2   FEASIBILITY

At this stage in the product development process, the proposed product idea must be examined for feasibility. Among the key questions to be answered at this stage are:

1.   What regulatory requirements must be met to offer this product? If this is a new field, are there barriers to entry? How easy is it to exit the new field?
2.   What education of sales representatives will be needed?
3.   Is the new product consistent with the existing distribution system?
4.   What are the target markets/demographics?
5.   What is the competition?
6.   What is the product's estimated "shelf life"?
7.   What effects will the new product have on the sales of existing products?
8.   Will additional sales aids be needed?
9.   How will availability of the product be advertised/publicized?
10.   What administrative capabilities must be added to administer this product?
11.   In light of the above, how much time/other resources are needed to bring this product to market?

The company may also wish to consider at this time whether to use consultants as a resource in product development, and there may also be consideration of using outside administrative facilities or even filling this marketing niche by using another company's product (i.e., being a "distributor" but not a "manufacturer.") Use of these outside resources may reduce the time required to market the product. Careful consideration should be given to the effect that use of outside resources will have on profit potential.

The key questions for any new product relate to the sales and profit potential. While it would be premature to suggest that those questions can be dealt with in any precise way at the feasibility stage, both the product actuaries and the marketing department should be prepared to give suggestions (with reasons) as to what they feel the sales and profit potential are, what the estimated shelf life is, and what effect the product will have on sales of existing products. This will be important information for top management to consider in deciding whether to take the product to the next step.

3.3   DEVELOPMENT

Once the product idea has passed the feasibility stage, more detailed actuarial work can begin.   The first step will be to arrive at detailed assumptions on all factors affecting "price".   Price means those financial elements of a product that are subject to competition.   For example, price for a deferred annuity product is the expected account values and surrender values at future durations.   For a traditional whole life product, it is the various elements in the premiums, dividends, cash values and death benefits that must be competitive in the marketplace.

A partial list of the assumptions affecting the price of a traditional whole life policy would include mortality, investment return, expenses, policy termination and loan experience, and the expected variation in each of these factors over the life of the policy.   The development phase is the stage at which various formulas for pricing (described in later chapters) are applied.   Most actuaries develop several sets of prices at this stage, representing the results of different assumption sets within the range of likely assumptions, and/or the results of different profit goals that might be considered.

A very important aspect of the development stage is the gathering of competitive information for comparison to the various test price sets.   The competitive information should relate to the kinds of products with which the new product is being designed to compete.   The actuary should have an idea, before proceeding further, what position in the marketplace is being sought for the new product.   For example, does it have to be absolutely the lowest priced, or is it acceptable to carry a price that is somewhere in the competitive range?   Sometimes, competitive positioning is accomplished not so much by price as by inclusion of attractive product features.

The final part of this stage will be the preparation of competitive price comparisons, with the assumptions, and resulting profit from each. Profit may be shown in terms of the return on investment, as a specific dollar level for the asset share at particular points in the life of the product, or in a variety of other ways, often depending on the particular company's traditions and preferences for profit goals.   Chalke [1] has pointed out that methods which produce profits per unit implicitly represent cost plus pricing.   He has also analyzed the arbitrary nature of cost allocation methods that attempt to allocate non-marginal costs per unit.   It is usually desirable to develop the expected profit from the entire expected sales of the block, since it may be desirable to work with the relationship between expected sales and profit at the next stage in development.

3.4 RECONCILIATION

Reconciliation is the stage at which the actuary presents the competitive comparisons, price sets and assumption sets to the marketing department, and often also to top management. The actuary needs to be thoroughly familiar with all the data at this stage, and to be able to respond to questions about the potential effect of changes in the assumptions. Quite often **sensitivity testing** is required at this stage. Sensitivity testing involves making changes in assumptions to determine the effect of the changes on the price and profit potential. One result of the reconciliation stage may be a request for an additional price set, based on a new assumption set (i.e., a return to the development stage).

Requests for re-development often result from the frustration of the marketing department over inability to arrive at an assumption set that will result in a product positioned in the market as the marketing department feels it should be. Top management needs to deal carefully with such requests to be sure that additional development work will be productive. Too many such returns to the development stage can add considerably to the cost of a product development project, as well as the time frame for its completion.

The reconciliation stage is complete only when there is agreement on:

1.   A set of pricing assumptions
2.   A set of prices based on these assumptions
3.   Expected profits

If the product will be sold using sales illustrations, the illustration actuary must be comfortable with the assumptions.

3.5 IMPLEMENTATION

Once the final assumptions and profit goals are decided, product implementation can begin. The first stage of product implementation is the completion of pricing. Usually, the pricing at the development and reconciliation stage is done only on a model basis: a set of ages, amounts, and other factors influencing price is taken as representative of the whole. At the implementation stage, therefore, it will be necessary to fill in the gaps. Rates for non-model ages must be calculated. Also, substandard rates, modal premium differentials, differentials for variations in specific geographic areas and the like are often left until this pricing stage.

This is also the stage at which prices must be tested to be sure they "work" at extreme ages and amounts. Since, in the normal case, sales at the extremes are rare and infrequent, profit levels are less important than for the range at which most sales are expected, but it is important that they not fluctuate drastically at the extremes. If there are ages in the premium structure that are unprofitable, they may attract more business than was expected. As a part of the final pricing, all nonforfeiture values that may appear in policy forms need to be established.

Most life insurance and annuities are sold through the use of a sales illustration that shows the price and development of guaranteed and non-guaranteed values year by year. Such illustrations must be certified by an **Illustration Actuary**, who attests that the assumptions used in deriving the illustrated values are appropriate. The sales illustration usually shows the premiums expected to be paid and the resulting benefits and values each year under a series of assumptions that are stated in the illustration. Often, the illustration shows more than one set of assumptions, and therefore more than one set of benefits and values. Making the necessary modifications to the illustration system for the new product is an important part of implementation. Preparation of other sales material such as sales brochures and rate cards or books must also be done.

Because it can be time-consuming, the preparation and filing with regulatory authorities of policy and application forms usually takes place simultaneously with final pricing. In fact, if there is agreement on the form and features, this can sometimes start while the final stages of price reconciliation are being completed. Approval from most of the fifty states usually requires at least three months, and can take much longer if the filing is at all unusual. Almost always, there are a few states in which approval takes much longer than the others. A year or more may be required to secure approval from all fifty states. If the product requires a prospectus, it must be developed and filed at this stage, as must the Illustration Actuary's certification.

While the approval process is going on, the company must develop sales, marketing, and advertising material. Administrative and sales personnel may need to be trained for the new product. If the new product requires changes in the accounting systems (statutory, tax, or GAAP), they need to be prepared and implemented at this stage. Usually the final stage in implementation is the preparation of administrative systems or modification of existing systems for the new product. The first stage of system development is usually modifications to the system that issues new policies. Simultaneously, or very soon after, modifications must be made to systems that bill and collect premiums, calculate reserves, calculate and credit dividends, and perform all the other administrative details necessary for an in force policy.

3.6   MONITORING

After the new product has been introduced and sales have begun, a program needs to be established for monitoring the sales, profits and assumptions on which the original development was based. All three parties to the development, the product actuary, marketing department and top management have a stake in understanding where and why there are deviations from the original plan. Not only will this information aid in making appropriate changes to the new product over time, but it should also sharpen the focus for development of other future products. The information may even be the source of additional product ideas.

REFERENCES

[1]   Chalke, Shane A., "Macro Pricing: Toward a Comprehensive Product Development Process," TSA XLIII, 1991, pp. 137-230.

REVIEW QUESTIONS

1.   In an insurance organization, who are the important parties to the product development process?

2.   What are the six stages of the product development process?

3.   Name three sources of product ideas?

4.   What questions must be answered at the feasibility stage?

5.   Define "price". What is price for a typical ART product?

6.   What is "sensitivity testing"?

7.   What is an illustration actuary, and what is the illustration actuary's role in the product development process?

8.   At what stage does the filing with regulatory authorities occur? What items may have to be filed?

9.   Why is it important to monitor deviations from the pricing assumptions?

CHAPTER 4
MEASURING PROFITABILITY

4.1   DEFINITION OF PROFIT

Dictionary definitions of profit generally focus on either a return on the capital invested in an enterprise or the excess of receipts over disbursements. This section of the text will generally focus on a definition of profit centered on the latter, i.e., the excess of receipts over disbursements. However, in a life insurance company, a large part of the disbursements, namely death benefits and cash values, do not take place until many years after the receipts (premiums and investment income). On the other hand, it is common for some of the disbursements, acquisition expenses, to take place before there are adequate receipts from which to pay them. Many ways of measuring profit that seek in one way or another to adjust for these problems are in common use.

In a life insurance company, profit is defined as receipts minus disbursements minus the increase in a reserve. The reserve is intended to include some provision for future death benefits (and sometimes, other disbursements) and may include some provision for spreading the high expenses encountered in the early policy years. If expenses in the first year exceed receipts, as they usually do, the reserve used to determine profit under some definitions can be negative, so that profits are not necessarily negative as a result of the high early expenses.

Since the amount of the reserves will directly affect the amount of profit reported to the public by the company, their calculation is a very important matter, and one of the most important responsibilities of a life insurance actuary. Over the long run, using different definitions of reserve will not affect the total profit, since ultimately all reserves are released when the last policy goes off the books. However, differences in the level of reserves will affect the incidence of profit, and thus its present value.

4.1.1   STATUTORY PROFIT

Income and disbursement items for statutory profits are defined in the
annual statement instructions prepared (in the U.S.) by the **National
Association of Insurance Commissioners (NAIC)**. As previously stated,
profit definitions do not vary greatly in the income and disbursement items
on which they are based, and use of the NAIC definitions is generally
accepted. The reserves on which **statutory** profits are based are the
reserves at or above the minimums established by law. The laws establishing minimum statutory reserves differ somewhat from state to state; usually
insurance companies hold reserves on the most conservative basis required
in any of the states in which they operate. It is important to note that the
law establishes a *minimum* level of reserves; it is almost always acceptable
to hold a higher reserve than the one specified in the statute. Therefore, a
company may choose to have lower early statutory profits than the
maximum that might be available to it if it held minimum reserves, but the
law, in effect, sets a cap on the amount of statutory profit that a company
may have each year. As a practical matter, most companies seek to
maximize their statutory profits because statutory profits are usually the
source of information used by the public to judge the company's financial
health.

Statutory profits are also important from the standpoint of a
company's ability to continue in business. The statutory profit is added to
statutory surplus each year, and the new resulting statutory surplus (after
other adjustments) is the basis for judging company solvency. In the early
years of a new product, statutory profits are usually negative, and this
places a "strain" on statutory surplus. The company must always be sure
it has enough capital available to cover the statutory surplus strain on new
products, or may have to limit the extent to which it can offer new products
because of the amount of capital it has available. Because statutory profits
(as limited by statutory reserves) place this restriction on the amount of
capital that must remain in the company, they also restrict the timing and
amount of profits that can be released to shareholders as dividends.

4.1.2   GAAP PROFIT

Like statutory profits, GAAP (Generally Accepted Accounting Principles)
Profits are defined as income less disbursements, less the increase in
reserves, but the GAAP reserve is defined differently from the statutory
reserve. There are several different definitions of GAAP reserves for

different kinds of products. Generally however, net GAAP reserves are equal to benefit and expense reserves less a deferral and capitalization of the acquisition costs. The deferred amount is called DAC (Deferred Acquisition Costs). The period over which DAC is amortized and the rate at which it is amortized each year are defined differently for different products, as described in more detail in the chapter on Reserves. Traditional GAAP reserves are calculated using a mortality and interest basis that represents the actuary's estimate of future experience, including some provision for adverse deviation (i.e., the mortality and interest chosen represent a somewhat conservative estimate of future mortality and interest experience). Usually, but not always, the mortality and interest rate chosen are less conservative than the least conservative basis defined in the law on which statutory reserves are based. GAAP reserves, therefore, are usually less conservative than statutory reserves.

This does not mean that GAAP profits are always larger than statutory profits, however. The adjustment term to statutory reserves (DAC) shrinks each year that a policy is in force. If a company's new business is not growing, the DAC for new policies added to the business in force will be less than the DAC being amortized for policies previously in force. In that case, total DAC will decrease, and the increase in GAAP reserves may be larger than increase in statutory reserves, reducing GAAP profits below statutory.

Ideally, in years when a company *does* add a large amount of new business, GAAP profits will be high. (Although this may not be true if there are large expenses of a type that cannot be amortized, or if the reserves contain large provision for adverse deviation.) In general, GAAP profits attempt to match the emergence of profit with those activities that will result in profit or loss. Because of this characteristic, GAAP profits are often considered a better indicator of a company's overall well-being than statutory profits. Stock companies' reports to stockholders refer to GAAP profits, and pay less attention to statutory profits. Mutual companies, however, have no stockholders or stockholder's reports, and mutual companies do not always calculate GAAP reserves or GAAP profits.[1] However, more Mutual companies are reporting on a GAAP basis in order to provide useful information to insurance company rating agencies.

---

1   Mutual companies that do not adopt GAAP will not receive an unqualified opinion from an accountant on their financial statements. However, many mutual companies do not need such an opinion.

4.2   PROFIT MEASURES

Companies generally seek to maximize profit, whichever way they may choose to define it. In addition to knowing how large overall profits are, most companies want to compare profits to their profit plans. There are a number of different ways in which a company may choose to measure the profits for comparison to plans. Many of these measures involve taking a ratio of profits to some other financial item.

4.2.1   PROFIT MARGIN

The **Profit Margin** in a policy or group of policies is defined as the present value of profits divided by the present value of premiums. Present value, for this purpose, involves interest, and assumption as to mortality and policy persistency. Profit margin is affected to a considerable degree by the choice of assumptions for the present value, and comparison of one company's profit margins with another's can be misleading unless there is some uniformity in the choice of assumptions. Unfortunately, there is no consensus on the appropriate assumptions, although many companies simply discount using the current rate of earnings on assets. Comparison of profit margins works best, however, when done internally. Profit margin is frequently used as the profit measure for term insurance.

4.2.2   RETURN ON INVESTMENT, INTERNAL RATE OF RETURN, RETURN ON EQUITY AND RETURN ON ASSETS

Return on Investment (ROI) is the ratio of the present value of profits to surplus. The **Internal Rate of Return (IRR)** is that interest rate at which the present value of profits at issue is zero. **Return on Equity (ROE)** is the ratio of profits to equity, which will usually include the amount needed to cover acquisition expenses, and may also include the company's target surplus (for example, for statutory risk-based capital requirements.) The **Return on Assets (ROA),** as the name implies, is a ratio of profits to the assets that the business has. It is most likely to be calculated for lines that generate fairly large amounts of assets, such as annuities. ROE or ROA can apply for a period of any length, but are most commonly applied to refer to a period of a single policy year. ROI is usually calculated for the life of the policy, but can also be referred to on a year-to-year basis. Thus, for example, an actuary might say "Product X has an ROI of 10%, but the ROI in the second year is only 2%."

Since ROI or ROE usually applies to a particular policy or line of business, and are calculated prospectively, the "surplus" referred to in the denominator of the ratio is not the company's total surplus, but that part of surplus needed to "support" the particular business on which profits are being calculated. ROI and ROE profit measures are suitable for all lines of business, but are especially likely to be encountered in lines that require a large amount of invested surplus. ROI, IRR, and ROE are all often used as profit measures for individual permanent insurance. Many companies use a single profit measure (such as ROE) for all lines of business, and compare the lines on that basis.

When ROE is used as a measure, most companies strive for a rate that significantly exceeds the rate available on fixed investments. Thus, if the rate of return currently available on fixed investments were 8% before Federal Income Tax, a pre-tax ROE of 15% might be expected. Note that, since ROE is defined as the ratio of profit to equity, the rate calculated depends not only on how much profit a company has, but also on how the company defines the equity invested in a particular product. Equity usually includes some measure of the risk-based capital that must be held for the product, as well as the investment in putting the business on the books.

4.2.3 OTHER PROFIT MEASURES

In addition to calculating ratios based on the total present value of profits, many companies compare the accumulated profits after set periods of time to other financial results. Thus, "accumulated profits equal to 5% of reserves after 20 years" might be one company's profit goal. Another goal might be to break even (i.e., to have accumulated profits that offset all early losses) after 10 years. Still another company might seek to achieve accumulated profit as a certain percentage of accumulated premiums or of insurance in force after a specified number of years. A profit as a percentage of insurance in force would be more likely to be a goal for a line such as term insurance, which involves little in the way of reserve or asset accumulation.

4.3   SOURCES OF PROFIT

Charles Dudley Warner once wrote: "Everybody talks about the weather, but nobody does anything about it." Fortunately this comment is not equally applicable to profit. In fact, it can be said that all, or almost all, of the efforts of a corporation should be focused on "doing something about" profit. In order to be able to control profit, it is essential to understand exactly where profit and loss come from. In an insurance company, analyzing the sources of profit and loss is one of the essential jobs of the actuary. To do so, the actuary relies on an understanding of the mathematical elements of the insurance contract, and especially of the reserve, since the increase in reserve makes such an important contribution to the annual profit.

4.3.1   GAIN FROM INTEREST, MORTALITY AND EXPENSE

The classical formula for profit (ignoring persistency) looks something like this:

$$Profit = (Gross\,Premium + PY\,Reserve) \times (1 + i')$$
$$- q' \times (Face - CY\,Reserve)$$
$$- Expense\,and\,Taxes - CY\,Reserve$$

(i' and q' stand respectively for actual interest and mortality rates and *PY* and *CY* stand for previous year and current year)

The actuary expands the terms for reserve and restates the formula as follows:

$$Profit = (Net\,Premium + PY\,Reserve) \times (i' - i) \qquad \text{(interest gain)}$$
$$+ (q - q') \times (Face - CY\,Reserve) \qquad \text{(mortality gain)}$$
$$+ (Gross\,Premium - Net\,Premium)$$
$$\times (1 + i') - Expense\,and\,Taxes \qquad \text{(expense gain)}$$

Where $CY\,Reserve = (PY\,Reserve + Net\,Premium)$
$$\times (1 + i) - q \times (Face - CY\,Reserve)$$

(The unprimed i and q are reserve interest and mortality.)

This gives a precise definition of three of the most important sources of profit for a life insurance company. Also, it gives the company management some indication of what it needs to "do something about" to get profits on track. For example if all the other sources of profit are on track, but the mortality gain is less than established in the pricing, management knows that the business is not being tightly enough underwritten, and can take appropriate action.

4.3.2 SURRENDER GAINS

Most actuaries add an additional term to the formula used in gains analysis in the form:

$$r' \times (CY\,Reserve - Cash\,Value) \qquad \text{(surrender gain)}$$

The "r'" function represents the actual rate of surrender. (In this analysis it is assumed that $r = 0$, i.e., that no surrender rate was assumed in gross premium development.)

4.3.3 ANALYSIS OF GAINS

Simply knowing the sources of gains or losses provides some useful information, but usually there is a need for more. For example, a management that learns expense losses are higher than anticipated will usually want to pinpoint with as much accuracy as possible the source of the excess expenses, so that a decision can be made on what actions to take.

To use another example, lower investment gains than expected could come from many sources other than an inability to find investments yielding the interest rate assumed in pricing. The shortfall could also be due to capital losses, to loan defaults, to later than expected payment of premiums or from an inability to invest funds as quickly as expected, to mention a few possible problems.

One source of gains that needs special attention in gains analysis is riders. Because riders are often priced using simplified pricing formulas, there is a tendency to overlook them or to apply oversimplified methods of gain analysis. The gains from riders, however, are subject to the same basic tools of analysis as the gains from policies and oversimplified analysis is often a mistake.

REVIEW QUESTIONS

1. How is profit defined for a life insurance company? Statutory profit? GAAP profit?

2. Do GAAP profits normally exceed statutory profits? Why or why not?

3. Define: profit margin; ROI; ROE; ROA; IRR.

4. Name four sources of gains. How are gains by source derived?

CHAPTER 5
ELEMENTS OF GROSS PREMIUM CALCULATION

In his landmark 1959 paper [1], James C. H. Anderson gave a very complete analysis of the approach to determination of profits resulting from given levels of gross premiums. Anderson was writing at a time when the use of computers was first becoming a practical reality for premium determination and testing, and his very complete formulas quickly gained acceptance, replacing the elegant but greatly simplified formulas of Cammack [2] and Hoskins [3]. Anderson covered the area of gross premium development so thoroughly that gross premium calculation in the 1990's, except for a few very simplified instances, is almost always done using what is referred to as "Anderson's Method," or "Anderson's Formula," even when one or two terms of the formula differ slightly from the specific terms used by Anderson.

Anderson [1] states: "For each individual buyer of life insurance there exists a theoretical premium rate. It is uniquely defined by the following parameters:

1. the probability of collecting premiums,
2. the interest earned on the accumulated funds,
3. the benefits paid on survival, death and withdrawal,
4. the expenses incurred, including taxes and reinsurance costs,
5. the charges assessed for contingencies,
6. the profit objectives adopted by the company, and
7. the basis of liabilities established for future benefits."

Anderson goes on to define a formula for the book profit each year. The book profit is set equal to the reserve at the beginning of the year, plus the premium less expenses, benefits, and any other payments (such as cash values or dividends), also appropriately discounted for probability of payment and interest to the time of payment, and less the reserve at the end of the year, discounted for a full year's interest and for the probability that a life will still be insured at the end of the year. The book profits for each year can then be discounted at a different rate of interest (whatever rate the company needs to earn on surplus invested in new business) to determine a present value of future profits. The use of a separate interest rate for accumulation of the book profits is more realistic than accumulating book profits at the same rate as policy cash flows.

Table 5.1, on the following page, shows a typical Anderson formula based on annual premiums. Most of this chapter will be spent in defining and discussing the various formula terms, sources of data and frequently encountered variations. Since it is impossible to cover all variations that may be encountered in practice, an important part of the discussion will center on the techniques of making changes in the formula to reflect practical variations. Anderson's formula, as stated, defines book profits in terms of a number of variables, gross premiums among them. Anderson's paper contains a mechanism for arriving at the gross premium that will produce a specified level of book profit. Since modern spreadsheet programs make it a relatively simple matter to adjust one variable in a formula to derive a desired value of another variable, however, there is no reason to describe that aspect of Anderson's work.

5.1   RESERVES

Anderson intended that the book profits be based on the statutory reserve, approximated by the terminal reserve on whatever basis the company is using for annual statement purposes. The term $_tV$, therefore generally will mean the terminal reserve on the annual statement basis. However, a few companies may want to define profits for gross premium determination or testing on a GAAP basis. In that case, the GAAP assumptions used by the company need to replace the statutory assumptions in the determination of terminal reserve. Expenses and other items used in the GAAP profit calculation need to be adjusted to a consistent basis. (As discussed under "Percentage of Premium Expenses," however, the creation of a Deferred Acquisition Cost (DAC) reserve offset, while intended to offset expenses, does not cause any movement in the expenses themselves.) Development of reserves is discussed more fully in Chapter 8.

Table 5.1
Formula for Book Profit

Formula	Explanation
$_tB = {}_{t-1}V$	Reserve at beginning of year
$+P \times (1 - c_t - p_t)$	Annual premium reduced by commission and percentage of premium expense
$- E_t / A$	Per policy expenses converted to unit value
$-(D_t + Q_t / A) \times v^{.50} \times q_t$	Death benefit plus death expenses converted to unit value payable (on average at mid year) at death
$-[.5 \times ({}_{t-1}CV +{}_tCV) + W_t / A]$ $\times v^{.5} \times w_t$	Cash Value (on average at mid-year) plus withdrawal expenses converted to unit value payable at withdrawal
$- {}_tS*(1 - q_t - w_t) \times v$	Survivorship benefit (e.g. dividend) payable at survival to end of year
$- {}_tV \times v \times (1 - q_t - w_t)$	Reserve at end of year if unit survives

5.2   PREMIUMS

The premium term (P) is the variable being solved for when Anderson's formula is used to derive a premium. Alternatively, actuaries sometimes begin the process using a premium level they would like to maintain and use the formula to verify that the resulting book profits are acceptable.

Premiums, as stated for the formula, are collected annually at the beginning of each policy year. If the premium is not normally collected exactly on the anniversary, adjustment can be made. For example if premium collection actually averages ten days after the anniversary, the premium term can be multiplied by $v^{(1/36)}$. In practice, few actuaries would bother to make such a small adjustment. Of more practical importance would be an adjustment to reflect frequent payment of premiums on a non-annual basis. If most premiums were payable monthly, for example, then the premium, P, should be replaced by

$$P' \times (1-(11/24) \times (q_t + w_t)) \times v^{(13/24)},$$

where P' is 12 times the monthly premium as charged. If premiums are payable monthly, then monthly lapse becomes possible, and adjustment needs to be made in the cash value term of the formula.

Most companies have some factor in their premium that varies by policy size. Since P is on a per unit basis, this factor needs to be included in the premium by first dividing it by the average policy size, A, and then adding the result to that part of the unit premium that does not vary by policy size. Derivation of a portion of the premium that should vary by policy size could be done by testing large and small average sizes to derive a premium for both that produces the desired profit margin. The difference between the premiums for the large and small test sizes can be used to derive the theoretical difference by average size. (As a practical matter, it may be desirable to use some size variation that differs from the theoretically appropriate one.)

5.3 COMMISSIONS AND OTHER PERCENTAGE OF PREMIUM SALES COSTS

Most life insurance and annuities are sold by agents who receive a commission as a percentage of premiums. Frequently, sales supervisors who recruited and trained the agent (often these individuals are called general agents or branch managers) also receive a percentage of the premium called an "override." Sometimes there are several layers of sales management receiving overrides. All these kinds of sales expenses are included in C_t the sales expense percentage of premium factor.

Almost always, the selling agent receives a commission in renewal years as a part of his compensation for the sale, and renewal overrides are also frequently encountered. For life insurance, the first year commission is often a fairly high percentage of the premium. New York law allows first year expenses of as much as 96%, but not all this is commission.

Companies licensed in New York must observe the New York limits even on business sold in other states. Renewal commissions and overrides are generally only a fraction of the commission and override paid in the first year. For annuities, the amount paid in the first year is usually fairly low (e.g., 3 or 4%) and in that case it sometimes happens that renewal commissions are paid at the same rate.

Many companies recognize that the selling agent may incur expenses in selling the business, and allow an additional percentage of the first premium as an expense allowance. Often, there may be no separation of the two amounts, but simply a payment of (say) 75% of first year premiums as a combination of sales compensation and expense allowance. Obviously, regardless of whether they are separated, all such amounts should be included in C_t for the year they are paid (or the year to which they are charged).

If the profits being derived or targeted are to be on a GAAP basis, then expenses must be charged by duration on the same basis as they are charged for GAAP purposes. However, if reduction is made in the reserve in early years to offset acquisition costs (i.e., if a DAC reserve offset is established), then that offset does the work of reallocating expenses, and there is no need to make separate adjustment to the expenses themselves.

It has recently become common to pay the selling or servicing agent a percentage of assets under management on annuities and life insurance policies (such as Universal Life) that have a separate asset or fund account. Such expenses, even though they may be for selling effort, are clearly not a part of the percentage of premium expense term, and provision for them will be described under "Percentage of Account Value Expense."

Some actuaries have suggested that the optimum premium for the market will be achieved if sales expenses are allowed to vary with the premium level, so that a level of commissions can be set that will produce desired levels of both premium and profit margin. Because of the New York limits, however, sales expenses can never exceed certain levels, even if raising them might theoretically bring more sales (in spite of the increased premium). On the other end of the scale, lowering commissions to zero would be unlikely to result in high sales, even with significantly lower premiums. In practice, an existing sales organization usually expects commissions to vary within a fairly small range, and is likely to have expectations (even for new products) that, if not met, can have a severely negative effect on sales. When the new product being developed is for an entirely new distribution method (for example, fee-based financial planners) there may be somewhat more flexibility, but even in that case there will be limitations imposed by the expectations of the new distribution system and the competition with other entities using such a system.

5.4   OTHER PERCENTAGE OF PREMIUM EXPENSE

Most companies have several kinds of expenses that vary with the amount of premium collected. Premium taxes are an obvious example. The expenses of running a billing and collection system usually do not vary by the amount of premium, but there may be exceptions. Any expenses considered to vary by the amount of premium should be included in the P_t factor.

5.5   PERCENTAGE OF ACCOUNT VALUE EXPENSE

As noted under "Sales Costs", it is now fairly common to provide "trailer commissions" as part of the compensation for selling a policy or contract. Trailer commissions are calculated as a percentage of the policy account value (usually a fairly low percentage, since they can become quite large as the account value builds.)

Such expenses are usually allocated directly as an additional term in the premium formula by a term in the form: $e_t'*AV_t$, where e_t' is the percentage payable in year t, and AV_t is the account value.

5.6   EXPENSE PER POLICY

A standard method of allocating expense in a life insurance company is to assign directly those expenses known to be associated with each of the following functions: Underwriting and issue, valuation and other ongoing administration, death claims, surrender claims, etc. After all of these expenses are assigned, there will still be a fair amount of costs, known as indirect costs, that are not assigned. These will include, for example, the costs of maintaining a Human Resources Department and other costs that the company has simply to stay in business. Usually, these indirect costs are added proportionately to the directly allocated costs, and the results divided by the number of policies in force, etc. to derive the expenses per policy. Usually the per policy expense, E_t, varies between the first and renewal years but is the same for all renewal years.

Because administrative expenses do increase with inflation, it is not uncommon to add a factor for inflation so that $E_t = (1+j)^t \times E$ where j is the expected rate of inflation and E is the observed renewal expense rate.

5.7   AVERAGE POLICY SIZE

In designing a new policy form, there is usually some decision made as to the market in which the form will be sold, and thus the average size, A, that is expected for the form. Since the average size will have an effect on the amount of expense charge per unit, there is frequently a tendency to inflate expectations of the average size. While the same average size is usually used throughout the book profit formula used in premium development, it would be possible to make an assumption that there was a different average size for first year lapses than for surrenders at the later durations.

5.8   DEATH BENEFITS

The amount of death benefit, $_tD$, is normally taken as $1,000, although it would not be unusual to work with other amounts where there is some other unit basis for a form. An example might be a decreasing term form providing a unit value of an annuity certain of $10 per month for twenty years from issue. For many types of insurance, $_tD$ does not vary by duration, but there are also coverages where it may increase or decrease.

5.9   DEATH CLAIM EXPENSE

The death claim expense, Q_t, is usually higher during the contestable period. After that, it does not normally vary by duration except for any inflation factor. Since death claim expenses are arrived at using the allocation process described for E_t, they are subject to the same arbitrary allocation of indirect expense.

5.10   INTEREST

The interest discount factor, $v = [1/(1+i)]$, included in the book profit formula will normally be based on the company's best estimate of the interest it expects to earn on the investments that will be made with the cash flows from the product. Note that some pricing formulas require a higher "hurdle" rate of interest on the investment of surplus in new business. This is described more fully in Chapter 10, Profit Margins, and is not a part of the descriptions in this chapter. Policy Loans are often made at rates different from the rate the company expects to earn on other investments, and in that case the interest rate will include an adjustment based on expected policy loan utilization to reflect this difference.

5.11   MORTALITY

The death rate, q_t, is based on the company's expectation of mortality for the form. It is not unusual to assume different rates of mortality at the same age for different forms when the forms are sold in different markets or underwritten differently. Many larger companies have developed their own mortality tables, which will be the source of q_t. Companies that do not have their own mortality experience frequently use the basic tables developed by the Society of Actuaries (for example, some percentage of the 1975-80 Basic Tables). Frequently, industry tables are used with an adjustment to reflect company experience. The basic tables vary mortality by both age and duration, as is normally the case in developing book profits. The actuary may decide to adjust mortality based on an estimate of future mortality improvements.

5.12   CASH VALUES

The cash or other nonforfeiture values, $_tCV$, will be those values that the company has developed for the form. Techniques of developing nonforfeiture values are covered in depth in Chapter 7.

5.13   SURRENDER OR CASH VALUE EXPENSE

The cash value or surrender expense, W_t, will be developed in the expense allocation process. If inflation is included in the development of E_t, it would be usual to include it in W_t as well. While expenses will be lower for withdrawals at durations where the cash values are zero, they may not be zero, and it would not be unusual to include a positive value of W_t at those durations.

5.14   LAPSE RATES

The rate of lapsation, w_t, normally varies more by duration than by issue age, but some variation by age is frequently encountered. Variation by distribution method or market is often significant. As with mortality rates, the source of data may be either the company's own experience or published information such as the Lapse studies prepared by LIMRA and published by the Society of Actuaries [4]. Variation of lapse rates from form to form and by market is to be expected.

5.15   SURVIVOR BENEFIT (DIVIDEND)

The formula for book profits includes a term representing a survivor benefit, $_tS$, that is payable to only those who survive the year. While many companies require survival to year-end for the payment of a dividend, there are also companies that pay pro-rata dividends on death, or sometimes on withdrawals. Variations like this will require appropriate modifications to the formula. Determination of dividends is discussed at length in Chapter 9.

5.16   OTHER VARIATIONS

Smaller companies, and even some larger companies for which it is a significant expense may choose to add a term for **reinsurance expense** to the book profit formula. This would consist of the charges made by the reinsurer for the reinsured situations (this might be only the larger size policies), with an appropriate reduction in the death benefit, $_tD$, for the reinsurer's payments.

Where the insurance being priced has a conversion feature, a term could be added with a conversion rate and the cost of conversion. Some have also argued that if the insurance being priced is likely to replace business now on the books it should include some term making up for the lost profits on the replaced business.

REFERENCES

1.   Anderson, J. C. H., "Gross Premium Calculations and Profit Measurement for Nonparticipating Insurance," TSA XI, 1959, pp. 357-394.

2.   Cammack, E.E., "Premiums for Nonparticipating Life Insurance," TSA XX, 1919, pp. 379-409.

3.   Hoskins, J. E., "A New Method of Computing NonParticipating Premiums," TSA XXX, 1929, pp. 140-166.

4.   TSA Reports, 1988-90.

REVIEW QUESTIONS

1.   Name six kinds of expense factors that are usually included in gross premium development.

2.   Other than expenses, what costs contribute to gross premiums?

3.   How is the sales force traditionally compensated for selling life insurance?

4.   Since the ultimate cost of insurance is independent of the reserve basis, why do reserves affect gross premiums?

5.   What effect would an offer to allow policy loans at low interest rates have on gross premiums?

CHAPTER 6
PREMIUMS FOR SUPPLEMENTAL BENEFITS

6.1   INTRODUCTION

While the preparation of gross premiums for life benefits may require the major share of the pricing actuary's attention, marketing of the new product may also require preparation of a great many additional premiums reflecting supplemental benefits included in the new product offering. Because these supplemental benefits will almost always have premiums lower than the basic benefit, and because they will be sold only to a portion of the buyers of the new product, there is a tendency to use simplified pricing methods with supplemental benefits. Supplemental benefits are almost never participating, and therefore, if there are no other non-guaranteed elements to provide margins for adverse experience, care is needed to assure that the price of supplemental benefits is adequately conservative. Conservative assumptions are the rule, in fact, for supplemental benefits, since price competition in life insurance usually is without consideration for the cost of supplemental benefits. This section will describe pricing mechanisms for commonly encountered supplemental benefits. The principles developed can be extended to the pricing of other less common benefits.

6.2   DISABILITY BENEFITS

Disability benefits in life insurance contracts usually cover either waiver of premiums, waiver of monthly charges (for non-traditional life) or provide an income benefit. The amount available as an income benefit tends to be severely limited, to avoid overinsurance and the kind of financial underwriting that is necessary for stand-alone individual disability income. Insurers are usually willing, however, to offer waiver of premium or waiver of monthly charges for any amount of life insurance that the insured qualifies for, without separate financial underwriting for the disability coverage.

Standard formulas for disability net premiums are given in *Actuarial Mathematics* [1], and these can be applied to the amount of premium to be waived. For policies without fixed premiums, the disability feature is often used to cover the cost of insurance for each month that the insured is disabled, and this can be calculated based on the same principles. Variations are made of course, for non-level waived premiums or costs of insurance. Another common benefit variation provides paid-up insurance for disabilities that continue to age 65. Once disability net premiums have been derived from first principles formulas, they are usually increased by a percentage loading to cover expenses. Common loads for such benefits range from 10% to 20% or more.

Disability experience may be obtained from the 1985 CIDA tables [2], or from the company's own experience. Because companies vary widely in definitions of disability as well as in underwriting and claims handling, use of the company's own experience is usually preferred for disability benefits. However, for many companies this is difficult because waiver is sold on only a fraction of policies, and the experience may not be adequate to be statistically significant.   Intercompany experience on disability waiver benefits is available [3], but its usefulness is limited by the lack of homogeneity among company practices for disability. A practical alternative is to compare company experience to the intercompany and use a modification of the intercompany.

6.3   ACCIDENTAL DEATH BENEFITS

It is fairly common to offer "double indemnity" benefits as a rider to a life insurance policy. Double indemnity benefits provide an extra death benefit equal to the face amount if the insured's death results from an accident. Less common, but sometimes offered are "triple indemnity" benefits, providing double indemnity plus an additional benefit equal to the face amount if the accident is of a specified type. The most common form of triple indemnity has a very restrictive definition of the specified type of accident; passenger in a common carrier. Another much less restrictive definition specifies any motor vehicle not operated as part of the insured's occupation. One other feature sometimes added to accidental death benefits in individual policies is a dismemberment benefit providing a benefit equal to the face amount if the insured accidentally loses two or more designated body parts in an accident. The dismemberment benefit is practically universal in group life accident benefits, but much less common in individual.

Accidental death benefits frequently are limited in duration, e.g., they may not cover accidents occurring after the insured's age 70. If there is a limiting age, the extra premiums for the rider are not charged after that age. Formulas for calculation of net premiums follow life insurance formulas for term insurance net premiums. Because accidental death rates peak in the early 20's, then decline to about 30 and remain more or less level until they begin to increase at age 60 and later, accidental death benefits which terminate at age 70 do not build much reserve, it is quite common to use a level charge at each duration, calculated as a level premium term to age 70.

Reserves are usually held on the 1959 Accidental Death Benefits Table [4] and this table is also frequently used as a source of data for premium calculation. Like many tables intended for valuation purposes, this table includes some margins for conservatism. There is also a more recent report of experience [5] which contains useful data regarding the additional cost of triple indemnity benefits.

6.4   TERM CONVERSION AND GUARANTEED INSURABILITY OPTION

Most term insurance policies include a conversion option permitting conversion to a whole life policy without submitting evidence of insurability, and the premium for the term policy must reflect the cost of this benefit, unless conversion is limited to a special "conversion policy" that is priced to cover the extra mortality. The policy may require that the election must be made before a specified age (such as 65), or it may be available for the entire term period. It is also common to offer a guaranteed insurability benefit to policies other than term insurance as an extra cost rider. A typical guaranteed insurability benefit allows the insured to purchase, without evidence of insurability, additional whole life policies up to $25,000 each at policy anniversaries nearest ages 25, 28, 31, 34, 37, and 40. Clearly, such options have additional cost, since insureds who are in poor health will be more likely to elect the purchase, and the mortality under the elected policies can be expected to be less favorable than under policies that have undergone the normal underwriting process. Offsetting the extra mortality costs, however, are the savings in underwriting costs and possibly in sales costs (if the company does not allow full commissions on the elected policies). Some companies design the rider so that it terminates on any option date when the insured does not purchase the additional coverage, and this helps to limit the anti-selection.

Pricing such options involves making assumptions regarding election rates, and also assumptions regarding the mortality on the elected policies. If available, the insurer's own experience is the best source of the assumption regarding election rates. Election rates from intercompany experience are available [6], but vary widely by company. Election rates at the last age at which conversion or election is available are always much higher than at earlier durations, and are usually treated separately. To calculate net premiums, the first step is to calculate the extra mortality at each election age by a formula such as:

$$\sum_{t=1} {}_tp^C_{[x]+r+t-1}(q^C_{[x]+r+t} - q^S_{[y]+t})AR_{[y]+t}v^t$$

The age at original issue is x, duration at election is r, the age at election is y, AR represents the amount at risk on the elected policy, the C functions have the mortality rates of converted policies and the S functions have standard mortality.

The extra mortality cost for each election age is then multiplied by the probability of election at that age (which includes the probability of surviving to that election age) and discounted for interest, and the result is summed for all election ages. The net premiums can then be converted to gross premiums using the companies standard expense assumptions, reduced by the underwriting savings and the savings, if any, on sales costs.

6.5   ACCELERATED DEATH BENEFITS

The simplest kind of accelerated death benefit pays an amount based on a percentage of the face amount (often 50%) to the insured if he can show that because of a medical condition his life expectancy is very short (usually the criterion is one year or less.) The insurer, of course, incurs some cost as well as some risk in making a determination of life expectancy. An eligible insured is paid the percentage of the death benefit reduced by interest from the date of payment to their life expectancy (i.e., their actual, shortened, expectancy based on increased mortality). The death benefit and the cash value are reduced by the percentage on which the payment is based. Another variation is to treat the amount paid out as a lien on the policy. Because this benefit is approximately actuarially equivalent to the regular death benefit, most companies offering this benefit do not charge for it. The charge, if any is the cost of administering the early payment.

A somewhat more complex accelerated death benefit pays a percentage of the face amount if the insured can show that he has one of a list of specified "dread diseases." A typical list of dread diseases might include: cancer, heart attack, coronary bypass, stroke, and end-stage renal disease, each carefully defined to exclude any forms of the disease that are not life-threatening. The life expectancy of an insured with one of these conditions could vary considerably from only slightly worse than an insured in good health to a period of one year or less, and therefore there is usually no interest discount applied to the early death benefit in a dread disease type benefit. Instead, a specific charge is made for the benefit. For example, if the amount of dread disease benefit is 50%, half the net premium for the plan could be calculated using standard mortality, and the other half using special "mortality" rates based on the rates of occurrence by age of the specified diseases. One source of data for the incidence rates of the specified diseases is the U.S. National Center for Health Statistics. Insurers with sufficient experience in the health insurance business may be able to develop incidence statistics from that experience.

Equivalently, it is common to derive an adjusted set of q's somewhere between standard and the special ones that will produce premiums and values equivalent to half of each. Death rates for specific diseases are available from various sources, including the U.S. National Center for Health Statistics. The adjusted q's are then used as the periodic mortality charge in a universal life policy. The extra premium for the benefit is the difference between the q's, or on a level premium basis, the level amount whose present value is equal to the present value of the difference in q's.

6.6   LONG-TERM CARE BENEFITS

Long-term care benefits sold as riders to life insurance policies usually represent a special case of the accelerated death benefit type plan, since the payment of the long-term care benefits is usually conditioned on some reduction in the face amount of the policy. As such, the pricing technique parallels that for dread disease riders. Special "mortality" rates are used which take into account the incidence of long-term care claims, i.e., nursing home confinement or need to utilize home health care. Long-term care experience has been published that can be used for this purpose [7].

While it would certainly be possible to offer long-term care as a rider that does not reduce the face amount, (similar to a disability income benefit) many states have been reluctant to approve such a rider as a life benefit, instead requiring that it must be filed and administered as a health insurance coverage and comply with burdensome regulations covering long-term care insurance. In fact, some states have required that even the "accelerated benefit" type long-term care rider must comply with the long-term care regulations if it is advertised, marketed or offered as such. Other requirements that an insurer may have to add to make the rider qualify as an accelerated death benefit include the requirement that the condition triggering the long-term care benefit must be expected to continue till death, and an optional lump sum payout instead of the normal monthly payments for long-term care. Since the tax deductibility of stand-alone long-term care has been clarified, it offers some advantages over long-term care as rider, and the future of long-term care riders to life insurance is uncertain.

6.7   OTHER BENEFITS

The pricing principles for some of the more common benefits have been illustrated. These can be extended to other, less common, benefits. For example, a few companies offer a Beneficiary Purchase Option, allowing the beneficiary named at issue to purchase insurance without evidence of insurability at the insured's death. Another benefit sometimes encountered is a Cost of Living Purchase Option, allowing the insured to increase the benefits by some percentage based on the increase in the cost of living at specified option dates. Both can be priced using the theory of select-and-ultimate mortality, as outlined for the Guaranteed Insurability Option.

REFERENCES

1. Bowers, et al., *Actuarial Mathematics,* Society of Actuaries, Schaumburg, IL, 1986.

2. "Report of the Special Committee to Recommend New Mortality Tables for Valuation", TSA XXXIII, 1981, pp. 617-670.

3. TSA, 1978 Reports.

4. Brodie and November, "A New Table for Accidental Death Benefits", TSA XI, 1960, pp. 749-765.

5. TSA, 1977 Reports.

6. TSA, 1982 Reports

7. "Long-term Care Valuation Insurance Methods", TSA XLVII, 1996, pp. 599-774. Also, TSA, 1993-4 Reports.

REVIEW QUESTIONS

1. Name three types of benefits offered as disability riders on life insurance policies.

2. What accident benefits are commonly offered with life insurance policies? How does the rate of accidental death by age affect the pricing and design of these benefits?

3. What basic theory is used in pricing term conversion and guaranteed insurability benefits? Name two other benefits for which this theory applies in the pricing.

4. Name three common types of accelerated death benefits.

5. Why is the future of long-term care benefits as a rider to life insurance uncertain?

SECTION III

CALCULATION OF
POLICY VALUES

CHAPTER 7
LIFE AND ANNUITY
NONFORFEITURE BENEFITS

7.1 NONFORFEITURE BENEFITS

The term "nonforfeiture" actually comes from the intention of early legislation which was designed to protect policyholders from the "forfeiture" of the equity they had built up in their contracts. The term equity refers to the policyholder's share of pre-funded mortality costs similar to, but not necessarily the same as, the statutory reserve required for the policy. The earlier requirements defined this equity as the policy reserve less some constant or some percent. In today's terminology this would be called a surrender charge. The complaint about this method was that it linked nonforfeiture values, which should represent a policyholder's equity in a policy, to statutory reserves which were intended to assure adequacy. The difference between the adequacy represented by the statutory reserves and the equity represented by the surrender value was often related to an estimate of the expenses incurred to sell the policy. Although the direct linkage was eliminated in the mid-1900's, nonforfeiture values and reserves were indirectly linked until the 1980's through the requirement that the same mortality and interest be used for calculated values.

Nonforfeiture benefits are actually the options available to policyholders which allow them to recover the equity that they have built up in insurance or annuity policies through the payment of premiums or the deposit of funds in excess of the insurance charges and expenses that are rightfully and legally chargeable to the policyholder.

Prior to the legal requirements for nonforfeiture values, the values of life insurance policies were at times determined by the price that a buyer was willing to pay for the rights to the benefits of the policy if that buyer was willing to continue premiums on the policy. This was one of the early functions of Lloyds and is not unlike the viatical settlement companies that have been springing up recently in the U.S. and now primarily buy the insurance policies of individuals with terminal illnesses (e.g., AIDS).

The adoption of nonforfeiture requirements by various states provided policyholders with some value for the premiums paid into their policies. Initially these requirements applied (for the most part) only to life insurance contracts, however, they were later extended to annuity contracts during the deferred period and more recently have been extended to long-term care contracts.

The requirements for nonforfeiture values generally can be expressed in the form of actuarial equations. They effectively transfer to the policyholder the rights to the accumulation of a defined net premium after the insurance company has recovered a defined cost allowance to cover acquisition and possibly other costs.

The policyholders can exercise their option on these rights by requesting cash or, in the case of life policies, other items of value such as the continuation of some insurance coverage through extended term insurance or reduced paid-up insurance. Such other options are calculated so that their actuarial value is equivalent to the cash value of the policy at the time the option is exercised.

Life insurance policies and deferred annuities in the accumulation phase may also offer to provide an income option through what is called a settlement option. Policies or contracts usually contain a set of guaranteed settlement options which guarantee monthly incomes, either for periods certain only, or for life with or without periods certain. Companies also offer current settlement options which are calculated using current (more favorable) mortality and interest assumptions. While "current" settlement option values are not guaranteed into the future, at the time of exercise, the then current values do become guaranteed for that policy. In most cases settlement options with life contingencies do not have surrender values.

Note that when establishing reserves for a series of policies it is a good idea to review the settlement options that have been guaranteed in that series of policies. Although guaranteed settlement options generally assume conservative levels of interest at the time of the product's design, interest rates have been known to change. In addition, the mortality assumptions may not have anticipated the improvements that have been realized in annuitant mortality, and this may more than offset any interest margins that might exist.

7.1.1   LIFE INSURANCE NONFORFEITURE OPTIONS

Upon discontinuance of premiums, traditional life insurance policies generally must offer the nonforfeiture option of cash and may also offer extended term, reduced paid-up, premium loans or monthly incomes as nonforfeiture options.   Universal life insurance policies allow more flexibility in premium payments and use instead a specified minimum cash value.   Traditional life insurance applications usually indicate a standard or default nonforfeiture option and the applicant may elect otherwise from other options presented on the application.   This standard option is generally extended term insurance but may be reduced paid-up or automatic policy loans.

The use of reduced paid-up as the standard nonforfeiture option from a policy design standpoint is recommended for those coverages where the mortality experience of those policyholders accepting the automatic option is expected to be considerably higher than normal.   This may occur, for example, on policy forms for which little or no underwriting is done.

The automatic policy loan for a premium can also be used as the automatic option.   Some insurance departments will not approve policy applications that provide a premium loan as the automatic option.   This option is the preferred choice, however, for certain life contracts designed for the corporate marketplace, which rely on the loan process to fulfill their intended purpose.

While the underlying assumptions may differ between nonforfeiture options, any nonforfeiture option chosen by the policyholder should have the same actuarial value as any other option available to the policyholder at the time of election.

7.1.2   LIFE INSURANCE MINIMUM NONFORFEITURE VALUES

Minimum nonforfeiture values for life insurance are regulated by the nonforfeiture law of the state in which a policy is issued.   These requirements are applied when a policy form is filed with an insurance department prior to its use.   The requirements may also be applied during a market conduct exam by an insurance department.   During a market conduct exam the insurance department reviews, among other things, the policy forms being sold and their compliance with the laws of the states in which they are sold.

These nonforfeiture laws, similar to valuation laws, are based on models established by the National Association of Insurance Commissioners (NAIC). The NAIC model sets forth a formula for minimum cash values and details any modifications to or exemptions from this formula. The model also addresses the application of the minimum cash value to the other nonforfeiture options that were described in preceding sections.

The language in the NAIC model nonforfeiture law can be translated into an equation in actuarial notation which describes the minimum cash nonforfeiture benefit value. The concept behind the formula is to allow the company to take credit for an allowance to cover excess initial expenses associated with the issuance of a policy and then to accumulate future adjusted net premiums. The **adjusted net premiums** are calculated to cover the cost of future guaranteed benefits plus the initial expense allowance.

The excess initial expenses which the allowance is intended to cover are incurred when the company places the new insurance policy on its books and may include items such as first year commissions, underwriting costs, medical exam costs and the cost of establishing the records for the new policy at the company. Note that this expense allowance, which under the current NAIC model equals $60 ($50 in New York) per thousand of face amount for a whole life policy, does not vary by company and may not completely cover a company's actual excess expenses incurred when placing a new policy.

An actuarial representation of the minimum cash value formula described in the current version of the NAIC model nonforfeiture law for a level premium whole life policy is shown below.

$$_tCV_x = A_{x+t} - P^A \times \ddot{a}_{x+t}$$

The adjusted premium, P^A, is defined as

$$P^A = (A_x + E^1)/\ddot{a}_x.$$

The expense allowance, E^1, is defined as

$$E^1 = 1.25 \times MIN[P^{WL}, .04 \times F] + .01 \times F,$$

and the nonforfeiture net level premium for a whole life policy, P^{WL}, is

$$P^{WL} = A_x/\ddot{a}_x.$$

F is the face amount if level; otherwise F is the average face amount over the first ten years.

Note that the rounding of results from this formula varies. There exists a rather extensive set of rounding rules for the 80 CSO calculated values, but in this day of rampant personal computing they seem to have been ignored. However, the rounding rules for 58 CSO were once religiously followed and it was common to be able to reproduce previously calculated values exactly.

Some companies provide nonforfeiture values greater than the minimum required by the above formula possibly for competitive reasons or in order to meet certain product design objectives. The methods that can be used to systematically provide values that are greater than the minimum include:

- Starting with a lower initial excess expense allowance.
- Amortizing the expense allowance over a shorter period of time.
- Grading to the statutory reserve over some period of time (this may be difficult if the interest rate used for the nonforfeiture benefit calculations differs from that used for reserves).

Whatever approach is used to arrive at nonforfeiture values, they should be financially sound.

The actuary should consider the level of nonforfeiture benefits and the type of benefits expected to be chosen in the pricing of the underlying product. One train of thought is that the nonforfeiture value should follow the asset share calculated for the product or the net GAAP reserve, i.e. the GAAP benefit reserve less the GAAP expense reserve.

The mortality table used for the calculation of minimum cash values is often the same as that used for reserving. Under current mortality tables there can be differences in the form of the table being used. For example an ultimate table can be used for cash values while reserves are based on select-and-ultimate. Another exception is in the case of policies which are subject to the Norris decision, i.e. policies issued on a group basis or as part of an employee benefit program. The Norris decision is a judicial finding that requires that nonforfeiture values must be the same for males and females. However, although there is an NAIC model which allows for the recognition of this decision for nonforfeiture values, that NAIC model does not allow the use of blended unisex mortality in the calculation of reserves.

Another difference in the calculation basis of minimum cash values and minimum reserves can be the rate of interest used in the formulae. The interest rates used for nonforfeiture values have been unlinked from those used for minimum reserves and are allowed to be as much as 125% of the dynamic interest rate used for reserves (rounded to the nearest quarter of a percent).

Not all life insurance policies require nonforfeiture values. For some forms of coverage the nonforfeiture values that would be produced by the formula described above are so small as to be immaterial. Therefore, the nonforfeiture law provides exemptions for some coverages including certain level or decreasing term policies. Exemptions are also provided for reinsurance, for group insurance and for policies that do not produce cash values which by formula are greater in any year than two and one-half percent of the policies' face amount in that year.

7.1.3   EXTENDED TERM

The extended term option provides for the continuance of the face amount of the base insurance policy (less any policy loans to avoid anti-selection) for as long as the cash value will allow after which time the contract expires without value. The term for which continued coverage is provided under the extended term option is usually calculated using a loaded mortality table, the Commissioner's Extended Term (CET) table.

The reason for the use of a loaded mortality table for the calculation and reserving of the extended term benefit is that when there is a choice between reduced paid-up and extended term, those insureds who expect their mortality to be higher than normal can be expected to select the extended term. They will do this in spite of its limited length of coverage because of the greater death benefit and their higher chance of qualifying for the death benefit prior to the expiration of the remaining term. Healthier insureds expect to live beyond the term period and would, thereby, receive nothing. Therefore, they often accept the lower face amount provided by reduced paid-up insurance discussed in the next section.

Extended term values are typically expressed in terms of years and days of coverage. The approach generally used to calculate the term for which coverage can be extended is to compare the nonforfeiture value available for a given attained age to a table of extended term net single premiums for different years of coverage commencing at that attained age. The number of years is then determined as the lowest number of full years for which the net single premium is less than the nonforfeiture value. Then the number of additional days is determined as the ratio of the remaining nonforfeiture value to the cost of one more year's extended term coverage times 365 days.

As with the calculation of the nonforfeiture values themselves, rounding varies. The extended term days are often rounded to the high day. The equations shown below describe the above process of calculating extended term values.

Select the number of years, "*n*," such that

$$ETP_{x+t:n} < {}_tCV_x < ETP_{x+t:n+1}.$$

Then calculate the number of days, "*d*", as

$$[({}_tCV_x - ETP_{x+t:n})/ETY_{x+t:n}] \times 365,$$

where ${}_tCV_x$ is the policy's cash value as of the date of nonforfeiture less any loan, $ETP_{x+t:n}$ is the net single premium for extended term coverage of *n* years from attained age $x+t$ for a face amount equal to the original face amount less any loan (in order to maintain the company's net amount at risk), and $ETY_{x+t:n}$ is the cost of one year's extended term coverage from $x+t+n$ to $x+t+n+1$.

7.1.4   REDUCED PAID-UP

Reduced paid-up coverage is exactly what the name implies. It is a continuation of the base policy with a reduced death benefit and generally without riders or supplementary benefits. The reduced face amount available under this option is generally calculated using the same mortality that is used for the base policy cash values.

Due to the lower face amount under this option relative to the face amount available under the extended term option and the resultant reduced anti-selection, the use of the base policy's valuation mortality assumption is more appropriate. However, it can be anticipated that both extended term and reduced paid-up business will exhibit higher mortality than the base policy since one potential cause of electing a nonforfeiture option is disability due to illness where no waiver of premium disability benefit was purchased. If large volumes of either nonforfeiture benefits are in place it may be appropriate to review the relationship of mortality experience to the underlying mortality table used for reserving.

The formula below shows the reduced paid-up (*RPU*) insurance calculation.

$$RPU = {}_tCV_x/A_{x+t}$$

RPU is the face amount of the reduced paid-up insurance, $_tCV_x$ is the policy's cash value as of the date of nonforfeiture less any loan, and A_{x+t} is the net single premium at attained age $x+t$ for the continuation of coverage under the original form of coverage.

7.1.5   AUTOMATIC PREMIUM LOANS

This option allows the continuation of the policy through the automatic borrowing (from the insurance company) of amounts of money which are used to pay the gross premium of the policy.

The cash surrender value of the policy is used as collateral for the loans and the loans will be made as long as there is sufficient collateral (i.e., cash value) to support the payment of additional premiums plus interest on outstanding loan balances. After the collateral is no longer sufficient to pay another premium, the small remaining collateral will be used to allow the policy to continue under extended term unless additional premium is paid. The automatic loan process varies from company to company. Some policies look to the collateral at the time that the loan is made while others look to the collateral at the end of the period for which the premium will be paid. In addition, some companies will allow only the payment of annual premiums under this method while others will allow the payment of the lowest modal premium available.

The automatic premium loan option has the advantages of keeping any supplemental benefits or riders that were attached to the base policy in force and keeping any loans on the base policy in place which is not the case for the reduced paid-up and extended term options.

This was a more popular option under the former income tax law, which allowed individuals to deduct the interest paid on policy loans from taxable income. The option is still somewhat advantageous to corporate policy owners, who may be allowed to deduct the interest paid on the loan. The disadvantage of this option is that it may use up the policy's value more rapidly than the extended term option. One advantage of this option to the selling agent is that generally companies continue to pay commissions on premium paid by automatic pension loan.

7.2 UNIVERSAL LIFE NONFORFEITURE REQUIREMENTS

7.2.1 FLEXIBLE PREMIUM UNIVERSAL LIFE NONFORFEITURE REQUIREMENTS

Due to the complex nature of universal life products, the standard nonforfeiture law is not readily applicable, therefore the NAIC developed a separate set of requirements for universal life, based on a retrospective accumulation of value unlike the standard nonforfeiture law for traditional life products which takes a prospective look at values.

The NAIC model regulation for universal life sets forth requirements for nonforfeiture values as well as minimum reserves. The regulation defines the minimum cash surrender values for flexible premium universal life as being equal to the accumulation of premiums paid less the accumulation of:

i. benefit charges: charges for mortality or supplemental benefits which are subtracted in the fund accumulation process.
ii. averaged administrative charges for the first year and any insurance-increase years: these are the average administrative charges over years 2 to 20, including charges per payment, per policy, per thousand or percent of premium administrative expenses. The excess first-year and increase year charges are addressed by (iv).
iii. actual administrative charges for years other than the first-year or increase years.
iv. the excess of first-year and increase-year expense charges over the averaged amount as described in (ii) but only to the extent that these excesses do not exceed the expense allowances defined below.
v. any charges for services made at the request of the policyholder excluding cash surrender or nonforfeiture requests.
vi. any partial withdrawals.

All accumulations use the actual rates of interest credited to the contract.

The expense allowance which is used above to limit the excess first-year and increase-year expenses is initially equal to the expense allowance defined in the standard nonforfeiture law for an endowment policy with a face amount equal to the initial (or increase in) face amount of the universal life policy, with the same premium-paying period and maturing on the same date.

To the extent that the initial and increase expense allowances exceed the excess first-year and excess increase expenses, an unused expense allowance results. This amount is amortized and is effectively used to limit the surrender charges which can be imposed on the universal life insurance product.

The expense allowance is amortized by the ratio of $\ddot{a}_{x+t:\overline{n-t}} / \ddot{a}_{x:\overline{n}}$, where x is the issue age for the amortization of the initial expense allowance the age at the time of increase for the amortization of the increase expense allowance, n is the premium-paying period remaining at the point-of-issue or increase, and t is the number of years from issue or increase for the amortization of the initial expense allowance or the increase expense allowance respectively.

7.2.2 FIXED PREMIUM UNIVERSAL LIFE NONFORFEITURE REQUIREMENTS

The requirements of the universal life model with respect to fixed premium universal life insurance policies are very similar to the requirements of the standard nonforfeiture law as described in Section 7.1.1 with the exception of the definition of the nonforfeiture net level net premium.

For fixed premium universal life, the nonforfeiture net level net premium is defined as the present value of future guaranteed benefits divided by an annuity of $1 per year for the premium paying period of the policy, i.e., $PVFB/\ddot{a}_x$, where the present value of future guaranteed benefits, $PVFB$, is determined by taking into account all guarantees made in the policy or by declaration by the company including interest guarantees, guaranteed mortality charges and expense charges.

7.3   ANNUITY NONFORFEITURE REQUIREMENTS

The NAIC has also provided a model nonforfeiture law for individual deferred annuities. This model requires that the minimum nonforfeiture values for individual deferred annuities be no less than the following defined net premiums accumulated at 3% per annum.

For flexible premium deferred annuities the defined net premiums are:

First Year: 65% of gross considerations less $30 per annum and $1.25 per consideration.

Renewal: 87.5% of gross considerations less $30 per annum and $1.25 per consideration.

Decreased by prior withdrawals accumulated at 3%, decreased by any indebtedness and increased by any additional amounts credited to the contract.

There is also a provision allowing the application of the first-year loading to renewal considerations which for any year exceed the sum of all amounts previously subject to the first-year loading to the extent those excess amounts are not greater than twice the amount already subject to first-year loading.

For contracts with a fixed schedule of premiums the minimum nonforfeiture value is calculated in a manner similar to flexible premium contracts, with the condition that the first-year net premium is equal to 65% of the net consideration after annual fees and collection charges plus 22.5% of the excess of the first-year net consideration over the lesser of the second and third-year net considerations. The annual contract charge is defined to be the lesser of $30 and 10% of the gross annual consideration.

For single premium deferred contracts the methodology required for determining the minimum nonforfeiture benefit is similar to that described for flexible contracts except that the defined net premium is equal to 90% of the net consideration where the net consideration is the gross consideration less a $75 charge.

The nonforfeiture law also includes a "smoothness" requirement which requires that annuity surrender benefits equal or exceed the present value of guaranteed benefits discounted at a rate 1% higher than the guaranteed rate. The effect of this provision is to require that as an annuity approaches maturity, surrender charges cannot decrease by more than 1% per year and must equal zero at maturity.

REVIEW QUESTIONS

1.   What are nonforfeiture benefits?

2.   What nonforfeiture benefits are commonly offered with life insurance policies?

3.   What are the advantages/disadvantages of the Extended Term?

4.   What are the advantages/disadvantages of the automatic premium loan option?

CHAPTER 8
STATUTORY, GAAP, AND TAX BASIS RESERVES

8.1   U.S. STATUTORY VALUATION

8.1.1   WHAT ARE STATUTORY POLICY RESERVES?

This chapter will address the underlying concept of life insurance and annuity policy reserves and other liabilities. In addition it will cover current valuation methods.

The most recent activity in the area of valuation of life insurance and annuities has been to require that actuaries consider the assets backing reserves when rendering an opinion on the adequacy of reserves. This is required for most life insurance and annuity business by the most recent version of the Standard Valuation Law (SVL) and the accompanying Model Regulation. The State of New York acted earlier than the NAIC in addressing this issue and adopted their own requirements in New York's Regulation 126. New York has since modified their requirements to mirror those of the NAIC model valuation law. This "asset adequacy analysis" as it is called is a topic that will be discussed in considerable detail later in this Chapter and in Chapter 12.

Let us address the issue of what exactly is a "reserve."

- To the actuary, a reserve is a calculation using present value formulae, a computer model or some type of scientific estimate which produces a number which represents the funds necessary to mature the company's obligation under a life insurance or annuity contract.
- To the accountant, a reserve is a statutory liability item which shows up on page 3 of the Life Insurance Company annual statement.

- To the life or annuity contract holder the reserve is a fund set aside to guarantee their future benefits.
- To the investment department a reserve is a liability item backed by assets which must be properly invested.

For an insurance company to be solvent the reserve liabilities produced by policies must be balanced by assets. These assets might include bonds and mortgages, a summary of which appears on the asset page of the Annual Statement. These bonds, mortgages and other company investments are what will actually provide the cash flows needed to guarantee the contract holder's benefits, not the reserve.

If the actuary must consider the assets backing reserves when expressing an opinion as to the adequacy of the reserves, then the actuary must consider the timing of receipts on those assets, including interest and principal, to cover the outflow on the reserves including surrenders and benefits. This exercise is called asset adequacy analysis, cash flow testing or comparing asset cash flows to liability cash flows.

This should not to be confused with the **matching** of assets and liabilities which often refers to a matching of the Macauley durations and which is not always considered to be as accurate as cash flow testing in determining the adequacy of the assets to mature the liabilities.

8.1.2   RESERVE METHODS

Some of the reserve methods used in the past include methods such as FPT (full preliminary term) and MPT (modified preliminary term) which are described in the older sections of valuation laws and in other actuarial text. The methods of most current importance are the CRVM (Commissioner's Reserve Valuation Method) method for life insurance and the CARVM (Commissioner's Annuity Reserve Valuation Method) for annuities. These methods are to be used with specified interest and mortality rates (see Chapter 12).

The CRVM required for life insurance allows an insurance company some relief from the additional first-year cost of acquiring an insurance policy by reducing the reserve that is required in the first year below that which would be required by a level reserving method such as the Net Level Premium (NLP) method of reserving.

The NLP reserving method does not make any allowance for the higher initial expenses typically encountered in the sale of life insurance. This method is described in formula form below for a level premium level face amount whole life policy.

$$_tV_x^{NL} = A_{x+t} - P^{NL} \times \ddot{a}_{x+t}$$

where:

A_{x+t} = the present value of benefits at the end of year "*t*" for issue age "*x*",

$\ddot{a}_{x+t}$ = the present value of an annuity due of 1 per year at the end of year "*t*" for issue age "*x*" ;

$P^{NL} = A_x/\ddot{a}_x$ and

$_tV_x^{NL}$ = the reserve at the end of year "*t*" for issue age "*x*"

The table below shows the implications of this first-year deferral of reserves on a life insurance company's income statement.

Year One Income Components	CRVM	Net Level
Premium Income	$ 100.00	$ 100.00
Investment Income	10.00	10.00
Total Income	110.00	110.00
Death Claims	$ 10.00	$ 10.00
Increase in Reserves	5.00	80.00
Expenses	90.00	90.00
Total Expense	105.00	180.00
Net Income	$ 5.00	($ 70.00)

The CRVM reduction in the first year reserve must be amortized over the premium-paying period of the policy. There is also a limit on the reduction of the first year's reserve. For any contract, this reduction cannot be greater than would be realized for a 20-pay life insurance policy issued at the same age.

The CRVM is, however, the minimum statutory formula reserving method and an insurance company is free to establish higher reserves such as net level reserves or to grade the first-year reduction in reserves under the CRVM method over a period shorter than the premium-paying period of the policy. Note that additional reserves my be necessary as a result of Asset Adequacy Analysis (See Chapter 12).

The CRVM method is expressed in formula form below for a level premium level face amount whole life policy.

$$_tV_x^{CRVM} = A_{x+t} - \beta_x^{CRVM} \times \ddot{a}_{x+t}$$

where:

$$\beta_x^{CRVM} = P^{NL} + (P^{NL} - c_x)/\ddot{a}_x$$

and

$$\alpha_x = \beta_x^{CRVM} - (P^{NL} - c_x)$$

β is the modified renewal net premium and α is the net premium for the first year. In cases where, due to premium paying period or variations in face amount or premium levels, the β_x^{CRVM} produced is greater than that for a 20-pay life policy, then the quantity $(P^{NL} - c_x)$ is to be replaced by $(_{19}P_{x+1} - c_x)$.

The above formula before the $_{19}P_{x+1}$ limitation produces what are known as full preliminary term reserves. The concept of full preliminary term reserves is that the insurer doesn't have to start accumulating funds to cover future benefits until after the first year. This results in the following formula for the modified renewal reserve premium.

$$\beta_x^{FPT} = P + (P - c_x)/\ddot{a}_x$$

For a method called the New Jersey method, the quantity $(P^{NL} - c_x)$ was amortized over a period equal to the lesser of 20 years and the premium paying period without any limit on the size of the amount to be amortized. This resulted in the following formula for β_x^{NJ} which was used for years two through twenty in reserve calculations with the net level premium being used for years beyond twenty if the premium-paying period went beyond twenty years.

$$\beta_x^{NJ} = P + (P - c_x)/\ddot{a}_{x:19|}$$

The Illinois method required that in cases where the β_x^{FPT} produced is greater than that for a 20-pay life policy then the quantity $(P - c^x)$ is to be replaced by $(_{19}P_{x+1}-c_x)$ as with CRVM but is then to be amortized over twenty years or the premium-paying period if less. This is shown by formula below for the case where $(P-c_x)$ is greater than $(_{19}P_{x+1}-c_x)$.

$$\beta_x^{ILL} = P + (_{19}P_{x+1}-c_x)/\ddot{a}_{x:20|}$$

However, whole life policies are not as common as they once were and actuaries should be aware of some of the complications of the CRVM method when applied to other forms of insurance including Universal Life and Annual Renewable Term insurance which are addressed later in this chapter.

8.1.3   MINIMUM RESERVES

The SVL contains provisions for a minimum level of reserves. This provision was once called and is still sometimes referred to as a "deficiency reserve" provision. The thrust of the provision is that the calculation of prospective reserves should not deduct future net premiums that exceed the gross premium. If the gross premium is less than the valuation net premium (i.e., "deficient") then a reserve for the present value of all such deficiencies must be established. Under the current SVL, the deficiencies are defined as a minimum reserve and are calculated using the method shown below.

$$_tV_x^{DEF} = (A_{x+t}^M - G_x \times \ddot{a}_{x+t}^M) - (A_{x+t}-P_x \times \ddot{a}_{x+t}),$$

where M refers to the minimum standards of mortality and interest, G refers to the gross premium and P refers to the net premium based on the mortality and interest specified in the policy.

In practice, actuaries may consider loadings added to the base gross premium such as "modal" loadings and policy fees in determining the compliance with this requirement unless that is not allowed by the state that the reserve opinion is expressed to (there is at least one state that has issued an interpretation on this method). The actuary is also generally permitted to consider any excesses on the premiums charged for supplemental benefit premiums in comparing gross premiums to minimum net premiums.

8.1.4   UNIVERSAL LIFE RESERVES

The concept of formula CRVM reserves is not readily applicable to Universal Life policies since these contracts usually allow flexible premium payments and variations in face amounts. There are a number of states that have adopted the NAIC model for Universal Life Policies which includes definitions of universal life CRVM reserves and cash values. These requirements will also apply to fixed premium universal life, sometimes called excess interest whole life, which as the name implies has fixed premiums but credits interest in excess of some guaranteed rate to a defined account value. The more common form of universal life is that which allows variations in the premiums as well as the face amount.

The mechanics of the universal life CRVM reserve requirements for flexible contracts are described below:

1.   Calculate a "**Guaranteed Maturity Premium**" (GMP). This is the level annual gross premium calculated at the date of issue that funds guaranteed policy benefits to the latest possible maturity date considering guaranteed interest, mortality and expense loadings.

$$GMP = (PVMC_x + (E_1 - E_R) + E_R \times \ddot{a}_x + {_n}E_x)/\ddot{a}_x,$$

where: $PVMC_x$ is the present value of future mortality charges.

E_1 is the first year expense charge.

E_R is the renewal expense charge. Although it is assumed to be level here, it may vary.

${_n}E_x$ is the present value of the face amount assumed to be endowed at maturity.

All present values are calculated using the statutory valuation basis except in those states which require the use of the policy guarantees in place of the statutory basis if more favorable. Although this formula makes the calculation seem straight-forward, it can be an iterative calculation due to the monthly calculation methods that are typically used and variations in face amount tied to the guaranteed accumulation value. I.R.C. Section 7702 can require increases in face amount to maintain the insurance qualification under the federal tax code. Also, some UL policies provide "option 2" universal life death benefits which are equal to the account value plus a fixed amount.

2.   Calculate the Guaranteed Maturity Funds (*GMF*'s) of the contract on each anniversary assuming that all *GMP*'s are paid, again assuming policy guarantees.

The *GMF* is an amount which together with future *GMP*'s will mature the policy based on all policy guarantees in place at issue. Present values are calculated using the valuation basis. The formula representation of *GMF* is shown below.

$$GMF_t = PVMC_{x+t} + E_R \times \ddot{a}_{x+t} + _{n-t}E_{x+t} - GMP \times \ddot{a}_{x+t}$$

Then, on the valuation date, the greater of the actual account value and the *GMF* on that date is projected forward assuming that all future *GMP*'s are paid and a present value of the future benefits generated (*PVFB_t*) is calculated using the valuation basis. Net level premiums are also calculated using the guaranteed benefit stream available from the date of issue, and the present value of these premiums using the valuation basis (*PVP_t*) on the valuation date is then calculated. The derivation of *PVP_t* is

$$PVP_t = P_x^{ULNL} \times \ddot{a}_{x+t},$$

where

$$P_x^{ULNL} = PVFB_0/\ddot{a}_x.$$

3. A reserve is then calculated using the *PVFB_t* and P_x^{ULNL} from above, a β_x^{ULCRVM} which is defined below and a defined "*r*" factor. The "*r*" factor is the ratio of the account value to the *GMF* on the valuation date (not greater than one).

$$\beta_x^{ULCRVM} = P^{ULNL} + (P^{ULNL} - c_x)/\ddot{a}$$

$$\alpha_x = \beta_x^{ULCRVM} - (P^{ULNL} - c_x)$$

$$_tV_x^{ULCRVM} = (PVFB_t - \beta_x^{ULCRVM} \times \ddot{a}_{x+t}) \times r$$

As the above demonstration shows, the drafters of the universal life reserve requirements have designed a method which takes the reserve calculations for universal life contract back to a form similar to that used for an ordinary life contract in applying the CRVM adjustment. The definition of Universal Life CRVM essentially modifies the spread between the account value of a Universal Life policy (net deposits accumulated at interest) and the reserve by varying the traditional CRVM first-year expense allowance for changes in the account value.

There has been considerable discussion on new methods for determining universal life reserves and a number of proposals have been made by the Life and Health Actuarial Task Force of the NAIC, however, nothing had come of those proposals at the time of this writing.

The description of the universal life reserve methodology above includes comments about cases where the policy guarantees may not be the same as the valuation basis. This is not uncommon and in several states this represents a potential valuation issue since those states require (either by regulation or by interpretation) that the policy valuation basis should be replaced by the policy guarantees if the guarantees produce higher reserves. The state of California, which has such a requirement, will allow the reserve to be estimated as the mean of the account value and the surrender value in lieu of using the policy guarantees to perform a full UL CRVM calculation.

It may be tempting to assume that the surrender value (account value less surrender charge) can be used as an approximation to Universal Life CRVM reserves. However, this can be an erroneous and deficient assumption depending on the design of the Universal Life policy and the premium payment pattern of the policyholders. This is due to the "*r*" factor's impact on the CRVM expenses allowance where the account value has fallen well below the GMF. In those situations where UL CRVM reserves are required, UL CRVM reserves should be calculated in order to determine if such an assumption is valid.

The universal life model also has a "deficiency" reserve or alternate minimum reserve requirement which applies in cases where the GMP is less than the valuation net premium calculated using the minimum valuation mortality and interest. In these cases the minimum reserve is equal to the greater of:

1.   The reserve calculated according to the method described above.
2.   The reserve calculated according to the method described above only using the minimum valuation mortality and interest and by replacing the valuation net premium (β_x^{ULCRVM}) with the GMP for each year in which the GMP is less than β_x^{ULCRVM}.

8.1.5   ANNUAL RENEWABLE TERM RESERVES

Applying the *CRVM* method to annual renewable term (ART) reserves may be complicated due to the annually changing pattern of the premiums.

Similar issues apply to other renewable term plans including 5-year and 10-year renewable term. Because of this, there have been different interpretations of the approach that should be taken in applying the CRVM method to ART.

One of these approaches, the **unitary method**, assumes that net premiums are a uniform percentage of all future gross premiums. The unitary method has led to what some regulators believe are inadequate reserves at the early durations of ART plans in those situations where the plans are structured to have very competitive gross premiums in the early durations and higher premiums in much later durations.

To combat this perceived abuse, several states have established requirements that a reserve should be established for the present value of the excess of the net premiums on the reserve basis over the gross premiums and that no credit is to be allowed for those durations in which gross premiums exceed net premiums.

NAIC Actuarial Guideline IV defines the reserving methodology to be used for 1958 CSO term life insurance policies without cash values. Guideline IV applies only to 1958 CSO term plans without cash values. Under this Guideline, minimum reserves, including deficiency reserves, must be calculated separately for successive periods of level premiums. This prevents large distant future premiums from depressing near-term net premiums, which would occur if the unitary method were used (i.e., if net premiums were a uniform percentage of all future gross premiums).

This guideline also has implications for reinsurers. If a reinsurer has the right to raise premiums to net valuation premiums, the reinsurer need not hold deficiency reserves, and the ceding company gets no such reserve credit. If reinsurance premiums are guaranteed, deficiency reserves may be needed.

Different companies have made different interpretations as to the reserving requirements for non-level premium policies valued using the 1980 CSO mortality basis. Some companies use a Guideline IV approach in valuing these policies. A few states have indicated that the Guideline IV methodology is the required approach regardless of the mortality table. However, many companies continued to use the unitary reserving methodology, where net premiums are defined as a constant percentage of gross premiums in all years.

At the NAIC meeting in March, 1995, the NAIC adopted Model Regulation XXX (Reg. XXX) entitled "Valuation of Life Insurance Policies Model Regulation, including the Introduction and Use of New Select Mortality Factors."

The main purpose of Reg. XXX is to address the regulators' concerns about the adequacy of reserves for term insurance policies with long-term level premium guarantees. Regulators also are concerned about "term-like" universal life products that they feel may have been developed to avoid the Reg. XXX reserve treatment of term and term Universal Life plans.

Reg. XXX addresses these concerns by requiring companies to hold, at each valuation date, the greater of the unitary reserves and the segmented reserves, for policies with non-level premiums and/or non-level benefits. Segmented reserve calculations are also required for universal life policies which provide "no lapse" guarantees in excess of five years or which may be kept in force after the fifth policy year by the payment of minimum premiums which are less than the one-year valuation premiums at the same duration.

Segmented reserves are defined similarly to unitary reserves, except that the segmented modified net premiums are a constant percentage of gross premiums for each policy segment defined by the contract segmentation method, as opposed to being a constant percentage of all gross premiums to expiry as under the unitary method. A new policy segment is defined each time the rate of change in gross premiums from one year to the next is greater than the rate of change in the valuation mortality rates from one year to the next. For a policy with guaranteed level premiums for the first ten policy years and significantly higher YRT premiums thereafter, segmented reserves calculated for the first segment (which would be ten years long) would ignore the gross premium level after policy year ten.

If the length of the first segment is five years or less, then companies may make use of a safe harbor exemption in Reg. XXX which allows companies not to replace net premiums with deficient gross premiums during the first segment in calculating deficiency reserves. Any deficiencies after the first segment must be reserved for issue. To make use of this safe harbor, companies must demonstrate annually that the reserves held for these policies are adequate.

Major Provisions of Reg. XXX. Reg. XXX applies to all life insurance policies (with or without cash values) issued after the effective date of the regulation, except for variable life insurance policies and except for re-entry term policies that were issued prior to the effective date of the regulation and guarantee the premiums for the new policy (i.e. the re-entry). In addition, Reg. XXX applies to group life insurance certificates which contain a stated or implied schedule of maximum gross premiums that would keep coverage in force for more than one year.

Reg. XXX makes available to companies **new base select mortality factors**, multiples of which may be applied to the 1980 CSO valuation tables when calculating both basic reserves and deficiency reserves. The new base valuation selection factors are fifteen years in duration and vary by issue age, sex, and smoking status. Reg. XXX allows the use of 150% of the new selection factors for the calculation of basic reserves and 120% of the new selection factors for the calculation of deficiency reserves. Reg. XXX also allows a company to modify the new base select mortality factors by using the new base select mortality factors for the first ten policy years (modified by either the 150% or 120% multiple) and then by grading from the tenth policy year factor to the factor at the beginning of the ultimate period in policy year 16. Companies may also use the current 1980 CSO ten-year selection factors.

Policy fees may be used in the calculation of deficiency reserves, even if policy fees were not used in the calculation of basic reserves. **Basic policy reserves** at each valuation date may not be less than the greater of:

1. The unitary reserves at that duration, and
2. The segmented reserves at that duration.

In addition, basic policy reserves at each duration may not be less than $\frac{1}{2} c_x$ (assuming mid-year issues and the use of mean reserves). Other rules apply for mid-terminal reserves.

All of the basic reserves must be calculated using the same valuation mortality and valuation interest basis. Note that it is possible that the reserves for a given policy may be based on unitary reserve calculations at some durations, and segmented reserve calculations at other durations.

Total reserves (including basic reserves, deficiency reserves, and supplemental benefit reserves which would expire upon contract termination) must be at least as great as the policy cash surrender value (including cash surrender value of the supplemental benefits but before any reduction for policy loans). As written in the regulation, this **cash surrender value floor** only applies to policies with non-level premiums and/or non-level death benefits.

Unitary reserves are calculated as the present value of future death benefits and pure endowments less the present value of future modified premiums, where present values are calculated to the mandatory expiry date of the policy. Modified net premiums are defined as a uniform percentage of the respective gross premiums, where that percentage is defined as the ratio of (a) the present value of future death benefits and pure endowments plus a CRVM expense allowance over (b) the present value of future gross premiums. Policy fees that are level over the premium-paying period of the policy may be ignored in calculating unitary reserves.

Segmented reserves are also calculated as the present value of future death benefits and pure endowments less the present value of future modified premiums, where present values are calculated to the mandatory expiry date of the policy. Modified net premiums are calculated in a similar manner to the unitary reserve modified net premiums, however, the segmented modified net premiums are calculated separately for each **policy segment** (i.e., segmented modified net premiums are calculated separately for each segment as a uniform percentage of the respective gross premiums for each segment). A CRVM adjustment is allowed in calculating the modified net premiums for the first segment only.

In calculating segmented reserves and net premiums, insurers are given the option to treat unitary reserves or cash values at the end of each segment as a pure endowment and to subtract the unitary reserves or cash values applicable at the beginning of each segment from the present value of future guaranteed benefits. Without this option, segmented net premiums would not properly reflect the pre-funding of reserves on cash value policies.

The "**contract segmentation method**" is used to define the length of each segment. This method compares the slope of the gross premium scale (defined as G_t in Reg. XXX) with the slope of the valuation mortality rates (defined as R_t in Reg. XXX), and defines a new segment at each duration in which the rate of change in gross premiums from one year to the next is greater than the rate of change in the valuation mortality rates from one year to the next (i.e., $G_t > R_t$). In determining segment lengths, the rules below need to be followed.

1.   The guaranteed gross premiums are used in determining the year-to-year slope of the gross premium scale.
2.   Policy fees can be excluded in calculating the year-to-year slope of the gross premium scale only if the fees are level for the premium paying period of the policy.
3. R_t is based on the valuation mortality rates used in calculating deficiency reserves.
4.   The new base select mortality factors may be used only during the first policy segment. If the first segment is less than ten years, then the ten-year selection factors currently defined in the Standard Valuation Law may be used from the end of the

first segment to the end of year ten. Note that unitary reserves must be calculated using the same valuation mortality rates as are used in defining segment lengths and in calculating segmented reserves, and because the selection factors that may be used depend on segment lengths, segment lengths must be defined before unitary reserves can be calculated.

5.   In calculating the ratio of valuation mortality rates from one year to the next, both the numerator and denominator of the ratio need to use the same mortality basis (and the same selection factor basis). This rule is important when changing from one selection basis to another (e.g., changing from new fifteen-year selection factors to the ten-year selection factors at the end of the first segment) or when changing from selection factors to ultimate valuation rates. (This rule is not explicitly stated in Reg. XXX, but was demonstrated in sample calculations that the ACLI distributed with an earlier version of the regulation and is incorporated in Reg. 147.)

6.   In any policy year, R_t may be adjusted by $\pm 1\%$, but R_t may not be less than one. This will result in the creation of one long segment when a product's ultimate gross premium rates are set equal to a constant multiple of the valuation mortality rates (i.e., $G_t = R_t$).

Deficiency reserves for each policy, if needed, are calculated as the excess of recalculated basic reserves (defined as "Quantity A" in Reg. XXX) over the originally calculated basic reserves. The recalculated basic reserves use the gross premiums (including policy fees) instead of the modified net premiums whenever the gross premiums (including policy fees) are less than the modified net premiums.

For policies where the first segment is not greater than five years, Reg. XXX provides a "safe harbor" that allows that, even if gross premiums are less than the modified net premiums, those gross premiums do not need to replace the modified net premiums during the number of years equal to the length of the first segment in calculating either segmented deficiency reserves or unitary deficiency reserves. Note that companies must still calculate deficiency reserves and fund for them from issue if there are any deficiencies after the first segment.

Companies making use of this deficiency reserve safe harbor must demonstrate each year that the reserves held for all such policies are adequate. For a company which issues a "Section 8" actuarial opinion, this demonstration would automatically be performed as part of the cash flow testing process. For a company which issues a "Section 7" actuarial opinion, the valuation actuary will need to demonstrate, based on the company's underwriting practices and mortality experience, that the reserves held for these policies are adequate.

Under Reg. XXX, deficiency reserves are to be calculated for a given policy year on the same basis as used in defining basic reserves for that policy year. If the basic reserve is equal to both the segmented reserve and the unitary reserve, then Quantity A must be calculated on a segmented basis.

For policies with an **unusual pattern of guaranteed cash surrender values**, an additional reserve test must be performed. The reserve generated by this additional reserve test acts as a floor against which the segmented/unitary reserve must be compared. The purpose of this additional reserve is to assure adequate funding for significant increases in guaranteed cash surrender values. As written in the regulation, this additional reserve test only applies to policies with non-level premiums and/or non-level benefits. A policy is considered to have an unusual pattern of guaranteed cash surrender values if one year's guaranteed cash surrender value exceeds the prior year's guaranteed cash surrender value by more than the sum of:

1.   110% of the scheduled gross premium for that year, plus,
2.   110% of one year's accrued interest (using the nonforfeiture interest rate underlying the guaranteed cash surrender values) on the sum of the prior year's guaranteed cash surrender value and the scheduled gross premium, plus,
3.   5% of the first policy year surrender charge, if any.

Reg. XXX defines the following reserve calculations for policies with an "unusual" pattern of guaranteed cash surrender values.

- Prior to the first occurrence of an "unusual" guaranteed cash surrender value, the minimum reserve test treats the policy as providing term coverage for "n" years followed by a pure endowment equal to the cash surrender value at the end of "n" years, where "n" equals the number of years from issue to the date the first "unusual" guaranteed cash surrender value is available. Reserves are calculated during this period by assuming a segment length of "n" and defining net premiums as a constant percentage of gross premiums. A CRVM expense allowance may be reflected in the calculation of these reserves.

- Reserves after the first "unusual" guaranteed cash surrender value are calculated by assuming a segment length of "*m*" and treating the policy as providing term coverage for "*m*" years followed by an endowment equal to the next "unusual" cash surrender value at the end of "*m*" years, where "*m*" equals the number of years between the prior "unusual" cash surrender value and the next "unusual" cash surrender value. The net premiums for this segment, calculated on a net level premium basis, are set equal to a constant percentage of the gross premiums during the segment. The constant percentage is defined as $[(a) + (b)] / (c)$, where:
  - (a) equals the present value at the beginning of the segment of the death benefits payable over the "*m*" year segment,
  - (b) equals (i) the present value at the beginning of the segment of the next "unusual" cash surrender value minus (ii) the prior "unusual" cash surrender value (this prevents the incorrect inflation of the net premiums for this segment by recognizing that a reserve already exists at the beginning of the segment), and,
  - (c) equals the present value at the beginning of the segment of the gross premiums payable during the segment.

Reg. XXX provides several optional exemptions from the segmented/unitary reserve requirements including:

- Optional exemption from calculating unitary and segmented reserves for YRT reinsurance.
- Optional exemption from calculating unitary and segmented reserves for attained-age based YRT life insurance.
- Exemption from unitary reserves for certain juvenile policies.
- Exemption from unitary reserves for certain *n*-year renewable term life insurance policies.

Provisions Applicable to Universal Life Policies. Reg. XXX defines possible additional reserves for fixed and flexible premium universal life policies with secondary guarantees that extend beyond the fifth policy year. For purposes of this section, a **secondary guarantee** includes:

1.   a policy which is guaranteed to remain in force at the original schedule of benefits in excess of five years subject only to the payment of premiums specified in the policy (commonly referred to as a "no-lapse" guarantee), and,

2.   a policy in which the minimum premium at any duration beyond the end of the fifth policy year needed to keep the policy in force on a guaranteed basis is less than the corresponding one-year valuation premium based on the maximum valuation interest rate and the 1980 CSO Table With or Without Ten-Year Select Mortality Factors.

The **minimum premium** for any policy year is the premium that would produce a zero account value at the end of the policy year, assuming a zero account value at the beginning of the policy year. The minimum premiums for all contract years are defined at issue based on the guaranteed policy cost factors.

The "**secondary guarantee period**" is the longest period for which the policy is guaranteed to remain in force subject only to one of the secondary guarantees. For example, if a policy has a ten year "no-lapse" guarantee, and if the same policy has minimum premiums during the first twelve years that are less than the first twelve one-year valuation premiums, then the secondary guarantee period for this policy would be twelve years.

Secondary guarantees that are unilaterally extended by the insurer after issue must be considered as having been made at issue and secondary guarantee reserves must be recalculated from issue to reflect such extensions.

Basic and deficiency reserves for policies with secondary guarantees greater than five years are to be calculated using the segmented reserve method, and *using the specified premiums, if any, or otherwise the minimum premiums* as the gross premiums both for determining segment lengths and for defining modified net premiums. Use the specified premiums for as long as they are specified, then use the minimum premiums if the secondary guarantee period is based on minimum premiums. During the secondary guarantee period, the reserves for these policies are the greater of the basic plus deficiency reserves for the secondary guarantee and the minimum reserve otherwise required for universal life policies.

New York Regulation 147 (Reg. 147). The New York counterpart to Reg. XXX, was adopted by the New York Insurance Department in November,

1994. Reg. 147 is similar to Reg. XXX in many respects. However, there are several significant differences and other minor differences between these two regulations. The significant differences include: (a) Reg. 147 was effective for issues on or after January 1, 1994 whereas Reg. XXX will not be effective until adopted by each state. In most states, Reg. XXX will not be effective for some time. (b) Reg. 147 defines reserving requirements for issues prior to the effective date of the regulation, whereas Reg. XXX is silent on this matter; and (c) Reg. 147 may define deficiency reserves on a different basis than was used in calculating basic reserves, whereas Reg. XXX defines deficiency reserves on the same basis used in defining basic reserves.

The New York Insurance Department historically has had an unwritten rule prohibiting the use of future premium sufficiencies to offset current premium deficiencies. The Department's unwritten position has been that companies should be following a Guideline IV approach in setting reserves for non-level premium policies valued using the 1980 CSO Mortality basis. Because of the Department's desire for a formal regulation to define the acceptable reserving methodology for non-level premium policies, and because of the slow pace at which the NAIC Model Regulation was developing, the New York Insurance Department drafted its own regulation (called Reg. 147).

Differences Between Reg. XXX and Reg. 147. The table on pages 102-103 summarizes all of the differences between Reg. XXX and Reg. 147.

8.1.6 COMMISSIONER'S ANNUITY RESERVE VALUATION METHOD

The method that is required by most state valuation laws to establish reserves for single premium and flexible premium annuities is the Commissioner's Annuity Reserve Valuation Method. Prior to the establishment of this method, companies typically held the surrender value as the required reserve and sometimes, in addition, an excess interest reserve to cover the guarantee of interest in excess of the valuation rate for some period of time beyond the valuation date.

The CARVM method incorporated the excess interest reserve into the basic reserve and also included in the basic reserve a mechanism for the funding of any steep drops in the surrender charges that are often associated with this type of product. The method requires that the reserve be the

Table 8.1
Reg. XXX / Reg. 147 Differences

Difference	Regulation 147	Regulation XXX
Effective date for new issues	January 1, 1994	Whenever adopted in each state (Note: few state have adopted XXX. A number of States have set up a mechanism whereby the rule is adopted when more than 51% of the States have adopted it.)
Reserving requirements for issues prior to effective date	Defined	Not discussed
Valuation mortality basis to be used in determining segment lengths	Basic valuation mortality	Deficiency valuation mortality
Optional calculation for segmented net premiums	Allows use of only unitary reserves	Allows use of either cash values or unitary reserves
Annual actuarial opinion-required for use of five-year deficiency reserve safe harbor	Not discussed	Required
Use of alternative sets of selection valuation factors	Requires superintendent approval, even if meeting safe harbor	Different safe harbor defined (grading from select to ultimate), no superintendent approval required

Difference	Regulation 147	Regulation XXX
Use of same selection factors in both numerator and denominator in calculating R_t	Required	Not discussed, but is consistent with sample examples previously distributed by ACLI
Rounding selection factors after applying 150% or 120% factor	Round to nearest integer	No rounding allowed
½ c_x floor and cash surrender value	Applies to all policies subject to Reg. 147	Applies only to policies with non-level premiums and/or non-level benefits
Additional reserve test for policies with a pattern of "unusual" cash surrender values	Applies to policies with non-level premiums and/or non-level death benefits and UL policies with secondary guarantee	Applies only to policies with non-level premiums and/or non-level death benefits
YRT reinsurance exemption	Restricts direct writer rein-surance credit to reserve level established by reinsurer	No discussion of direct writer reinsurance credit
Jumping-juvenile exemption (refers policies that increase in face amount at, say age 21)	Based on guaranteed premiums	Based on current premiums

Difference	Regulation 147	Regulation XXX
Possible additional universal life reserves	Calculate possible additional reserves separately for "no-lapse" guarantee and minimum premium guarantee; must be calculated on both a unitary and segmented basis	Calculate possible additional reserves together for "no-lapse" guarantee and minimum premium guarantee; calculate on a segmented basis only
UL secondary guarantees made after issue	Not discussed requirements apply	Secondary guarantee reserve
Immediate payment of claims reserve	Methodology defined for all policies (new and in force)	Not discussed in Reg. XXX, but requirement contained in recently adopted NAIC Actuarial Guideline XXXII
Basic reserving methodology for universal life policies	Reg. 147 formally adopts UL CRVM methodology defined in NAIC Universal Life Model Regulation; also allows "California" safe harbor	Not discussed in Reg. XXX, but already covered in NAIC Universal Life Model Regulation

greatest of the present values at the appropriate valuation rate of the future guaranteed surrender values of the annuity contract.

$$V_t^{CARVM} = MAX[CV_t \times (1+i)^{-0}, CV_{t+1} \times (1+i)^{-1}, CV_{t+2} \times (1+i)^{-2},$$

$$CV_{t+3} \times (1+i)^{-3}...]$$

Contingent Surrender Charges. An issue that has been raised by several states in connection with this method has to do with what is referred to as contingent surrender charges. This definition includes surrender charges which are waived for one reason or another. Most of the states concerned about this issue consider contingent surrender charges to be only those surrender charges subject to some type of "bail-out" provision, i.e., a provision that allows the annuitant to surrender the contract without the imposition of a surrender charge in the event that the credited rate on the contract drops below some index or a fixed rate. A few of these states define a contingent surrender charge to be a surrender charge that is subject to any contingency, e.g., a waiver of the surrender charge upon entry into a nursing home.

The states that are concerned about contingent surrender charges do not allow the account value of the annuity contracts being reserved to be reduced by contingent surrender charges in the calculation of CARVM reserves. This used to be a problem only for those companies domiciled in those states but with the adoption by many states of the 1990 valuation law which requires the actuary to opine on the adequacy of reserves according to the laws and regulations of the state in which an opinion is being filed, the contingent surrender charge issue has become a larger issue.

A related reserve issue is the waiver of surrender charges on partial withdrawals. It is not uncommon to allow 10% of the account value to be withdrawn in any year (typically after the first year) without the imposition of a surrender charge. For annuities with this feature the benefits available in the CARVM calculation should be grossed up to take into account the waiver of a portion of the surrender charge. This is generally accomplished by reducing the surrender charge applied by the proportion of the account value subject to free withdrawal.

For example in the case of a 10% free partial withdrawal in year t

$$CV_t = AV_t - .90 \times SC_t$$

Continuous CARVM. Another issue raised by several states in connection with the interpretation of CARVM is the "continuous" CARVM issue. Initially CARVM was applied primarily using a policy-year to policy-year calculation where the value for a particular policy year being discounted back was the guaranteed surrender value at the end of that policy year. A number of regulatory actuaries felt that the valuation actuary should be discounting back to the valuation date the surrender value on the first day of the following policy year. This generally produces higher reserves since the surrender charges typically change on the policy anniversary. This continuous method requires taking the present value at whatever time during the future, (whether or not on an anniversary) produces the highest value, so it may also be interpreted to take into account any other changes in the surrender value during the policy year but not at the end of the policy year, e.g., the waiver of surrender charges during some "window" period of time in contracts referred to as CD (certificate of deposit) annuities.

8.1.7   OTHER STATUTORY RESERVE ISSUES

Immediate Annuities and Supplementary Contracts. Immediate annuities and supplementary contracts are typically the same type of animal. The difference in nomenclature and the location of their respective reserves in the life insurance company annual statement results from the source of the funds applied to purchase the immediate or deferred annuity. Funds received directly from an individual result in the classification of immediate annuity while funds transferred from another product will be classified as supplementary contracts due to the issuance of an additional or supplementary contract to define the annuity.

The reserves required are present values of guaranteed benefits using the appropriate annuitant mortality and rate of interest. (See Chapter 12 for a discussion of required interest and mortality rates for annuities.) The benefit structure can include annuities without life contingencies which can range from funds left on deposit for supplementary contracts to multi-year payouts of level or varying amounts. Contracts with life contingencies can range from life only annuities to annuities with various periods certain and may include multiple lives.

In cases where the annuity payments are not level and/or where substandard mortality was used in the pricing of the contract the actuary is guided by Actuarial Guidelines IX, IXA and IXB of the NAIC examiner's handbook which are summarized on the following page.

Guideline IX. "Form Classification of Individual Single Premium Annuities for Application of the Valuation and Nonforfeiture Laws." For the purposes of the SVL and SNFL, an individual single premium annuity is classified as immediate, as opposed to deferred, provided the first annuity payment is not more than thirteen months from issue date, succeeding payments are no less frequent than annually, and guaranteed payments in any year are not greater than 115% of guaranteed payments in preceding year.

Guideline IXA. "Use of Substandard Annuity Mortality Tables in Valuing Impaired Lives Under Structured Settlements." For substandard structured settlement annuities (structured settlements are defined in the guideline) where there are medical records to justify higher assumed mortality, minimum reserves are those which would be calculated by a constant addition to mortality rates such that the adjusted life expectancy is greater than or equal to the actual life expectancy and such that reserves grade to standard reserves at the end of the mortality table. This results in a decreasing extra percentage mortality.

Guideline IXB. "Clarification of Methods for Deferred Annuities and Structured Settlements Contracts." Guideline IXB expands upon Guideline IX and provides direction as to what to do if an annuity fails Guideline IX. If the first payment is deferred more than 13 months (and there are no cash settlement options), use the deferred annuity valuation interest rate based on the issue year method and a guaranteed duration equal to the years from issue to first payment. At the time payments begin, use the immediate annuity valuation rate for the year of issue, the year of premium receipt, or the year payments begin (but apply consistently). For "lumpy" payment patterns (i.e., individual contract with payment more than 115% of previous year's payment, and an issue year block with payment greater than 110% of previous year's payment) some options are defined that involve either splitting the block into smooth and lumpy pieces, or calculating graded interest rate reserves.

Another Actuarial Guideline, Guideline XXXIII, was adopted by the NAIC to define the valuation methods to be used for annuities that have multiple benefit streams. This Guideline is summarized below.

Guideline XXXIII. "Determining Minimum CARVM Reserves for Individual Annuity Contracts." This guideline clarifies the application of

CARVM to individual annuities with multiple benefit streams, where these benefit streams can include whole or partial withdrawals, annuitizations, death benefits, or other benefits such as nursing home related withdrawals without the application of a surrender charge.

The CARVM reserve should be the largest of the present values of all possible benefit streams. The valuation rate for each benefit stream is determined from the Plan Type and guarantee duration applicable to each benefit stream. In the case of the annuitization benefit stream, since there will probably be no cash surrender options, the Plan Type is "A" and the guarantee duration is determined as the time from the original issue date to the date that annuitization is assumed to occur.

A company may still make an election at the time of issue to value annuities with cash settlement options on a change in fund basis. However, annuity benefit streams with no cash settlement option must be valued on an issue year basis. If preferential annuitizations (annuitizations at a current settlement rate) are guaranteed, the reserve may not be less than 93% of the current accumulation fund.

This revised version of the Guideline is effective on December 31, 1998 for all contracts issued on or after January 1, 1981. The prior version was effective on December 31, 1995. Both versions included the option for a three-year grade in of any additional reserve requirements at the discretion of the state of domicile.

Curtate Reserves vs. Continuous Reserves. The actuary valuing traditional or fixed premium UL policies will also have to be aware of the frequency of compounding of the interest used in the calculation of the present values of future benefits and future net premiums.

If future benefits are assumed to be paid at the end of the policy year ("curtate" interest for benefits), the actuary should establish a reserve for the company's actual practices, which are typically to pay benefits immediately and to allow interest on benefits from the date of death to the date of payment. The reserve for immediate payment of claims is generally approximated as one-half of the applicable valuation rate times the reserves.

Reserve for Non-deduction of Deferred Fractional Premiums (and Refund of Unearned Premium). If future premiums have been assumed to be paid annually, then since it is general practice (and may be required by law) to refund any unearned premium at the date of death and not to deduct the portion of the annual premium that was unpaid at the date of death, the actuary should establish an additional reserve. This reserve is often referred to as the non-deduction (and refund of premium) reserve and is often approximated as one-half of the net premium times the reserve for the term portion only of the underlying plans (for practical purposes an average reserve per thousand is generally used in lieu of a term only reserve).

Type of Reserve Factor Applied. The actuary should also understand whether the valuation system being used is calculating interpolated reserves or applying mean reserve or mid-terminal reserve factors. The formula representations of these different reserve factors are shown below.

Interpolated Reserve:

$$_tI_x = (1-R) \times {_t}V_x + R \times (P_x + {_{t+1}}V_x)$$

where R is the fraction of the policy year which has passed as of the valuation date. This factor also assumes the receipt of a full annual premium.

Mean Reserve:

$$_tM_x = .5 \times ({_t}V_x + P_x + {_{t+1}}V_x)$$

This factor assumes a mid policy year valuation and the receipt of a full annual premium.

If mean or interpolated reserve factors are being used and premiums are assumed to be annual, then a net deferred premium asset should be calculated and the actuary should address the adequacy of the loading in the gross deferred premiums to cover the commissions and other costs of collection inherent in those premiums (in any case the actuary should address the adequacy of the loading in any due premiums to cover their costs of collection). If the loading is not sufficient to cover the costs of collection an additional liability should be established and reported on page three of the NAIC Life Insurance Company Annual Statement.

A sample calculation of the adequacy of the cost of collection of due and deferred premiums is shown on the following page.

Gross due and deferred premiums	$100,000
Less:	
Net due and deferred premiums	90,000
Loading	10,000
Average commissions on collections @ 6%	6,000
Average premium tax @ 2.5%	2,500
Administrative cost of collecting premium	2,500
Total cost of collection	$11,000

An additional reserve of $1,000 would be required to recognize the excess of the $11,000 cost of collection over the $10,000 loading.

Mid-Terminal Reserve:

$$_tMT_x = .50 \times (_tV_x + _{t+1}V_x)$$

This factor assumes a mid policy year valuation. This method should be accompanied by an unearned premium liability for any due or collected modal premiums (i.e., monthly, quarterly, semi-annual or annual premiums) which provided coverage beyond the valuation date, an advance premium liability for any modal premiums which were collected prior to their due date and a net due premium asset for any modal premiums which were due as of the valuation date.

Supplemental Benefit Reserves. The SVL defines the bases for some of the supplemental benefits which are sold with life insurance policies. These typically include accidental death benefits (ADB) and waiver of premium (WP) benefits.

ADB benefits are typically reserved for using the 1959 ADB table combined with a current mortality table and rate of interest. WP benefits are typically reserved for using the 1952 Disability table also combined with a current mortality table and rate of interest. The WP benefit will have both an active life reserve for possible future disabilities and a disabled life reserve for disability claims which have already occurred and for which a reserve must be set up to fund the waiver of premiums under that disability. However, the actuary may find the need to approximate the premium-paying reserves for these supplemental benefits. It is not uncommon to see reserves for ADB or active life WP approximated as one-half of the gross premium. In considering the adequacy of an estimate of this nature the actuary should consider the materiality of the reserve, the premium-paying period of the underlying benefit in relation to the benefit period, and the extent to which the benefit costs increase with duration.

Payor Death and Disability. When insurance is sold on the life of a minor that sale may include the addition of benefits that will continue the premiums (possibly only to some age, e.g., 21) on the policy in the event of the death or disability of the payor, typically a parent. Benefits of this nature may also be included in family policies, which package coverage of a primary insured with coverage on a spouse and/or children.

Benefits of this nature necessitate both active life reserves and reserves on the occurrence of the insured event. The reserves for the continuance of premiums on the occurrence of the insured event will of course depend on whether it is death or disability. In the case of death the reserve would be an annuity for the premium payable for the period payable using the age and sex of the beneficiary. Variations on this can be found in cases where the premiums are paid for the life of the beneficiary and a net single premium is held as the reserve for the insurance on the beneficiary. Another variation is the use of an annuity calculated without life contingencies. This can be done either as a conservative approximation or due to lack of age and sex information on the beneficiary.

In the case of disability, the reserve is generally calculated as a disabled life reserve with a benefit equal to the premium insured and a benefit period equal to the period for which premiums are to be continued.

Substandard Extras. During the underwriting process for a policy the insured may be assessed a surcharge due to anticipated excess mortality. Such a surcharge is referred to as a substandard extra. Substandard extras come in several varieties including permanent or temporary extra charges which can take the form of either percentage extras or flat extras. The type of extra being used will depend on the company's practice and the impairment of the insured.

Reserves for this additional mortality rating should theoretically take into consideration the additional mortality rating but as a practical matter an unearned premium reserve is often held, typically assumed to be one-half of the extra premium charged.

Last-to-Die Policies. Reserves for last-to-die policies are usually calcula-ted using the Frasier assumption that reserves do not change on the first death. Since this assumption also necessarily affects nonforfeiture values as well as reserves, it is usually stated and described in the policy form.

Excess of Cash Value over Reserve. After the actuary has followed the required valuation formulae for traditional and universal life, there is still the possibility that the cash value of a given policy may exceed the calculated reserve for that policy. Such a reserve must be calculated on a seriatim (policy-by-policy) basis and there is no offset allowed for those policies where the cash value is less than the reserve.

Group Conversions, Term Conversions and Guarantee Purchase Options. Although not as common as it was in the past, policyholders under group life policies and many term life insurance policies have the option to convert their coverage to a whole life form of coverage. Another somewhat comparable benefit is the guarantee purchase option which allows the policyholder to purchase additional (typically whole life) coverage at the occurrence of specific events such as marriage, childbirth or on certain policy anniversaries.

A policyholder electing any of the options described above might be selecting against the company due to information which the policyholder has, probably relating to the underwriting risk of the policyholder. Due to the probability of anti-selection and the resultant additional mortality, the actuary should establish a reserve for the excess mortality inherent in the elected options and should also consider establishing a reserve to fund the possible election of these options.

Reserves for benefits of the type described can be calculated as the present value of the excess of the mortality expected under these elected options over pricing mortality. These election reserves can then be pre-funded by accumulating pre-election reserves in relation to the probability of the options being elected.

Variable Life Products. Variable life product reserves are addressed by the NAIC model on variable life products which has been adopted by many states. The reserves for these products begin with a reserve for a compar-able non-variable product and then must be adjusted for the variable nature of the product.

This variable nature can manifest itself as sudden large drops in cash value or account value for the product. Meanwhile, the insurance company is probably still on the hook for the face amount available prior to the drop in value or there may be some other minimum death benefit guarantee (GMDB) in place. The insurance company's net amount at risk in this situation has increased and some reserve considering the possibility of this increase is required.

The reserve required by the model is the greater of:

- The full term cost for a period of one year (or the guarantee period if less) of the excess of the GMDB over the otherwise payable death benefit following a one-third drop in the value of the current assets in the separate account followed by a net investment return equal to the investment rate assumed in the contract; and

- A component designed to protect against an extended period of poor investment performance by requiring the funding of the GMDB by level payments over the future premium-paying period of the contract. (Note that this alternative applies only to fixed premium variable life products. The minimum reserve for flexible premium products is a term reserve equivalent to that defined by the first alternative above. Since the timing of future premiums is uncertain, a reserve of the second type described above cannot be calculated for flexible premium variable products.)

A term **"residue"** is defined as the prior year's reserve under this alternative and is accumulated forward using a **"Fackler type accumulation"**: that is interest at the valuation rate is added to last year's reserve, the cost of excess mortality (GMDB less DB) is deducted and a net premium as defined below is added. The reserve for the current year-end is also the residue for the following year. The formula for this iteration is shown below.

$$V_{t+1} = R_{t+1} = R_t \times (1+i) - MAX(0, GMDB - DB) \times q + P_{GMDB}(t),$$

where $R_0 = 0$.

$P_{GMDB}(t)$ is the level premium designed to fund the excess death benefit that occurs in year t and is equal to the level premium required to fund the excess, if any, of the net single premium for this excess death benefit over the "residue." The actuarial notation for this is shown below.

$$P_{GMDB}(t) = \{MAX[0, GMDB(t) - DB(t)] \times A_{x+t} - R_t\} / \ddot{a}_{x+t}$$

An earlier version of this model law required a reserve that was equal to the accumulation of the level cost assigned to the GMDB less actual claims paid and subject to the minimums described above. This approach was dropped due to the many variations in the assignment of the level cost of the GMDB. This method, however, is sometimes used for variable annuity minimum death benefit reserves.

Group Life. The present SVL doesn't provide much guidance on the reserving of group life products. As a matter of fact, some products are structured as group products to alleviate the reserve requirements that would apply if they were individual policies. The typical approach is to reserve for group ordinary (i.e., life and term) using the same method and tables that would be used for individual products. Exceptions to this will be found in those few states where a group life valuation mortality table has been specified.

The reserve for true group one-year term coverage will typically be established as the unearned premium for that coverage.

Practical Issues. In the past actuaries calculated reserves by hand on paper with or without the aid of calculators. Many of the current reserve formulae, reporting requirements and even some of the programs being used to calculate reserve factors or to apply them to inventories of inforce have been designed around older methods of reserve calculation.

Presently, however, it is the rare actuary that doesn't have access to a PC, workstation or other computer with programs or spreadsheets to calculate any imaginable reserve factors needed. These factors can then be manually coded (heaven forbid) or electronically uploaded or transferred to the computer system that is used to apply these reserve factors to the policy inventory that is being valued.

Given the state of automation of reserve calculations it is critical that today's actuary have an overall understanding of the reserve methods and interest rate and mortality table requirements as well as some knowledge of the underlying reserve formulae. It is also more important that the actuary perform reasonability checks including the trending of reserves by year for certain blocks of business since processing mistakes are more likely to occur than technical calculation errors once computer systems have been tested.

Documentation. One last practical issue that should be considered is documentation. Whatever work an actuary does in connection with statutory reserve determination, whether it is calculating approximations to certain reserves, making adjustments to system output or coding base reserve assumptions and methodology, all work should be documented. The actuary's work will be reviewed by one or more of the following: the CPA firm auditing the company, the IRS, a State Insurance Department actuary, another actuary following the actuary in later years and probably the actuary him or herself in later years. Therefore, it is essential that appropriate documentation be maintained to leave a trail that can be followed by someone reviewing the work that was done. In addition, depending on the type of work being done there may be actuarial standards of practice, valuation laws or regulations that require adequate documentation.

8.2   U.S. TAX RESERVES

Prior to the early 1980's, tax reserves in the U.S. were equal to statutory reserves with the possible addition of an allowance to adjust CRVM reserves to approximate net level reserves. This adjustment was referred to as "the 818(c) adjustment" because of the IRC section describing it. This adjustment gradually became the topic of many disputes between life insurance companies and the IRS due to product designs which maximized the tax benefits of reserving on a CRVM basis and using this tax allowance. In addition, congress and the IRS thought that life insurance companies were not paying enough taxes. So a number of changes were made to life insurance company taxation in the early 1980's including, in 1983, the requirement that reserves used in the calculation of taxable income for life insurance and annuities be computed on a basis defined by the IRS.

This new tax reserve basis required the use of the commissioner's methods, i.e., CRVM and CARVM. In addition, mortality tables were specified and interest rates were initially defined using statutory definitions and later redefined as the applicable federal rate (AFR). The mortality table and interest rate initial definitions were based on "prevailing" state requirements which were defined as the mortality and highest interest rate requirements in place in 26 or more states at the beginning of the contract year in which the policy was issued. The tables on pages 116 and 117 provide some of the prevailing rates. The IRS also issued a regulation in 1983 addressing lines of business for which there were no prevailing tables. The tables required to be used in the calculation of tax reserves for taxable years beginning after December 31, 1983 are described on pages 118-119.

Table 8.2
Prevailing Tables and Interest Rates

| Year(s) | Ordinary Life | | | | Individual Annuity | | | | Group Annuity | |
| | Interest | Tables | | | Interest | | | Tables | Interest | Tables |
		Life	Disa.	Indust.	Immed.	SPDA	Other			
1948-59	3.5%	41CSO	1926 DT	41CSI	3.5%	3.5%	3.5%	37SA	3.5%	37SA
1960-61		58CSO								
1962			Period 2					A49		GA51
1963-73				61CSI						
1974								71IAM		71GAM
1975-79	4.0%				6.0%	4.0%	4.0%		6.0%	
1980-81	4.5%				7.5%	5.5%	4.5%		7.5%	
1982		80CSO								
1983-84	Dynam.				Dynam.	Dynam.	Dynam.		Dynam.	
1985-87								83A		83GA

Year(s)	Ordinary Life					Individual Annuity				Group Annuity	
	Interest	Tables				Interest			Tables	Interest	Tables
		Life	Disa.	Indust.		Immed.	SPDA	Other			
1988	7.77%					7.77%	7.77%	7.77%		7.77%	
1989	8.16%					8.16%	8.16%	8.16%		8.16%	
1990	8.37%					8.37%	8.37%	8.37%		8.37%	
1991	8.42%					8.42%	8.42%	8.42%		8.42%	
1992	8.40%					8.40%	8.40%	8.40%		8.40%	
1993	8.10%					8.10%	8.10%	8.10%		8.10%	
1994	7.45%					7.45%	7.45%	7.45%		7.45%	
1995	6.99%					6.99%	6.99%	6.99%		6.99%	
1996	6.63%					6.63%	6.63%	6.63%		6.63%	
1997	6.33%					6.33%	6.33%	6.33%		6.33%	
1998	6.31%					6.31%	6.31%	6.31%		6.31%	

Table 8.3

Tables to Be Used When There Is No Prevailing Table

Type of Contract	Table
Group term life insurance (active life reserve)	1960 CSG Mortality Table
Group life insurance (active life reserve); ADB	1959 ADB Table
Permanent and paid-up group life insurance (active life reserve)	Same tables as are applicable to males for ordinary life insurance
Group life insurance (active life reserve); disability income benefits	The tables of period 2 disablement rates and the 1930 to 1950 termination rates of the 1952 Disability Study of the Society of Actuaries
Group life insurance; survivor income benefits insurance	Same tables as are applicable to group annuities
Group life insurance; extended death benefits for disabled lives	1970 Intercompany Group Life Disability Table
Credit life insurance	1958 CET Table

Type of Contract	Table
Supplementary contracts involving life contingencies	Same tables as are applicable to individual immediate annuities
Noncancellable accident and health insurance (active life reserve); benefits issued before 1984	Tables used for NAIC annual statements of December 31, 1983
Noncancellable accident and health insurance (active life reserve); disability benefits issued after 1983	1964 CDT Table[1]
Noncancellable accident and health insurance (active life reserve); accidental death benefits issued after 1983	1959 ADB Table
Noncancellable accident and health insurance (active life reserve); after 1983 other than disability and accidental death	Tables used for NAIC annual statement
Noncancellable accident and health insurance (claim reserves); disability benefits for all years of issue	1964 CDT Table[1]
Noncancellable accident and health insurance (claim reserves); all benefits other than disability for all years of issue	Tables used for NAIC annual statement

[1] In 1988 an update to this list of tables was provided which required that the 1985 CIDA tables be treated as new prevailing tables as of December 26, 1989 for individual disability.

The prescribed tax reserves were therefore, CRVM or CARVM reserves calculated using the prescribed tables and interest and were calculated net of any due and deferred premiums. The IRS requires that the tax basis reserves be equal to the greater of the net surrender value of the contract and the reserves determined under the federally prescribed basis. In addition, the tax reserve is not allowed to be greater than the statutory reserve.

When a new prevailing table is adopted, the company has three years in which to start using the table in the calculation of tax reserves and for other than annuity contracts, the company is allowed to use the prevailing interest rate for the previous year on a contract-by-contract basis.

Companies are allowed to carry the statutory as the tax reserve for certain supplemental benefits including guaranteed insurability, accidental death benefits and waiver of premium. Care must be taken when performing the cash value comparison test when supplemental benefits are involved. The IRS defines a category of supplemental benefits as "qualified supplemental benefits". These are supplemental benefits for which a defined separate premium is charged and where the cash value under the base contract is not available (except through automatic premium loan) to fund the supplemental benefit. For qualified supplemental benefits, the cash value comparison test is made excluding any reserve for the supplemental benefits. For supplemental benefits which are not qualified supplemental benefits, the cash value comparison test is made including any reserve for the supplemental benefits with the reserve for the base policy. An example of the implication of this distinction is shown below.

TAXATION OF QUALIFIED vs. NON-QUALIFIED SUPPLEMENTAL BENEFITS

	Qualified	Non-Qualified
Base Policy Prescribed Reserve	$3,800	$3,800
Supplemental Benefit Reserve	50	50
Tax Reserve Compared to Cash Value	3,800	3,850
Cash Value	4,000	4,000
Tax Basis Reserve	4,050	4,000

8.3   U.S. GAAP VALUATION

8.3.1   GAAP FOR LIFE INSURANCE COMPANIES

In addition to calculating financial results for the statutory annual statement, most life insurance companies also calculate an additional set of financial results based on Generally Accepted Accounting Principles (GAAP). GAAP financial results differ from statutory results in a number of important respects. Life insurance GAAP accounting standards were first introduced with the publication of *Audits of Stock Life Insurance Companies* (The Audit Guide) in 1972.

Life insurance GAAP accounting standards are now codified in Statements promulgated by FASB. There are three Statements specific to the life insurance industry, all of which provide a specific exemption for mutual insurance enterprises:

- SFAS 60, *Accounting and Reporting by Insurance Enterprises*. Published in 1982, SFAS 60 extracted the specialized life insurance accounting practices from the Audit Guide.
- SFAS 97, *Accounting and Reporting by Insurance Enterprises for Certain Long-Duration Contracts and for Realized Gains and Losses from the Sale of Investments*, was adopted in 1987. SFAS 97 defines accounting standards for investment contracts, limited-payment contracts and universal life-type contracts.
- SFAS 113, *Accounting and Reporting for Reinsurance of Short-Duration and Long-Duration Contracts*, was adopted in 1992.

Mutual companies were also exempt from SFAS 12, *Accounting for Certain Marketable Securities*. However, SFAS 12 has been superseded by SFAS 115, *Accounting for Certain Investments in Debt and Equity Securities*, which does apply to mutual companies.

With exemptions from certain GAAP standards in hand, most mutual companies adopted the position that their statutory statements were "in conformity with generally accepted accounting principles." They essentially ignored *all* FASB Statements, instead of those for which they were specifically exempt. This position went virtually unchallenged for 20 years.

8.3.2   SFAS 60 AND THE BASICS OF GAAP RESERVES

SFAS 60, which is applicable to traditional, non-participating contracts, is a "premium-based" model and earnings emerge in relation to gross premiums (i.e., Deferred Acquisition Cost (DAC) is amortized instead of being expensed as with statutory accounting). SFAS 97, described later, is applicable to annuities and universal life-type products. SFAS 97 is a "margin-based" model and earnings emerge in relation to estimated gross profits.

GAAP reserves differ in two important ways from the reserves that the company calculates for its statutory financial statements:

- GAAP reserves are calculated on an interest and mortality basis selected by the actuary, not a basis specified by law. Also, GAAP reserves include specific provision for lapses and payment of cash values or other nonforfeiture benefits.
- GAAP reserves include a specific provision for amortization of a part of the cost of acquiring the policy called Deferred Acquisition Cost (DAC). Deferrable acquisition costs include only those expenses that are directly related to the production of new business. The reserve offset arising from DAC is calculated on the same basis as the benefit reserve. Acquisition costs are almost always heaviest in the policy's first year, but can also be present in years after the first. For example, the extra commission costs arising from a heaped commission scale (a scale with higher commissions in the early renewal years) are usually included in DAC.
- The assumptions used for calculation of GAAP reserves usually include some provision for **adverse deviation** (that is, a margin for conservatism) but are usually not as conservative as those required for statutory valuation.

8.3.3   SFAS 60

The mechanics of calculating GAAP reserves is generally very similar to that for calculating statutory reserves. A **Benefit Net Premium** is calculated as a level percentage of gross premiums equal to the present value of death benefits, cash values and all other benefits provided by the policy.

Once the assumptions for amortization of benefits and expenses are established at the issue of a policy, they are **locked in** under SFAS 60.

Changes in experience do not lead to any changes in the GAAP assumptions. An exception to this rule is loss recognition resulting from gross premium valuation when the premiums and investment income don't support the claims and expenses.

8.3.4 SFAS 97

Statement 97 establishes GAAP accounting standards for universal life insurance contracts. The statement also establishes accounting standards for limited-payment insurance contracts and investment contracts and amends Statement 60, Accounting and Reporting by Insurance Enterprises with respect to the reporting of realized gains and losses on investments. Statement 60 will remain in effect for those contracts not covered by Statement 97.

The key points contained in Statement 97 include:

- The retrospective deposit accounting method, which establishes the account balance as the benefit liability, must be used for universal life contracts.
- Deferred acquisition costs (DAC) of universal life contracts are to be amortized based on a constant percentage of the present value of **estimated gross profits (EGP)**.
- For universal life policies the revenues are the mortality and other charges to the policy account value, rather than the premium receipts. Premium receipts represent an increase in the policyholder's account balance. Any front-end fees (extra charges in the first year) are deferred and amortized using the same methodology as for DAC.
- Gains or losses resulting from replacement of other life insurance with universal life are to be recognized at the time of replacement.
- For limited-payment contracts revenue and income recognition are to take place over the period that benefits are provided, not just the time that premiums are payable.
- Contracts without significant mortality or morbidity risks, e.g. most deferred annuities, are not to be accounted for as insurance contracts. Payments received are to be reported as liabilities and accounted for in a manner consistent with accounting for interest-bearing or other financial instruments.

- Realized investment gains and losses are to be reported on a pretax basis as a component of other income and shall not be deferred to future periods. (This also extends to some unrealized gains under SFAS 115, as is explained further on.)
- There is no provision for adverse deviation in the assumptions.
- If actual experience differs from earlier assumptions, allows for retrospective unlocking of assumptions.

8.3.5   GAAP ACCOUNTING FOR MUTUAL LIFE INSURANCE ENTERPRISES

Since life insurance GAAP accounting standards were first codified in the early 1970's, mutual life insurance companies and fraternal organizations have been granted exemptions from certain standards. They have routinely included a statement in their Audit Opinions that their statutory financial statements are "in conformity with generally accepted accounting principles."

The **Financial Accounting Standards Board** (FASB) clarified, with the promulgation of Interpretation 40 in 1993, that mutual life insurance enterprises are exempt only from three specific GAAP accounting standards, namely Statements 60, 97 and 113. Mutual companies who wish to publish GAAP financial statements must follow all other GAAP standards, including (but not limited to) the following:

- SFAS 106, *Employers' Accounting for Postretirement Benefits Other Than Pensions*
- SFAS 109, *Accounting for Income Taxes*
- SFAS 115, *Accounting for Certain Investments in Debt and Equity Securities*

Interpretation 40 does not address how mutual companies should account for their business; it merely states that mutual companies will no longer be able to portray their statutory statements as being in conformity with GAAP. The result of Interpretation 40 is that it makes it difficult for mutual companies to obtain a clean GAAP opinion since neither SFAS 60 nor SFAS 97 provide specific accounting standards for their participating business. FASB addressed this issue by urging the Mutual Life Task Force of the American Institute of Certified Public Accountants (AICPA) to resurrect its project on developing mutual company GAAP accounting standards.

AICPA SOP. Interpretation No. 40, published in 1992, clarified FASB's position regarding mutual company GAAP financial statements. However, it did not remove the exemptions to SFAS 60, 97, and 113, and it did not provide any alternative authoritative guidance for mutual companies to follow. To rectify this situation, FASB urged the AICPA to resurrect its Task Force on mutual company GAAP and bring it to an expeditious conclusion. FASB made its request to the AICPA in August, 1992, the same time that it first proposed Interpretation No. 40.

The AICPA responded with a Statement of Position (SOP) pertaining to "Accounting For Certain Insurance Activities of Mutual Life Insurance Enterprises." The SOP was released as an Exposure Draft on March 24, 1994 with a 90-day comment period.

The SOP applies to the following entities which are specifically exempt from the provisions of SFAS 60, 97, and 113:

- mutual life insurance companies,
- fraternal benefit societies,
- assessment enterprises, and
- wholly-owned stock subsidiaries of mutual insurance enterprises.

The SOP accounting standards apply only to long-duration participating life insurance products that have the following characteristics:

- They are expected to pay dividends to policyholders based on the actual experience of the insurer.
- They pay annual dividends in accordance with the Contribution Principle, that is, dividends are determined in a manner that distributes divisible surplus in approximately the same proportion as the policies are considered to have contributed to that surplus.

"Long-duration" contracts, as defined in the Audit Guide, include whole life, endowment, and most contemporary term products. "Short duration" contracts include non-renewable and non-convertible term contracts of less than five years, group term life and credit life.

Products issued by mutual companies that do not meet the criteria defined by the SOP (including all non-life products and life products that do not pay dividends) use the appropriate principles from SFAS 60 and SFAS 97 as their GAAP accounting basis.

SFAS 60, which is applicable to traditional, non-participating contracts, is a "premium-based" model and earnings emerge (i.e., DAC is amortized) in relation to gross premiums. SFAS 97, which is applicable to annuities and universal life-type products, is a "margin-based" model and earnings emerge in relation to estimated gross profits.

After reviewing both premium-based and margin-based accounting models, the AICPA Task Force concluded that a margin-based model is more appropriate for the participating business of mutual life insurance companies. Along with being margin-based, the SOP model is similar to SFAS 97 in that:

- It requires *retrospective unlocking* of assumptions (SFAS 60 requires assumptions to be "locked in" at time of policy issue, except when future losses are anticipated);
- Assumptions are to be based on best estimates, with no provision for adverse deviation.

However, because of the differences between participating and universal life-type business, there are also several differences between the SOP and SFAS 97 models, such as:

- *DAC Amortization Basis*: The SOP defines "Estimated Gross Margins" (EGM) as the basis for amortizing DAC. These are different from the "Estimated Gross Profits" defined by SFAS 97.
- *DAC Amortization Rate*: Under the SOP, the interest rate for amortizing DAC is the net investment income rate the company assumes it will earn. Under SFAS 97, DAC is amortized at the interest rate credited to policyholder balances.
- *Policyholder Balance*: This is the amount against which a policy's investment earnings are measured. Under the SOP, this balance is equal to a net level premium reserve and, for limited payment contracts, an unearned premium reserve (both of these items are described below). Under SFAS 97, this balance is the account value of a universal life contract.
- *Income Statement Items*: Gross premiums under the SOP are included as revenue (except in the case of limited-payment contracts), whereas they are treated as deposits under SFAS 97. The total amount of death and surrender benefits are included as expenses under the SOP; under SFAS 97, the amounts reported for these benefits are reduced by reserves released.

Estimated Gross Margins (EGM's). EGM's form the basis for amortizing DAC and the Terminal Dividend Liability (described below). Unlike Estimated Gross Profits under SFAS 97, EGM's are comprised of familiar items from the traditional income statement. EGM's are comprised of the following components:

- Premiums: Except for limited payment contracts, these are the gross premiums the company expects to receive. For limited payment contracts, these are net premiums, and any excess of gross over net premiums is brought into income in a constant relationship with insurance in force.
- Deferred Revenues: This is the deferred income from limited payment contracts described above.
- Investment Income: This amount is the investment income on prior year Policyholder Balances and current year cash flow (including realized capital gains, but not unrealized capital gains). Cash flow excludes Terminal Dividends and Deferrable Expenses.

less

- Policy Benefits: These include the total Death and Surrender Benefits that are expected to be paid.
- Expenses: These are recurring administration expenses and acquisition costs that are not deferrable.
- Increase in the Net Level Premium Reserve: This reserve is calculated using a traditional statutory approach, with interest and mortality assumptions defined by the SOP as follows:
  (a) The interest rate is the **dividend fund interest rate**. This is the interest standard, determined at policy issue, against which interest gains are measured in the dividend calculation (for many companies, this will be their statutory valuation interest rate). If this rate cannot be determined, then the guaranteed cash value interest rate should be used instead.
  (b) Mortality rates are the same as those used in calculating guaranteed cash surrender values.

- Annual Policyholder Dividends: These are annual cash dividends. Terminal Dividends are not included. In general, for the purposes of calculating EGM, dividends should be assumed to be paid in cash. However, if the design of a certain product anticipates a specific dividend option (such as PUAs), the EGM of the dividend option should be included as part of the policy's EGM.

plus

- Other Expected Assessments and Credits

Liability for Future Policy Benefits. The SOP defines the GAAP benefit reserve as the sum of the following:

- Net Level Premium Reserve: This is the statutory-type net level reserve defined above.
- Unearned Premium Reserve: This is the outstanding deferred revenue attributable to limited-payment contracts. This reserve, along with the Net Level Premium Reserve, comprise the Policyholder Balance.
- Terminal Dividend Liability: The SOP views Terminal Dividends as expenses that should be recognized over the life of a book of business in proportion to EGM.
- Loss Recognition Reserves: Reserves for any probable future losses (defined in Paragraphs 35 to 37 of SFAS 60).

Retrospective Unlocking. This concept was first introduced in SFAS 97, and it is included as part of the SOP. It requires companies to periodically evaluate and revise their EGM when experience or other evidence suggests it is appropriate to do so. For example, a change in the dividend scale would usually be considered to affect EGM enough to require unlocking of assumptions. These changes in EGM affect both past and future DAC amortization amounts. The changes in the amount already amortized (the retrospective adjustments) are charged or credited to earnings in the year the adjustment is made.

Relationship With SFAS 115. SFAS 115 established new rules that require companies to present investments in marketable equity securities and many debt instruments at fair market value. This requires companies to consider unrealized gains and losses, and report them, net of taxes, according to how the assets are characterized (described below). Unrealized gains that are reported as adjustments to equity are brought into the income statement when they are realized. SFAS 115 applies to:

- Marketable equity securities whose fair market value can be readily determined.
- All debt securities whether marketable or not.

SFAS 115 defines three classes of securities: **Held to Maturity (HTM)**, **Available for Sale (AFS)**, and **Trading**. HTM assets (applicable only to debt instruments) are still reported on an amortized cost basis; assets in the other two categories must be reported at fair market value. Unrealized gains and losses from AFS securities are reported as a change in equity, while those from the Trading category are recognized as income.

The relationship between the SOP and SFAS 115 lies in the DAC amortization. The Securities Exchange Commission (SEC), which has authority over financial statements for companies with publicly traded securities or variable life insurance, has ruled that, for margin-based GAAP standards, unrealized gains and losses produced by SFAS 115 should be included as a component of EGM (or EGP under SFAS 97). Thus, in determining the net effect on equity, unrealized gains (losses) are offset by an accelerated (reduced) amount of DAC amortization.

The amount of DAC amortization included in the income statement is not affected by the SEC decision; the inclusion of unrealized gains on AFS securities in the EGM (or EGP) is an adjustment to equity. This requires companies to maintain two DAC amortization schedules. One is required for the income statement (where unrealized gains are excluded), and the other, a **"Shadow DAC"** which includes unrealized gains as if they were realized, is required to make the proper adjustments to the balance sheet.

8.3.6 Amendments to SFAS 60, 97, and 113

Concurrent with the publication of the SOP Exposure Draft, FASB released an Exposure Draft of Amendments to SFAS 60, 97 and 113. The AICPA requested changes in the Statements in order to maintain consistency between the provisions of the SOP and the Statements promulgated by FASB. The Amendments to SFAS 60, 97 and 113 are:

- Remove the mutual company exemptions that currently exist in SFAS 60, 97 and 113;
- Instruct mutual companies to apply the accounting standards of SFAS 60 and 97 to their contracts, except for those contracts that are within the scope of the SOP (the SOP

requires mutual companies to apply the SOP accounting standards to those contracts defined by its scope);

- Permit stock companies to apply the accounting standards of the SOP to business they may have that is within the scope of the SOP. (A stock company is not required to apply the standards of the SOP; however, if it elects to do so, the SOP standards must be applied to all of its business that is within the scope of the SOP.)

Necessity For GAAP Statements. Mutual companies are generally not required to prepare GAAP financial statements. Their regulatory requirements are fulfilled when they file their statutory annual statements with the various State Insurance Departments. They can most likely publish Annual Reports to policyholders that exclude the Audit Opinion language that the financial data is "in conformity with generally accepted accounting principles" without causing a significant stir among policyholders.

Why then, should mutual companies put forth the significant time, expense and resource commitment to prepare GAAP financial statements? Following are some of the more compelling reasons for doing so.

- SEC Requirements: Mutual companies that issue variable products are required to file their financial statements with the SEC. The SEC usually requires GAAP financial statements; however, given the current lack of authoritative GAAP accounting standards for mutual companies, the SEC allows mutual companies (and their wholly-owned stock subsidiaries) to file statutory financial statements. (SEC Regulation S-X, Rule 7-02(b)). Mutual company GAAP accounting standards will be in place once the SOP and the Amendments to SFAS 60, 97, and 113 are finalized. When this occurs, the current SEC exemption for mutual companies will be eliminated. Mutual companies will then be required to prepare GAAP statements in their filings with the SEC.
- Demutualization: GAAP financial statements are a prerequisite for companies to demutualize. If an Initial Public Offering (IPO) is part of the company's demutualization strategy, the disclosure document (S-1) must include audited GAAP results for the three most recent years, as well as two additional years of unaudited GAAP results. The SEC also requires annual reporting of GAAP earnings for publicly-owned companies.

The SOP does not apply to stock insurance companies (other than stock subsidiaries of mutual companies). On the surface this would appear to create a discontinuity in accounting for participating business as companies converted from mutual to stock ownership. However, the amendments to SFAS 60, 97 and 113 provide a solution to this potential problem. The amendments include a provision that allows (but does not require) stock companies to apply the SOP accounting standards to their contracts that fall within the scope of the SOP. Therefore, a mutual company that prepares GAAP financials in preparation for demutualization would be able to use the same accounting basis for its participating business after its conversion.

Another issue related to demutualization is the data-gathering process. Much of the same effort in collecting data for a GAAP conversion is also required for demutualization. A well-planned and documented effort during the GAAP conversion may save a significant amount of effort if the company later pursues demutualization.

- Directors: Statutory financial statements are a constant source of frustration for many mutual company Boards of Directors. Statutory statements, with their inherent conservatism and focus on solvency, do not provide enough depth of information for directors to make sound business decisions.

  Directors have increasingly demanded more meaningful financial data. With no GAAP standards in place, companies have responded by preparing "management GAAP" or "modified GAAP" statements to meet this demand. With new accounting standards in place, directors will likely demand actual GAAP statements.

- Audit Opinions: Mutual companies publish Annual Reports based on statutory financial data for the benefit of their policyholders and other interested parties. These reports include an Audit Opinion from an independent accounting firm stating that the financial data has been prepared "in conformity with generally accepted accounting principles." With FASB's adoption of Interpretation No. 40, companies will no longer be able to state that statutory results are in conformity with GAAP. Companies that do not conform with GAAP standards will be required to include in their Audit Opinions a statement that their financial results "do not fairly represent the financial position of (company name) and are not in conformity with generally accepted accounting principles."

The language change in the Audit Opinion will likely have little effect on most policyholders. However, financial statements are scrutinized more closely in the upscale markets, especially in sales to corporations. Mutual companies operating in these markets will find themselves at a competitive disadvantage if they lack a clean Audit Opinion.

- Rating Agencies: Organizations that rate life insurance companies analyze numerous sources of data. A company that does not have a GAAP financial statement with a clean Audit Opinion may be viewed negatively relative to its competitors by some of the rating agencies.

Impact on Mutual Companies. The level of effort mutual companies must expend to implement GAAP standards depends on the magnitude of their past GAAP efforts. In general companies can be categorized as follows:

- Companies with no GAAP financials.
- Companies with "Management GAAP" financials.
- Companies with GAAP financials based on SFAS 60 principles.

Companies with no GAAP financials. These companies have always presented statutory financial statements as being prepared in accordance with generally accepted accounting principles. They have had little internal or external pressure to prepare statements on any other basis.

Companies in this category are likely to be fraternal organizations and smaller mutuals. Unless they have an immediate compelling reason to do otherwise, these companies will likely defer their GAAP conversions until a more urgent need develops.

For those that do convert, the task will require a tremendous expenditure of time and resources. The SOP and SFAS 60, 97, 106, 109, 113, and 115 (among others) will have to be implemented simultaneously. This process will require a significant amount of education and an organized effort among Accounting, Actuarial, Tax, Systems, and Investment Valuation resources.

Companies with "Management GAAP" financials. Recognizing the short-comings of statutory accounting principles, these companies developed internal statements that emulate GAAP in one way or another. The primary purpose of these statements is to provide management with more meaningful information with which to make corporate decisions; compliance with actual GAAP principles was often a less important concern.

These companies may find significant differences between their "Management GAAP" and actual GAAP financials. Those that find it necessary to convert to actual GAAP may undergo a transition period, during which time they will prepare "GAAP" statements on both bases. This situation will most likely occur in those companies that use "Management GAAP" financials as a basis for compensation or performance measurement.

Companies with GAAP financials based on SFAS 60 principles. These companies have already developed GAAP financials that they believe are in compliance with all existing accounting standards. However, since there are no standards for participating business, most companies applied modified SFAS 60 principles to this block of their business.

These companies have a significant investment in their current GAAP systems. GAAP financials are important to these companies, and they would prefer to maintain their current approach (as evidenced by their comments to the SOP Exposure Draft). The SOP will affect the GAAP profits of these companies, and it will force them to retool their systems to gather the data they need in order to comply.

Conclusion. The development of GAAP accounting standards for mutual insurance companies fills a hole that has existed since the Audit Guide was published in 1972. With standards in place, there will inevitably be an increase in demand by regulators, directors, CEOs, and the general public for mutual companies to produce GAAP financial statements.

The GAAP conversion process will require a significant commitment of time and effort, especially for companies with little, if any, GAAP financial reporting experience. The focus of this effort will certainly be on adopting SFAS 60, 97 and SOP accounting standards, but a more-than-trivial effort will be required to adopt other standards. SFAS 106, 109 and 115 are just three examples of other GAAP accounting standards that must be addressed as part of the conversion process.

REVIEW QUESTIONS

1. What is a reserve? Is it an asset or a liability? Please explain.

2. Discuss the reasons for using CRVM instead of Net Level reserves.

3. Why would a company want to carry reserves greater than the minimum required, and how might they calculate these reserves?

4. What is XXX?

5. How and why do tax reserves differ from statutory reserves?

6. How and why do GAAP reserves differ from statutory reserves?

7. Why should Mutual Life Insurance companies use GAAP accounting?

CHAPTER 9
DIVIDENDS AND OTHER
NON-GUARANTEED ELEMENTS

9.1 DIVIDENDS

The payment of dividends on life insurance has been common almost since the beginning of life insurance in North America. Many of the earliest life insurance companies on this continent were mutual companies, and paid dividends in some form almost from the time of their charters. (Most of the early dividends were probably proportional to premiums, as is common for casualty insurance dividends.)

Life insurance contracts usually extend over many years, and it is impossible for the issuing company to predict the actual cost of insurance on a reasonably accurate basis. Therefore, individual life insurance currently being issued almost always involves some kind of dividend or other non-guaranteed element. The company can then base its **guaranteed** premiums on a reasonably conservative set of assumptions, and refund any overcharge as a dividend. This has the advantage, from the company's standpoint, of reducing the level of risk that the company must take in issuing the policy. Policyholders also benefit from this arrangement (i.e., redundant premiums and resulting dividends) since they are spared the cost of the surplus an insurer would have to hold to cover the additional risk of fully guaranteed costs.

True **non-participating** life insurance (i.e., insurance for which the original guaranteed premiums are charged without an offer or expectation of any return or reduction in cost) was once quite common, but virtually disappeared in the late 1970's when dramatic fluctuations in interest rates began to make it impossible to guarantee long-term costs at levels reasonably related to market interest rates.

9.2   THE MUTUAL COMPANY PHILOSOPHY

Mutual life insurance companies were the original issuers of **participating** life insurance (insurance on which dividends are paid) and in some jurisdictions (e.g., New York and Massachusetts) they are not permitted to issue individual life insurance on any other basis. Mutual companies differ from stock companies not only by this requirement that all policies be participating, but also in the form of their ownership. In practice almost all life insurance issued by mutual companies is participating, even where this is not required. Mutual companies are not owned by stockholders, or any outside agency. In most cases, the managers of a mutual company will consider that the policyholders (who are responsible for electing directors on a periodic basis) are the company owners, even in situations where this may not be technically correct. For example, in some cases the ownership is technically vested in the management, with policyholders in a special debtor relationship. [1]

The special relationship of the management to policyholders in the mutual company gives rise to the mutual company philosophy. The important element of this philosophy, from the standpoint of dividend distribution, is the expectation of **equity** in dividend distribution; the distribution of gains to the sources from which they arose. This is also sometimes referred to as the "**Contribution Principle**."

Traditionally, mutual companies have managed their dividend scales more actively than stock companies. For example, in the period 1982 to 1992, when interest rates first rose to record highs and then began a gradual but continuous decline, there were several stock companies that did not deviate from the dividend scales originally illustrated on 1982 issues .[2] During the same period, almost all mutual companies went through the process of raising dividends, and later cutting them.

9.3   THE CONTRIBUTION FORMULA

The contribution formula was devised to calculate dividends based on three of the most important sources of gain and loss for life insurance companies, mortality, investments and expenses. At one time, dividends were determined entirely by use of the formula for many companies, but this would be quite unusual at the present time. Quite often, however, dividends are determined by some other method (such as the asset share method) and a contribution formula is devised to fit the dividends as determined.

The contribution formula is sometimes called the "three-factor method" because the formula for dividends consists of three terms. Each of the three terms compares the experience of the company with the assumptions used in setting gross premiums and reserves. They are: an investment earnings term (called "Factor i" in the discussion that follows), a mortality term ("Factor m") and an expense term ("Factor e").

9.3.1 THE INVESTMENT FACTOR

Factor i of the contribution formula is intended to return as dividend those elements of surplus gain that are related to investment income. It is usually calculated as:

$$(i' - i) \times (P +_{t-1}V) \tag{9.1}$$

where i is the interest rate used in calculating reserves, i' is a (usually higher) rate representing the actual returnable investment earnings, and $P +_{t-1}V$ is the initial reserve for policy year t. If the contribution formula were used directly to calculate dividends, it would probably be more appropriate to have the interest return (i.e., the $(i' - i)$ term) multiplied by an asset share or fund. In practice, however, many companies find it convenient to use either net level or modified initial reserves in this term. The investment interest rate i' is the element of this term subject to variation to fit the desired dividend schedule. If dividends were being developed directly, it would equal the companies net investment earnings rate, less any amount held back as a required surplus contribution, plus adjustment for capital gains.

As is true in the example shown, Factor i is usually the largest part of the total dividend especially at the later durations. Also, it is important to note that for permanent life insurance, Factor i increases in size with duration (assuming a constant difference between i' and i). This is not generally true of the other two factors. Elements of company gain or loss that are not strictly related to investments (especially federal income tax) are sometimes charged directly against this factor because their incidence by duration follows a similar pattern.

9.3.2   THE MORTALITY FACTOR

Factor *m* of the contribution formula returns those parts of the gain that depend upon mortality. Factor *m* is usually calculated as:

$$(q_{x+t} - q'_{x+t}) \times (1000 - {_t}V) \tag{9.2}$$

Where q_{x+t} is the mortality rate based on the mortality table used in establishing reserves, q'_{x+t} is the (usually lower) mortality rate actually being experienced, and $(1000 - {_t}V)$ is the **net amount at risk**, i.e., the amount the insurance company stands to lose if the insured dies, calculated as the difference between the reserve and the amount of insurance payable at death. Dividend factors are usually calculated per $1000 of insurance face amount, so for a policy with level death benefit equal to the face amount, the net amount at risk is $1000 less the reserve per thousand $({_t}V)$. Some approximation for the net amount at risk is often used for policies with non-level face amounts. As with the investment element, the use of the death benefit less an asset share or fund would probably give a more theoretically correct net amount at risk, but this refinement has little practical effect, and is seldom used. While the difference between the mortality rates in this formula may increase or decrease with duration, the net amount at risk on a whole life policy always decreases at the advanced ages, and therefore so does the mortality factor in the dividend.

In the example shown, valuation mortality has been calculated using 1980 CSO Non-Smoker Table B. Experience mortality was based on a modification of this table. In practice, most insurance companies have either a table of their own construction or some percentage of a standard table (perhaps varying by age, plan and duration) to represent experience mortality.

9.3.3   THE EXPENSE FACTOR

The final term in the three-term contribution formula, Factor *e*, is intended to return any excess of loading in the policy gross premium over the expenses needed to sell, issue and administer the policy. Factor *e* is usually calculated as:

$$(1 + i') \times [G \times (1 - r_t) - P - E_t] \tag{9.3}$$

where G is the gross premium, P is the valuation net premium, r_t is the percentage of premium expense at duration t, and E_t is the expense per \$1000 of face amount at duration t. While there may be many expenses that do not actually vary by either the amount of premium or the face amount, an attempt is usually made to allocate all expenses to one factor or the other. To the extent that they are not allocated to Factor i, the contributions to required surplus, to taxes, and where applicable the dividends to stockholders are usually charged to this term.

9.3.4 OTHER ADJUSTMENTS TO THE CONTRIBUTION FORMULA

However theoretically correct a company may make its dividends by using the contribution formula, it is likely that the total dividends that the formula will distribute will differ from the company's **divisible surplus;** the amount of dividends the company's board of directors has established to be distributed for the year. To adjust for this, the final contribution formula dividends may be of the form:

$$(1-a)(Factor\,i + Factor\,m + Factor\,e) - b \qquad (9.4)$$

where a and b are constants (of course, either or both may be zero) that adjust the total contribution formula dividends to the divisible surplus.

An argument can be made that equity is preserved with non-zero values of a and b as long as they do not vary by series, but are the same for all policies. However, all values of a and b other than zero diminish the ability of the dividend scale to allocate the correct reward to true sources of gain, and most actuaries look on adjustments like this as a practical expedient only and attempt to keep a and b near zero to the extent possible.

The process of dividend determination is fundamentally retrospective, in that dividends are determined based on past experience. However, once dividend experience has been established and current dividends have been determined, it is usual to project dividends for at least twenty years into the future. An important test of a dividend scale is the company's ability to maintain it in future years if experience does not change.

Table 9.1, on the following page, shows an example of contribution formula dividends projected twenty years from issue. In the example shown, experience interest is 5.5%, valuation interest is 4.5%, and valuation mortality is 1980 CSO Table B Non-Smoker. Experience mortality was calculated as 50% of this table at the first duration, 51% at the second

Table 9.1
Dividends Calculated on the Contribution Formula
Whole Life, Non-Smoker, Age 35

t	r_t	E_t	$1000q_x$	$_{t-1}V_{35}$	Factor i	Factor m	Factor e	Dividend
1	95.00%	$5.00	1.68	0.00	$0.11	$1.47	($16.35)	$0.00
2	10.00%	2.00	1.78	9.34	0.20	1.49	(0.87)	0.82
3	10.00%	2.00	1.89	19.01	0.30	1.52	(0.87)	0.94
4	10.00%	2.00	2.03	29.02	0.40	1.55	(0.87)	1.08
5	10.00%	2.00	2.17	39.37	0.50	1.58	(0.87)	1.21
6	8.00%	2.00	2.34	50.07	0.61	1.61	(0.58)	1.64
7	6.00%	2.00	2.51	61.11	0.72	1.63	(0.29)	2.06
8	4.00%	2.00	2.70	72.52	0.83	1.65	0.00	2.48
9	4.00%	2.00	2.91	84.28	0.95	1.66	0.00	2.61
10	4.00%	2.00	3.13	96.42	1.07	1.66	0.00	2.73
11	4.00%	2.00	3.38	108.94	1.19	1.66	0.00	2.85
12	4.00%	2.00	3.64	121.83	1.32	1.64	0.00	2.96
13	4.00%	2.00	3.93	135.12	1.46	1.61	0.00	3.06
14	4.00%	2.00	4.25	148.81	1.59	1.57	0.00	3.16
15	4.00%	2.00	4.58	162.89	1.73	1.50	0.00	3.24
16	4.00%	2.00	4.97	177.39	1.88	1.43	0.00	3.31
17	4.00%	2.00	5.41	192.28	2.03	1.49	0.00	3.51
18	4.00%	2.00	5.92	207.57	2.18	1.55	0.00	3.73
19	4.00%	2.00	6.50	223.21	2.34	1.62	0.00	3.95
20	4.00%	2.00	7.14	239.21	2.50	1.68	0.00	4.18

duration, and so on, up to a level of 100% in the fifty-first and later years. The gross premium is $13.73 (130% of $10.56, the net level premium). As a final adjustment, dividends were adjusted by adding .6202 to the value of E_t shown.

9.4 DIVISIBLE SURPLUS AND THE DIVIDEND LIABILITY

Establishment of both the amount of dividends to be distributed and the way in which they will be distributed is the responsibility of the insurance company's management and board of directors. While it is not always strictly necessary to do so, almost all companies employ an actuary, either as a consultant or company employee to assist them in determining dividends.

An actuary so employed will usually prepare a report to management indicating how the dividends were calculated and comparing the **policy factors** (generally, items determined at policy issue) and **experience factors** (items determined based on recent experience) on which the dividends are based. *Actuarial Standard of Practice No. 15* sets forth the appropriate contents of such a report. The company management is, of course, free to modify the actuary's suggestions in any way it deems appropriate, as long as there are no overriding legal restrictions. Often, as indicated, the management may modify the amount to be distributed (i.e., the divisible surplus) to meet the company's financial goals. When management does so, the actuary may modify some of the experience factors (such as i', q'_{x+t}, r_t or E_t) or make use of the adjustments described in the preceding section.

As a standard practice of life insurance accounting, life insurance companies set up a **dividend liability** at the end of each year equal to the total amount of dividends the company's dividend scale will distribute over the coming year with appropriate adjustment for persistency if, as is usually the case, payment of the dividend is contingent on the policy being in force on its anniversary. An advantage of the contribution formula for dividend determination is that the dividend liability is fairly easy to determine from other values in the year-end financial statement (Premiums, Reserves, and Face Amounts in force).

One disadvantage of the contribution formula, even with asset share tests, is that it does not result in regular emergence of additions to surplus.

Cody [3] has developed a five-factor formula that results in steady and regular additions to surplus on a GAAP basis. The extra terms adjust for gains on surrender and amortization of initial expenses.

9.5   THE ASSET SHARE METHOD

Dividends for almost all participating policies at the present time are developed on some form of the asset share method. In its simplest form, the asset share method consists of developing target asset share amounts at specified durations and then determining the annual dividends that will produce these target amounts. As easy to describe as this simple form of the asset share method is, it has several important disadvantages. Since negative dividends are not practical, it may be impossible to exactly meet any arbitrarily established targets for all plans and issue ages. It would be difficult, as well as illegal (except for assessment companies) to require the policyholder to pay more than the premium to keep the policy in force for any year. Moreover, prospective policyholders (and the company's sales force) have definite pre-established ideas about what a dividend scale should be like. In particular, they expect that dividends will begin by, at the latest, the end of the second policy year, and that they will increase with duration for any policy form that has cash values that increase with duration. Some companies also pay dividends in the first year, even though the asset share is almost never positive earlier than the third or fourth year.

For these reasons, the asset share method is usually applied in very general terms, with a few, usually long-term, targets, and a formula (very often the contribution formula) fitted to the durations for which there are no targets. Some companies will say that their dividend formula is "the contribution formula with asset share tests," while others say they use "the asset share method with a contribution formula fitted." In practice, these are by far the most common dividend methods. Table 9.2, on the following page, shows dividends developed on the asset share method using a target asset share of 104% of CRVM reserves at the end of twenty years. Two dividend scales were calculated meeting this target. The first is a "pure" asset share scale, the formula being $Dividend = Dividend_{t-1} \times (1.1)$. (Dividend A) The second scale uses a contribution formula with policy factors as defined for this policy (4.5% 1980 CSO Table B with 25% loading in the gross premium) and the same experience factors as are used in developing the asset share. (Dividend C) In spite of the use of the same experience factors as are used for the asset share, the contribution formula requires modification to fit the asset share because:

- The contribution formula includes no factor for persistency.
- An adjustment is required to compensate for the large negative dividend that the contribution formula would generate at the end of the first year.
- The asset share developed is more than 100% of the reserve.

In the example shown, the adjustment to the contribution formula was made as a constant deduction from Factor *e*, in this case a constant amount of $.6202 at all durations.

Table 9.2
Asset Share Method - Dividend Examples

Duration	Dividend A	AS-Reserve B	Dividend C	ModAS-Rsv D	DivC-DivA
1	$0.00	($5.95)	$0.00	($5.95)	$0.00
2	1.01	(6.01)	0.82	(5.81)	(0.18)
3	1.11	(5.74)	0.94	(5.32)	(0.17)
4	1.22	(5.48)	1.08	(4.85)	(0.14)
5	1.34	(5.27)	1.21	(4.41)	(0.13)
6	1.47	(4.79)	1.64	(3.99)	0.16
7	1.62	(4.05)	2.06	(3.62)	0.43
8	1.78	(3.03)	2.48	(3.28)	0.69
9	1.96	(2.05)	2.61	(2.99)	0.65
10	2.16	(1.02)	2.73	(2.64)	0.57
11	2.37	0.04	2.85	(2.21)	0.48
12	2.61	1.13	2.96	(1.69)	0.35
13	2.87	2.21	3.06	(1.05)	0.19
14	3.16	3.28	3.16	(0.28)	0.00
15	3.48	4.29	3.24	0.67	(0.24)
16	3.82	5.25	3.31	1.83	(0.52)
17	4.21	6.24	3.51	3.22	(0.69)
18	4.63	7.25	3.73	4.88	(0.90)
19	5.09	8.29	3.95	6.88	(1.14)
20	5.60	9.34	4.18	9.28	(1.42)

9.6   OTHER METHODS OF DIVIDEND DETERMINATION

Some companies calculate an **Experience Premium (EP)** for each age based on actual mortality and expense experience, and then calculate the dividend as:

$$({}_{n-1}V+P)^*(i'-i)+(GP-EP)(1+i') \tag{9.5}$$

This method, called the **Experience Premium Method**, has the advantage of leveling out the last two terms of the contribution formula, and always produces dividends that increase with duration if a policy has level premiums and reserves that increase with duration. By a similar procedure, (i.e., by including interest experience and surrender gains as well as mortality and expense in the experience premium) it is possible to derive a level percentage of premium (perhaps varying by age or plan, but not by duration) and distribute dividends on this basis. This is called the **Percentage of Premium Method**. The Percentage of Premium Method is rarely used for life insurance or annuities in the United States and Canada. Another method rarely used on this continent, but once common in the United Kingdom is the **Reversionary Bonus Method**. In the Reversionary Bonus Method, the divisible surplus is distributed as a uniform percentage of face amount to each policyholder.

9.7   TERMINAL DIVIDENDS

In addition to the amount paid annually, some companies pay an additional amount when the policy terminates by death or surrender. This may be considered the excess of the asset share over the sum of the reserve that will be released at termination and the amount that a terminating policy should contribute to surplus for the benefit of future policyholders. Often, the terminal dividend is calculated as a percentage of the reserves or asset share. For example, using the asset shares developed in this chapter (which reached 104% of reserve after twenty years), terminal dividends might be calculated as 1% of the reserves beginning in the fifteenth year. Another method of calculating terminal dividends would be to pay any excess of the asset share over 103% of the reserve as a terminal dividend. This latter formula will give terminal dividends that are steeper by duration.

Nearly a century ago, it was common to pay dividends on a policy only once every ten years. Policyholders who terminated before every tenth duration received nothing, and those who persisted received very large dividends (sometimes called "tontine dividends"). The New York law requiring annual distribution of surplus was introduced to curb these tontine dividends, which were perceived as an abuse. Since similar effects could result from the use of terminal dividends, the New York Insurance Department will not approve terminal dividends that ever exceed more than about 3.5% of the face amount, and requires that the progression by duration be smooth.

9.8   DIVIDEND OPTIONS

Once a dividend is due to a policyholder, the policy usually provides that it may be:

- Taken as cash.
- Used to pay premium.
- Left with the company to accumulate at interest.
- Used to purchase paid-up insurance (called **dividend additions**) at the net valuation rate.

In addition to these four options, which are legally required to be offered in many jurisdictions, many companies also offer an option which allows the policyholder to use some or all of the dividend to purchase one-year term insurance. A common form of "fifth dividend option" allows the use of the dividend to purchase a combination of term insurance and paid-up additions equal to the reserve (or, sometimes, the cash value). Thus, this option is similar to option B on a universal life policy.

The option was used at one time for "minimum deposit" insurance, where the amount paid each year was the premium plus loan interest less the dividend and increase in the loan value, thus resulting in a maximum policy loan each year. Using this option, the insured can enjoy a more-or-less level amount of insurance for many years even though the policy has a maximum policy loan against it. Usually, the option fails at extreme ages, and dividends are no longer sufficient to maintain insurance up to the amount of the reserve. Moreover, changes in the tax law have made minimum deposit insurance much less attractive than when policy loan interest was deductible for tax purposes.

9.9 DIVIDEND ILLUSTRATIONS

Since dividends significantly reduce the actual cost of insurance, a prospective insured has a legitimate concern with the level of dividends he can expect to receive on his policy. It is very nearly universal practice for projected future dividends to be illustrated in some form as a part of the sale of a participating policy. Quite often this is in the form of a table of future dividends (sometimes applied under one of the dividend options) together with future premiums, cash values and amounts of insurance. When applicable, terminal dividends are usually shown too, sometimes separately, and sometimes combined with cash values under a heading such as "cash available at termination."

9.10 EQUITY AMONG CLASSES

As mentioned earlier, equity in dividend distribution is a legal requirement in many jurisdictions, and the *Actuarial Standards of Practice* make it a professional imperative for the actuary developing a dividend scale. Problems can arise, however, from the fact that actuaries do not all agree on the definition of equity, and also from the fact that different companies are free to choose different sets of dividend classes, in accordance with each company's objectives.

At one extreme, each policy's costs would be entirely borne exactly by that policy and only that policy, thus destroying the advantage of insurance. At the other extreme, all costs would be spread over all policies. Neither extreme would satisfy a practical definition of equity. In very general terms, some ways in which companies define equity, and attempt to maintain it between classes might include:

1. Investments: While a few companies may still spread all investment earnings over all business (as was once common), most companies now use a variety of different experience rates for different classes of business. Distinctions by class for the purpose of applying experience interest rates might include:

    (a) Policies with loans: If the loan interest rate is less than the experience rate for other investments, many companies use a lower rate proportional to the amount of loan. While it was once held that only distinctions existing at issue constitute legitimate dividend classes [4], the very high rates that became available on non-loaned assets in the early 1980's made the equity of this rule more questionable. The equity was questioned because, in effect, this rule results in policies without loans subsidizing policies with loans through the dividend scale. Most companies have now abandoned this rule as it regards policy loans.

(b) Ranges of issue years: Allocation of investment earnings by ranges of issue years for dividend purposes is usually described as "an investment year method dividend formula." The principles used to establish the rates by range of years are usually based on averaging of the rates that the company has determined by investment year for the allocation of earnings by line of business.

(c) Policies with differing investment objectives, e.g., qualified pension business, or a special line of annuities. In some cases, a separate investment segment is formally established for such issues.

2. Mortality: Most companies distinguish experience mortality by issue age, sex, and smoking habits. Experience mortality is allocated by age using some graduated mortality table. (It would not be sensible to penalize policyholders at a single issue age because of a large claim at that age.) Many, but not all, companies also distinguish by policy duration to reflect the effect of selection. Policies in separate underwriting classes (e.g., guaranteed issue, term conversion or substandard) often have separate experience mortality factors. If material changes in underwriting have taken place over the years, there may be distinctions by broad ranges of issue years.

3. Expenses: It is very common to spread at least some part of the expense to all policies in proportion to the amount in force. Expenses that depend on premium (commissions, premium taxes, etc.) are usually allocated directly in proportion to premium. Series of issues that have a way of varying premiums by size (policy fees, amount bands, etc.) usually will have administrative expenses up to the level charged directly in the premium allocated per policy with the remainder allocated in proportion to amount of insurance. Since the dividend scale can almost never bear the high level of expense in the first

    policy year (i.e., without creating large negative dividends), it
    is common to amortize some or all of the excess first-year
    expense.

4. Retained Surplus: A company may have higher surplus needs
    for some policies than for others.[1] For example, since policy
    loans require less risk-based-capital than other investments, it
    would be reasonable to have lower retained surplus goals for
    loaned policies than for unloaned.

5. Withdrawal Experience: Classes frequently recognized as
    having differing withdrawal experience include:

    (a)   Term (versus permanent) insurance

    (b)   Pension issues

    (c)   Ranges of issue years

    (d)   Series priced for and/or sold in different markets

    (e)   Loaned business

6. Riders and Other Policy Variations: It is quite well established
    that it is both equitable and legal to charge through the
    dividend scale for losses on riders[2] (i.e., by paying lower
    dividends to policies that include the rider). It is also usual to
    charge by lowering the dividend for policies that have
    unusually favorable settlement options, unusually favorable
    renewal or conversion privileges (on term), etc.

As long as distinctions between classes reflect actual experience
differences which may reasonably be expected to be consistent from year-
to-year, they are usually considered equitable. In general, making more
distinctions will make a scale more equitable. As has been pointed out,
however, one limit in establishing the number of dividend classes arises
from the principle that it is not logical to make distinctions that cost more
to make than the benefit available from the distinction to the more favored
class [5].

---

1   Some actuaries argue, however, that distinction among classes in the amount of
retained surplus is inherently inequitable. D. Hagstrom, "Insurance Company Growth," TSA
XXXI, explores this issue.

2   In the case Rhein vs. New York Life, it was established that the company was
justified in paying lower dividends to policies that carried an unprofitable disability rider.

9.11   INDETERMINATE PREMIUMS

Indeterminate premium policies have a premium which the company retains the right to redetermine from time to time, subject to a maximum indicated in the policy, and sometimes limits imposed by the regulatory authorities. Most such policies are issued by stock companies and are non-participating except for the premium redetermination feature. However, some mutual companies issue indeterminate premium policies, usually for term insurance. As required by most mutual company charters, such policies will be participating, but in most cases, the company will reflect experience by adjusting the premium and does not normally expect to ever pay any dividends. Adjustments to the premiums are made on a class basis, based on expected future experience, in accordance with *Actuarial Standard of Practice #1.* Unlike dividends, the adjustments do not distribute past gains or attempt to recover past losses.

9.12   NON-GUARANTEED ELEMENTS IN UNIVERSAL LIFE

Universal life policies are usually sold with an illustration projecting the current mortality, interest and expense elements, and also the guaranteed elements, together with the anticipated results on both the current and guaranteed basis. Such illustrations are, of course, subject to the Life Insurance Illustrations Model Regulation as described in Section 9.14. In addition, most state laws governing universal life require that similar illustrations be prepared either once a year or as often as the current experience elements are changed on a given policy. As with indeterminate premium, some universal life insurance is technically participating, sold by companies that never expect to pay any dividends, but to re-price through the non-guaranteed elements.

Since the policyholder normally sees each of the experience elements separately, there may be some effort to make each element meet policyholder expectations on its own. This is in contrast to participating life insurance, for which all elements are combined in a single dividend and information about the elements contributing to the dividend is not normally available to the policyholder. Also, each universal life element is usually separately capped, and thus it may be necessary to charge excess expense losses, for example, through the mortality element. The charge of one element's costs through a term nominally associated with another element may be either because the cap prevents charging the costs in the expected way, or because the company management has chosen to reallocate costs to meet what the management perceives as policyholder expectations.

9.13   DETERMINATION OF NON-GUARANTEED ELEMENTS

From the actuary's point of view, determination of the non-guaranteed elements in universal life or indeterminate premium policies is governed by *Actuarial Standard of Practice #1,* The Redetermination (or Determination) of Non-Guaranteed Charges and/or Benefits for Life Insurance and Annuity Contracts. Determination (or redetermination) is normally a prospective process, in contrast with the process of dividend determination, which is normally retrospective. Asset share tests of some kind are almost always used to verify that the elements determined can be justified over the next several years if there is no change in the underlying experience (or the anticipated experience, in the case of a new issue)

As with dividend determination, the actuary responsible for the determination of non-guaranteed elements prepares a report indicating the contract factors (interest, mortality and expense factors guaranteed at issue) and the anticipated experience factors. It is usual to test the effect of deviations from the anticipated future experience (sensitivity testing) and include a description of the results in the report.

9.14   LIFE INSURANCE ILLUSTRATIONS

The NAIC Model Regulation on Life Insurance Illustrations includes extensive requirements on the dividends and other non-guaranteed elements that may be illustrated. This model regulation was approved by the NAIC in 1995, and the actuary's responsibilities under this regulation are the subject of Actuarial Standard of Practice Number 24 (December 1995). The regulation is now in effect in a sufficient number of jurisdictions that most companies are now following it. The regulation provides the following:

- For appointment of an Illustration Actuary who is responsible for annual certification of the company's **Disciplined Current Scale** (of dividends or other non-guaranteed elements), the Illustration Actuary must meet certain requirements to demonstrate his competency for this responsibility.

- The rules for determining the assumptions on which the Disciplined Current Scale should be based. In general, assumptions are to be not more favorable than the company's actual experience, with no anticipation of future improvements in experience, although expected future deterioration should be recognized. The expense assumption may be based on the company's actual expenses (either "fully allocated," i.e., with all actual historical expenses charged to a line of business, or "marginally" allocated, with the indirect expenses such as corporate overhead not allocated only to the extent that they don't exceed the **"Generally Recognized Expense Table,"** (**GRET**) or they may be based on the GRET. GRET provides a level of expenses approved each year by the NAIC and which is intended to approximate average expenses for all companies in the industry with similar distribution systems. GRET was introduced to prevent smaller companies from being unable to compete due to economies of scale. One exception to the requirement for use of historical experience is a rule allowing reflection of actual changes in practice that have taken place but whose effect on experience has not yet manifested itself, such as the introduction of new underwriting standards or staff reductions before they have direct effect on mortality or expense rates.

- A set of procedures under which the Disciplined Current Scale must be tested. The test consists of an accumulation at interest and persistency of the actual cash flow for the policy including the Disciplined Current Scale under the designated set of assumptions. The test is passed if, for every duration after the fifteenth, the accumulated cash flows exceed the "illustrated policyholder values." Generally, the illustrated policyholder value is the cash value. A second test (waived for policies without cash values) is also required to be sure that the Disciplined Current Scale is not "lapse supported." This test is the same as the other, with all the same assumptions, except that persistency for every duration after the fifth is assumed to be 100%. This test is also passed by having the accumulation exceed the illustrated policyholder values for every duration after the fifteenth. The twentieth duration can be substituted for the fifteenth on survivorship life for both tests.

In the absence of the NAIC Model Regulation, state laws on dividend illustrations usually require:

1.   The illustration must state which elements are not guaranteed.
2.   If non-guaranteed elements or results based on them are shown, guaranteed elements or results must also be shown and given at least equal emphasis.
3.   **Interest-adjusted cost indices** must be shown. An interest-adjusted cost index evaluates the level annual value of projected cash flows for ten or twenty years at a specified rate of interest, usually 5%.
4.   Dividends illustrated must be on the *current dividend scale*.

Since the law requires that illustrated non-guaranteed elements be based on the current scale, a natural tension exists between the desire to make dividends as high as possible so that illustrations will be competitive and the need to keep them low to prevent dissipation of surplus. Usually, one or more classes of existing business differ materially from the new business being illustrated in such basics as plan of insurance, underwriting, valuation assumptions, loading, and so on.

REFERENCES

[1]   Black and Skipper, *Life Insurance*, Eleventh Edition, Prentice Hall, Des Moines, 1987, pp. 507.

[2]   *Best's Review*, August 1993.

[3]   Cody, Donald D., "An Expanded Financial Structure for Ordinary Dividends," TSA XXXIII, 1981, pp. 313-338.

[4]   Winters, Robert C., "Philosophical Issues in Dividend Distribution," TSA XXX, 1978, pp. 125-138.

[5]   Jackson, R.T, "Some Observations on Ordinary Dividends," TSA XI, 1959, pp. 764-796.

REVIEW QUESTIONS

1. What is "The Mutual Company Philosophy"?

2. Name the three factors in the contribution formula and give their formulas.

3. What are two common adjustments to the contribution formula?

4. What is the Asset Share method of dividend distribution? How can it be combined with the Contribution Method?

5. What are terminal dividends, and how can they be calculated?

6. What are the four common dividend options? What is the "fifth dividend option"?

7. What is a Disciplined Current Scale? What two tests must it generally meet?

8. Name six ways in which companies sometimes make distinctions among classes for dividend purposes.

9. How do adjustment of indeterminate premiums and calculation of other non-guaranteed elements differ from dividend determination?

SECTION IV

PROFIT TEST
CALCULATIONS

CHAPTER 10
PROFIT TESTING

10.1   INTRODUCTION TO PROFIT TESTING

Profit testing is an essential part of the pricing process. After a product suggestion has had a tentative price developed, and the set of pricing assumptions has been determined, the profit testing process begins. In most cases, the first time a profit test is applied to the set of tentative prices and assumptions, it yields a different profit margin than the company's target.

Profit testing mechanisms should, therefore, be flexible, since the next step is the consideration of what changes can be made in prices, assumptions, or plan design that will help the company meet their product needs at their desired level of profit. An early step in profit testing is a "sensitivity analysis." Sensitivity analysis uses the pricing model that has been chosen to estimate the effects on prices or profits of making small changes in assumptions generally varying major assumptions one at a time. The pricing model is run initially for the base scenario and then run separately for each variation in assumption. It is not unusual to have many different sets of prices and assumption scenarios tested before a final pricing level is agreed upon.

Profit testing must also be fairly complete. If there are "weak points" in the set of profit tests (i.e., classes or ages where the desired profit level is not achieved), those are the ages or classes that are most likely to attract higher than expected sales. Profit testing cannot afford, therefore, to overlook them.

These requirements of good profit testing methods, flexibility and completeness, tend to be antagonistic to each other. The more complete a profit test is, the less flexible, and vice versa. This text will describe several methods of profit testing that strive to maintain a balance between the two.

10.2   LOADED NET PREMIUMS

Loaded Net Premiums (sometimes called **Hoskin's Method**) is more a method of developing gross premiums than a profit testing method. Essentially, a net premium providing for mortality, surrender benefits and required profit at various durations is calculated at realistic interest, mortality and surrender assumptions. To this net premium is added a percentage load (plus, often a level amount) intended to represent the expenses. The expense load may be arrived at in many ways (including estimates and approximations) but generally the present value of the load is intended to be equal to the present value of expected expenses at the interest, mortality, and surrender assumptions on which the net premium is based.

Loaded net premiums are not developed in detail for every age, sex and mortality class, but for selected ages in each class, and the loading formula is then applied to all ages based on the selected ages. This method develops premiums and profits in detail for selected cells, and premiums and profits for the line as a whole are estimated from those for the known cells. Loaded Net Premiums is therefore referred to as a "Cell-Based" method.

10.3   THE ASSET SHARE METHOD

The Asset Share method of profit testing is another cell-based method. For each age and class tested, an asset share is calculated at each duration, for as many durations as are needed to ascertain whether profit goals are being met. (It is not unusual, for example, to have profit goals that apply up to the twentieth or thirtieth duration, but no further.)

Under the Asset Share method, test premiums are the first step, and the amount of profit resulting from the test premiums at each duration is derived. Adjustments are then made to the assumptions and the test premiums until the desired profit is arrived at. For the asset share method, asset shares are calculated on a "profits retained" basis. That is, the profit or loss each year is accumulated using the same survival rates and interest rates as are used to derive asset shares, so it is treated as if it were retained in the asset share and accumulated with other cash flows.

10.4   ACCUMULATED BOOK PROFITS

Accumulated Book Profits is a variation on the Asset Share method. Therefore, it is also a cell-based model. Using test premiums, asset shares are calculated for each duration in a given cell. However, profits and losses are not treated as retained, but are paid into a separate fund called the profit account, where they are accumulated using the same survival rates as the asset share, but with a separate, higher interest rate called the **hurdle rate**.

The hurdle rate is set by the company as representing the cost that it must pay for the use of capital, and may be higher for kinds of policies thought to be riskier. If the accumulation within the policy (that is, the net rate the company thinks it can earn on its investment portfolio) is at an interest rate of 7%, it would not be unusual to find a hurdle rate in the range 10-15%. A profit goal in this case might be "break even after 20 years, with a 12% hurdle rate."

10.5   MODEL OFFICE METHOD

The Model Office Method is a non-cell-based variation on either the Asset Share or the Accumulated Book Profits Method. While individual asset shares are prepared for each of the individual cells, the profit goals and tests are not applied to the individual cells, but to the universe of individual cells, with each cell weighted by the amount of business that the company expects to be present in it. Normally, as a practical matter, some attention is given to the individual cells to verify that profits within each cell do not deviate too far from the stated goal for the product as a whole. Profits significantly lower for individual cells could cause the profit goal for the product as a whole to be compromised if more than the expected proportion of business is sold in those cells.

10.6   MACRO PRICING

Macro Pricing [1] refers to a process of pricing that is project-based; it extends to all products in the project. The goal of macro pricing is to maximize total profit for the project. Those responsible for marketing are asked to project, for each of several different test price levels, how much business will be produced, and a total amount of profit for each of the different price-production sets (scenarios) is calculated using a model office. Each of the scenarios has a different, but internally consistent set of assumptions: rate level, level of sales, expenses. For example, one scenario might have price set at $12.35, and the predicted resulting sales volume equal to $10 million, with expenses totaling $60,000. Another scenario might have price at $11.85, sales volume at $20 million, and expenses at $100,000. One might expect the second scenario to result in a larger profit.

In macro pricing, only marginal expenses, i.e., those expenses that are related to amount of business, are considered, since the conclusions arrived at in the macro pricing process depend on the amount of business. Assuming that all other assumptions have been fine tuned, the company chooses the price level with the largest profit potential. Those expenses which are not marginal are allocated to a corporate level where they become an offset to profit.

10.7   APPLICABILITY OF THE METHODS

In general, the methods described above are listed in increasing order of complexity. The level of importance of a particular product effort will be the most important factor controlling the choice of method, with the more complex methods being reserved for the more important product efforts.

Hoskin's method generally is used only in instances where the product is not expected to generate very much business (such as an infrequently encountered rider). Hoskin's method is also often used to generate additional premium adjustments (such as substandard extras) where the main pricing has been done using a more complex method.

The Asset Share and Accumulated Book Profit methods are the work horses of product development, and are used in most day-to-day product development work. In fact, Model Offices and Macro Pricing are simply continuations of one of these two methods. In present day actuarial practice, the Accumulated Book Profit method is usually chosen in almost all instances where the product requires a substantial investment by the company in the early years, since it gives the company an indication of the cost and return on that equity investment. The asset share method is more applicable to products where there is little early-year investment. One example of such a product would be front-loaded universal life, although this product is not now often encountered.

Most companies that price using ROE goals include some measure of the capital needs associated with a product in the equity used to determine ROE. This amount for capital needs, called "target surplus" may be based on the statutory risk-based capital requirements. It may also be based on the company's own assessment of capital needs, taking into account the requirements of the agencies that rate insurance company financial strength.

When an important product is being priced for an environment with considerable variability, it is useful, and usual to use the model office method. One example of this is annuity pricing, where interest scenarios are tested in a model office. Annuities priced using a "most likely" asset share frequently do not include enough margin to cover the deviations in interest rate that are likely as experience with the product unfolds.

Macro Pricing, then is usually reserved for major product efforts. For example, it is usual for a company to periodically re-price its entire life insurance line, and macro pricing would be the expected approach to such an effort. Macro pricing is also applicable when a decision has been made to enter for the first time a line of business in which the company has not previously been active.

It is possible that option-pricing techniques from mathematical finance concepts can be used to arrive at a "direct solution" for the price of certain products; for example, the minimum guaranteed death benefit offered with many variable annuity contracts could be priced this way.

REFERENCES

[1]   Chalke, Shane A., "Macro Pricing: Toward a Comprehensive Product Development Process," TSA XLIII, 1991, pp. 137-230.

REVIEW QUESTIONS

1. What are the requirements of a profit-testing method, and how are they achieved?

2. Describe the following profit-testing methods, and indicate their differences and similarities:
    Loaded Net Premiums
    Asset Share Method
    Accumulated Book Profits
    Model Office Method
    Macro Pricing

3. What is target surplus, and how is it determined?

4. Indicate what factors determine the choice of a pricing method.

CHAPTER 11
PROFIT TESTING EXAMPLES

11.1 CELL-BASED METHODS; ASSUMPTIONS

Tables 11.1 through 11.5 show examples of asset shares calculated for a participating whole life policy. These examples represent a profit margin run for the cell being explored; age 35, male, non-smoker. Reserves have been calculated on the 1980 CSO Table at 4.5%, Commissioners Reserve Valuation Method. Cash Values are the minimums on the Standard Nonforfeiture basis using the same 1980 CSO Table at 4.5%.

Dividends have been calculated using a contribution formula. Each year's dividend was calculated as 84% of the difference between the expected investment earnings rate (7%) and the valuation basis 4.5% applied to the initial reserve each year, plus the net amount at risk each year times the difference between dividend and valuation mortality rates, plus the difference between the gross and net premiums less the year's expenses. The dividend in the first year is taken as zero. For this test, the premium has been set at $13.50 per thousand. The test is for a block of insurance with total face amount of $1,000,000.

In this test, to simplify the example, all events have been assumed to occur on an annual basis. Premium payments are annual on the first day of the year. Surrenders all occur on the last day of the year, if the insured is then living. Death rates are on an annual basis, but are assumed to occur at the midpoint of each policy year (i.e., the approximate equivalent of assuming they occur uniformly throughout the year.) Expenses are assumed to be payable on the first day of each year, coincident with the premium. The expenses assumed have been calculated as an amount per $1,000 of face amount. In practice, of course, some expenses are per policy, so an implied assumption has been made about average size. To test the effect of a smaller average size, the expense per $1,000 would be increased.

For simplicity, the example differs from the profit testing usually encountered in practice in several ways. In practice, separate death and surrender expenses are usually calculated and assumed to occur simultaneously with the event with which they are associated. Also, in practice, profit testing often utilizes a continuous model.

The assumptions used are summarized in Table 11.1. Cash values, reserves, and dividends have been calculated as described. The expense rate has been calculated as 100% of the premium plus $6 per thousand in the first year. Subsequent years are 8% of the premium plus $0.30 per thousand, with the non-premium based expense increasing at the rate of 1% for each year after the first.

The lapse rate begins at 20% in the first year and decreases to 4% a year in the ninth year and later. At age 100, all policies are assumed to terminate for their cash value ($1,000 per thousand of face amount). Valuation mortality, as indicated, is the 1980 CSO male table. The experience mortality was taken as 85% of the 1975-80 basic table, with a mortality improvement factor of 1% per year for each year after the first. (i.e., the basic table mortality rates were multiplied by a factor of 85% times 99% raised to the power of the policy duration.) The dividend mortality was taken as 85% of the basic table, without any projected further improvements.

The persistency column shows the proportion of original issues that persist at the end of each policy year. It was calculated as:

$(1 - experience\ mortality\ rate) \times (1 - lapse\ rate) \times previous\ year\ persistency$

Many actuaries prefer to run profit margins to a duration where less than 5% of the policies persist. Since that does not happen until the 44th year in this example, these runs all extend to age 100. It is not uncommon, however, to artificially terminate the run at duration 20 or 30 by assuming that all policies receive their cash value at that duration. Alternatively, each policy can be terminated for its asset share at whatever terminal duration is chosen.

11.2   PROFITS RETAINED; STATUTORY BASIS

Table 11.2 shows an asset share profit margin run for the policy based on statutory reserves. The profits and losses are all assumed to be *retained* in the cell. Therefore, the accumulated profit or loss is added to the reserve and the other income and disbursements when interest earnings are calculated.

Most of the amounts are calculated by multiplying the appropriate value by the persistency. For example, the premium in the fourth year is .54981 times 13,500. Cash values were assumed to be paid to all who terminated during a year, but did not die. Thus, for example, the cash value paid in the third year is $7,781.31 times .655163 times .16 times $(1-.00084)$. The Federal Income Tax was estimated as 34% of the statutory profit. In practice, there would usually be additional adjustments, including an adjustment to the statutory reserve, some allowance for DAC tax, which moves part of the taxes from the later durations into earlier ones, and, if the insurer is a mutual company, the equity tax. These refinements were ignored in these examples to simplify them, but are not usually ignored in practice, since they can materially affect the results.

This asset share has been run for 65 years, to the policy's maturity at age 100. Almost certainly, the results at the earlier durations will be of more interest to the company management than those at the later durations. For example, this calculation indicates that the policy will "break even" (have a positive accumulated profit) after 10 years, and that total profits on this million dollar block of business will accumulate to $3.908 at the end of 20 years, roughly 7.85% of the $49,767 of reserve on the $189,556 of insurance still in force at that duration. The profit margin, the ratio of the present value of profits at the assumed interest rate of 7% to the present value of premiums over the policy life, is 5.66%. These are the kind of results that would probably be of most concern to this insurer's management.

Results at the very high durations are usually of little interest, because the likelihood of anything close to the original assumptions being maintained over so long a period is infinitesimally slim. Also, at the high durations, little business is left in force, and the results have less effect on the company's total profits than they do at the early durations.

11.3   GAAP RESERVES

Table 11.3 illustrates the development of GAAP reserves for this block of business. As is usual for GAAP reserve calculations on traditional life insurance, interest and mortality assumptions have been chosen that are more conservative than the assumed experience level, but less conservative than the statutory assumptions. In this case, the interest rate has been calculated starting at the assumed level of 7% in the first year, and then decreasing .05% per year to an ultimate level of 5%. The GAAP mortality is the 1975-80 Basic Table, not the discounted percentages of that table assumed for experience purposes. No change was assumed from the assumed experience level of lapses.

Of the total first-year expense (100% of premium plus $6), 90% of premium plus $3 is assumed to represent deferrable acquisition costs. No part of the renewal expense represents deferrable acquisition costs. This is a simplified example. In practice, there is usually some part of the expenses in the first few renewal years that represents deferrable acquisition costs.

The present value of the benefits for each policy year represents the payments to those who die or lapse each year, multiplied by persistency and interest at the assumed GAAP rates. Note that the assumed GAAP persistency factors differ slightly from the experience persistency factors because the GAAP mortality is more conservative than experience mortality. The benefit reserves do not make any provision for interest.

The benefit net premium is calculated as the sum of all the present values of benefits divided by the present value of 1 per year. In the same way, the expense net premium is calculated as the present value of deferrable expense divided by the present value of 1 per year. Reserves were calculated using a retrospective accumulation formula, but they could also have been calculated from a prospective formula, and the resulting reserve, of course would be equal. The final GAAP reserve is equal to the sum of the benefit reserve and the expense reserve (or DAC). Note that the GAAP reserve is negative at the end of the first year, and is *not* adjusted to zero. A comparison of the GAAP reserves with the statutory reserves in Table 11.1 will indicate that the GAAP reserve is always less than statutory at all durations.

11.4   GAAP PROFIT MARGIN

Table 11.4 is a profit margin example using GAAP reserves. All of the income and disbursements are identical to those in Table 11.2. This includes the investment income and the federal income tax, which will not differ just because of the assumed different reserve method.

The annual profit each year on the GAAP basis is generally higher through the first fifteen durations (minor exception at durations three and four). At durations sixteen and higher the statutory gains are higher. Since the income and disbursements are equal each year, and since both the

GAAP and statutory reserves are fully released at attained age 100, the accumulated value of all the profits is equal on the GAAP and statutory bases. The present value is higher on the GAAP basis, however, since the GAAP profits develop earlier.

11.5 RETURN-ON-EQUITY

Table 11.5 shows an example of a return-on-equity calculation using a hurdle rate of 12.5%. All income, disbursements and reserve are equal to those in Table 11.2, except for investment income. Investment income, in this case, does not include the interest on the accumulated profit, since that is accumulated at a different rate, namely the hurdle rate of 12.5%. The profits accumulated at that rate are shown in the accumulated profit column.

Since the profits excluding investment income on the accumulated profit become negative at the later durations, the determination of whether or not there will be an ultimate profit or loss depends on reaching a sufficiently high level of accumulated profit in the middle years to cover the losses at the later durations (i.e., to "get over the hurdle"). A profit margin of this kind is very sensitive to the choice of hurdle rate. Table 11.5A shows that the accumulated profits at a rate of 13% (just slightly higher) do not clear the hurdle.

REVIEW QUESTIONS

1. From the data shown in Table 11.1, derive Table 11.2 using the methods and information described in the text.

2. From the interest, mortality and lapse rates shown in Table 11.3, the cash values and other information in Table 11.1, and the $15.15 of deferrable expense per thousand, derive the other columns of Table 11.3.

3. Derive Table 11.4 from the data you prepared for Tables 11.2 and 11.3.

4. Using only the data in Tables 11.1 and 11.2, derive Tables 11.5 and 11.5a. (It is suggested that the student use a worksheet program, such as Lotus or Excel, for these derivations)

Table 11.1
Profit Margin Assumptions - Age 35 Whole Life
Gr Premium = $13.50   Net Reserve Premium = $12.43

Profit Margin Year	Cash Value BOY	Reserve BOY	Dividend Rate	Expense Rate	Lapse Rate	Valuation Mort Rate	Experience Mort Rate	Dividend Mort Rate	Persistency EOY
1	0.00000	0.00000	$0.00	19.50000	20.00%	0.2110%	0.0570%	0.0570%	79.9544%
2	0.00000	0.00000	$1.46	1.38000	18.00%	0.2240%	0.0707%	0.0714%	65.5163%
3	0.00000	10.72353	$1.55	1.39500	16.00%	0.2400%	0.0958%	0.0978%	54.9810%
4	7.78131	21.79433	$1.75	1.41075	14.00%	0.2580%	0.1130%	0.1165%	47.2302%
5	19.35957	33.21268	$1.98	1.42729	12.00%	0.2790%	0.1290%	0.1343%	41.5090%
6	31.28150	44.96994	$2.25	1.44465	10.00%	0.3020%	0.1439%	0.1513%	37.3043%
7	43.54902	57.06802	$2.54	1.46288	8.00%	0.3290%	0.1609%	0.1709%	34.2648%
8	56.14575	69.49076	$2.83	1.48203	6.00%	0.3560%	0.1775%	0.1904%	32.1517%
9	69.09455	82.38198	$3.11	1.50213	4.00%	0.3870%	0.1984%	0.2151%	30.8044%
10	82.38198	95.36462	$3.42	1.52324	4.00%	0.4190%	0.2174%	0.2380%	29.5079%
11	96.02371	108.81793	$3.77	1.54540	4.00%	0.4550%	0.2368%	0.2618%	28.2605%
12	110.00948	122.61052	$4.07	1.56867	4.00%	0.4920%	0.2610%	0.2916%	27.0593%
13	124.35764	136.76051	$4.34	1.59310	4.00%	0.5320%	0.2908%	0.3281%	25.9014%
14	139.07055	151.27021	$4.61	1.61876	4.00%	0.5740%	0.3222%	0.3672%	24.7852%
15	154.16120	166.15242	$4.90	1.64569	4.00%	0.6210%	0.3559%	0.4097%	23.7091%
16	169.61887	181.39659	$5.82	1.67398	4.00%	0.6710%	0.3253%	0.3783%	22.6867%
17	185.45202	197.01105	$6.22	1.70368	4.00%	0.7300%	0.3561%	0.4182%	21.7017%
18	201.62194	212.95763	$6.64	1.73486	4.00%	0.7960%	0.3898%	0.4624%	20.7524%
19	218.10907	229.21705	$7.10	1.76761	4.00%	0.8710%	0.4256%	0.5100%	19.8375%
20	234.88104	245.75736	$7.60	1.80199	4.00%	0.9560%	0.4642%	0.5619%	18.9556%
21	251.90113	262.54237	$8.10	1.83809	4.00%	1.0470%	0.5054%	0.6180%	18.1054%
22	269.16679	279.56956	$8.60	1.87599	4.00%	1.1460%	0.5513%	0.6809%	17.2854%
23	286.66430	296.82539	$9.07	1.91579	4.00%	1.2490%	0.6010%	0.7497%	16.4942%
24	304.41313	314.32907	$9.53	1.95758	4.00%	1.3590%	0.6564%	0.8271%	15.7305%
25	322.41560	332.08290	$9.96	2.00146	4.00%	1.4770%	0.7179%	0.9138%	14.9929%
26	340.67193	350.08706	$10.41	2.04753	4.00%	1.6080%	0.7861%	1.0107%	14.2800%
27	359.15400	368.31386	$10.86	2.09591	4.00%	1.7540%	0.8620%	1.1195%	13.5907%
28	377.82705	386.72900	$11.35	2.14670	4.00%	1.9190%	0.9441%	1.2385%	12.9239%
29	396.63792	405.28006	$11.91	2.20004	4.00%	2.1060%	1.0309%	1.3660%	12.2790%
30	415.52295	423.90425	$12.48	2.25604	4.00%	2.3140%	1.1248%	1.5054%	11.6553%
31	434.43323	442.55333	$13.08	2.31484	4.00%	2.5420%	1.2261%	1.6575%	11.0519%

Profit Margin Year	Cash Value BOY	Reserve BOY	Dividend Rate	Expense Rate	Lapse Rate	Valuation Mort Rate	Experience Mort Rate	Dividend Mort Rate	Persistency EOY
32	453.33452	461.19356	$13.63	2.37658	4.00%	2.7850%	1.3364%	1.8250%	10.4680%
33	472.22993	479.82799	$14.15	2.44141	4.00%	3.0440%	1.4574%	2.0103%	9.9028%
34	491.12606	498.46313	$14.62	2.50948	4.00%	3.3190%	1.5892%	2.2143%	9.3556%
35	510.03943	517.11526	$15.08	2.58096	4.00%	3.6170%	1.7328%	2.4387%	8.8258%
36	528.96168	535.77616	$15.57	2.65600	4.00%	3.9510%	1.8877%	2.6835%	8.3128%
37	547.83318	554.38700	$16.14	2.73480	4.00%	4.3300%	2.0529%	2.9478%	7.8165%
38	566.56669	572.86177	$16.82	2.81754	4.00%	4.7650%	2.2269%	3.2300%	7.3367%
39	585.04092	591.08083	$17.60	2.90442	4.00%	5.2640%	2.4135%	3.5360%	6.8732%
40	603.11585	608.90611	$18.40	2.99564	4.00%	5.8190%	2.6157%	3.8709%	6.4257%
41	620.70075	626.24813	$19.16	3.09143	4.00%	6.4190%	2.8374%	4.2415%	5.9937%
42	637.76236	643.07408	$19.83	3.19200	4.00%	7.0530%	3.0798%	4.6504%	5.5767%
43	654.32146	659.40447	$20.35	3.29760	4.00%	7.7120%	3.3455%	5.1026%	5.1745%
44	670.44387	675.30419	$20.74	3.40848	4.00%	8.3900%	3.6332%	5.5973%	4.7871%
45	686.23046	690.87274	$21.04	3.52490	4.00%	9.1050%	3.9426%	6.1353%	4.4144%
46	701.73610	706.16421	$21.34	3.64715	4.00%	9.8840%	4.2731%	6.7167%	4.0567%
47	716.94529	721.16334	$21.70	3.77550	4.00%	10.7480%	4.6233%	7.3406%	3.7144%
48	731.79655	735.80947	$22.19	3.91028	4.00%	11.7250%	4.9883%	8.0002%	3.3880%
49	746.16189	749.97639	$22.79	4.05179	4.00%	12.8260%	5.3703%	8.6998%	3.0778%
50	759.89432	763.51916	$23.35	4.20038	4.00%	14.0250%	5.7872%	9.4699%	2.7837%
51	772.92571	776.37055	$23.82	4.35640	4.00%	15.2950%	6.2384%	10.3114%	2.5056%
52	785.26300	788.53744	$24.13	4.52022	4.00%	16.6090%	6.7228%	11.2243%	2.2437%
53	796.98769	800.10019	$24.29	4.69223	4.00%	17.9550%	7.2393%	12.2086%	1.9980%
54	808.22437	811.18167	$24.29	4.87284	4.00%	19.3270%	7.7866%	13.2643%	1.7687%
55	819.13847	821.94502	$24.17	5.06248	4.00%	20.7290%	8.3544%	14.3752%	1.5561%
56	829.93235	832.58982	$23.98	5.26161	4.00%	22.1770%	8.9306%	15.5219%	1.3605%
57	840.84637	843.35310	$23.74	5.47069	4.00%	23.6980%	9.5147%	16.7042%	1.1818%
58	852.17597	854.52621	$23.50	5.69022	4.00%	25.3450%	10.1064%	17.9223%	1.0199%
59	864.28087	866.46392	$23.28	5.92073	4.00%	27.2110%	10.7053%	19.1760%	0.8742%
60	877.60752	879.60649	$23.29	6.16277	4.00%	29.5900%	11.3109%	20.4655%	0.7443%
61	892.49642	894.28975	$23.70	6.41691	4.00%	32.9960%	11.9229%	21.7906%	0.6294%
62	909.11723	910.68100	$24.70	6.68376	4.00%	38.4550%	12.5408%	23.1515%	0.5284%
63	927.29611	928.60879	$26.21	6.96394	4.00%	48.0200%	13.1643%	24.5480%	0.4405%
64	946.35433	947.40378	$27.55	7.25814	4.00%	65.7980%	13.7931%	25.9803%	0.3646%
65	965.09010	965.88077	$14.05	7.56705	100.00%	100.0000%	14.4267%	27.4482%	0.0000%
66	1000.00000	1000.00000							

Table 11.2
Profits Retained

Profit Margin Year	Premium Collected	Statutory Basis Reserve BoY	Profit Retained Inv Income	Dividend Pd	CV Pd	Death Bft Pd	Expenses Pd	Income	Disburse-ments	Increase in Reserve	Profit before FIT	FIT	Profit after FIT	Accummu-lated Profit	Att Age BOY
1	13500	0	-440	0	0	570	19500	13060	20070	0	-7009	-2383	-4626	-4626	35
2	10794	0	335	957	0	565	1103	11129	2625	7026	1478	502	975	-3651	36
3	8845	7026	769	854	815	628	914	9614	3210	4957	1447	492	955	-2696	37
4	7422	11983	1094	825	1488	621	776	8516	3710	3704	1102	375	727	-1969	38
5	6376	15686	1338	823	1771	609	674	7714	3877	2980	857	291	566	-1403	39
6	5604	18667	1538	840	1805	597	600	7142	3842	2622	677	230	447	-956	40
7	5036	21289	1717	870	1673	600	546	6753	3688	2522	542	184	358	-598	41
8	4626	23811	1892	909	1418	608	508	6518	3443	2637	437	149	288	-310	42
9	4340	26448	2077	959	1057	638	483	6418	3137	2928	353	120	233	-77	43
10	4159	29376	2286	1010	1181	670	469	6444	3330	2733	381	130	252	175	44
11	3984	32110	2482	1064	1295	699	456	6466	3514	2540	411	140	271	446	45
12	3815	34650	2667	1101	1402	738	443	6482	3684	2356	442	150	292	738	46
13	3653	37006	2840	1124	1501	787	431	6493	3843	2175	475	162	314	1052	47
14	3497	39181	3003	1143	1592	835	419	6499	3989	2000	510	173	336	1388	48
15	3346	41181	3155	1163	1676	882	408	6501	4128	1826	546	186	360	1749	49
16	3201	43008	3302	1320	1753	771	397	6503	4241	1688	574	195	379	2128	50
17	3063	44695	3437	1349	1823	808	387	6499	4367	1520	612	208	404	2532	51
18	2930	46215	3561	1378	1886	846	376	6491	4486	1353	652	222	431	2962	52
19	2802	47568	3677	1408	1941	883	367	6478	4600	1184	694	236	458	3421	53
20	2678	48752	3782	1440	1990	921	357	6460	4708	1014	738	251	487	3908	54
21	2559	49767	3878	1466	2031	958	348	6437	4803	851	784	266	517	4425	55
22	2444	50617	3965	1486	2065	998	340	6410	4888	690	831	283	548	4973	56
23	2334	51307	4043	1496	2092	1039	331	6377	4958	539	880	299	581	5554	57
24	2227	51846	4113	1499	2113	1083	323	6340	5017	392	930	316	614	6168	58
25	2124	52238	4176	1494	2128	1129	315	6299	5066	250	983	334	649	6817	59
26	2024	52488	4230	1486	2137	1179	307	6254	5109	107	1038	353	685	7502	60
27	1928	52595	4278	1476	2140	1231	299	6206	5146	-36	1096	373	723	8226	61
28	1835	52559	4318	1467	2136	1283	292	6153	5178	-181	1156	393	763	8989	62
29	1745	52378	4351	1462	2126	1332	284	6096	5204	-327	1218	414	804	9793	63
30	1658	52051	4377	1455	2110	1381	277	6035	5223	-470	1283	436	846	10639	64
31	1573	51581	4397	1445	2088	1429	270	5970	5231	-610	1349	459	890	11529	65
32	1492	50970	4409	1427	2060	1477	263	5901	5226	-742	1417	482	935	12465	66
33	1413	50228	4416	1401	2026	1526	256	5829	5209	-866	1487	506	981	13446	67

Profit Margin Year	Premium Collected	Statutory Basis Reserve BoY	Profit Retained Inv Income	Dividend Pd	CV Pd	Death Bft Pd	Expenses	Income	Disburse- ments	Increase in Reserve	Profit before FIT	FIT	Profit after FIT	Accumu- lated Profit	Att Age BOY
34	1337	49362	4418	1368	1988	1574	249	5755	5179	-983	1558	530	1029	14474	68
35	1263	48379	4415	1331	1945	1621	241	5678	5139	-1093	1632	555	1077	15551	69
36	1191	47286	4407	1295	1898	1666	234	5599	5093	-1201	1707	581	1127	16678	70
37	1122	46085	4396	1262	1845	1707	227	5519	5041	-1308	1785	607	1178	17857	71
38	1055	44778	4382	1234	1788	1741	220	5437	4983	-1412	1865	634	1231	19088	72
39	990	43366	4364	1210	1727	1771	213	5355	4921	-1514	1948	662	1286	20374	73
40	928	41852	4343	1183	1662	1798	206	5271	4848	-1611	2034	691	1342	21716	74
41	867	40241	4320	1149	1593	1823	199	5187	4763	-1697	2122	721	1400	23116	75
42	809	38544	4295	1106	1520	1846	191	5104	4663	-1771	2211	752	1459	24576	76
43	753	36773	4269	1053	1446	1866	184	5022	4548	-1829	2303	783	1520	26096	77
44	699	34944	4244	993	1369	1880	176	4942	4418	-1871	2396	814	1581	27677	78
45	646	33073	4220	929	1291	1887	169	4866	4276	-1900	2490	847	1643	29320	79
46	596	31173	4199	866	1212	1886	161	4795	4125	-1917	2587	880	1707	31028	80
47	548	29256	4182	806	1133	1876	153	4729	3967	-1925	2687	913	1773	32801	81
48	501	27331	4169	752	1053	1853	145	4671	3803	-1922	2790	949	1841	34642	82
49	457	25409	4162	701	974	1819	137	4620	3633	-1909	2897	985	1912	36554	83
50	416	23499	4161	650	896	1781	129	4577	3457	-1888	3008	1023	1985	38539	84
51	376	21612	4168	597	820	1737	121	4543	3274	-1854	3123	1062	2061	40600	85
52	338	19758	4182	541	745	1684	113	4520	3084	-1806	3242	1102	2140	42740	86
53	303	17952	4205	485	673	1624	105	4508	2888	-1744	3365	1144	2221	44960	87
54	270	16207	4239	430	604	1556	97	4509	2686	-1669	3492	1187	2305	47265	88
55	239	14538	4285	376	538	1478	90	4524	2481	-1582	3624	1232	2392	49657	89
56	210	12956	4343	326	477	1390	82	4553	2274	-1483	3761	1279	2483	52140	90
57	184	11474	4415	281	420	1294	74	4599	2069	-1375	3905	1328	2577	54717	91
58	160	10099	4502	240	367	1194	67	4661	1869	-1262	4055	1379	2676	57393	92
59	138	8837	4603	204	320	1092	60	4741	1675	-1147	4212	1432	2780	60173	93
60	118	7690	4720	173	277	989	54	4838	1493	-1033	4379	1489	2890	63063	94
61	100	6657	4853	149	238	887	48	4954	1323	-925	4556	1549	3007	66070	95
62	85	5732	5001	131	204	789	42	5086	1166	-825	4745	1613	3132	69202	96
63	71	4907	5166	115	174	696	37	5237	1022	-734	4949	1683	3266	72468	97
64	59	4173	5346	100	147	608	32	5405	887	-652	5171	1758	3413	75881	98
65	49	3521	5541	0	3120	526	28	5590	3673	-3521	5438	1849	3589	79470	99

Table 11.3
GAAP Reserves
Gross Premium = $13.50 Benefit Net Prem = 6.892 Expense Net Prem = 2.647

Attained Age BOY	Interest Rt	Deferrable Expense Rt	Lapse Rate	Mort Rate	Persistency	PV of Benefits in year	Benefit Reserve BOY	PV of Deferrable Expenses	Expense Reserve BOY	Total GAAP Reserve BOY	Policy Year
35	7.00%	15.15	20.00%	0.0670%	79.9464%	0.6477	0.00	15.15	0.00	0.00	1
36	6.95%	0	18.00%	0.0840%	65.5010%	0.6069	8.36	0.00	-16.73	-8.38	2
37	6.90%	0	16.00%	0.1150%	54.9576%	1.3025	18.85	0.00	-18.39	0.46	3
38	6.85%	0	14.00%	0.1370%	47.1987%	1.7334	29.89	0.00	-20.06	9.83	4
39	6.80%	0	12.00%	0.1580%	41.4693%	1.8192	40.96	0.00	-21.66	19.30	5
40	6.75%	0	10.00%	0.1780%	37.2559%	1.7215	52.05	0.00	-23.12	28.93	6
41	6.70%	0	8.00%	0.2010%	34.2065%	1.5368	63.15	0.00	-24.32	38.83	7
42	6.65%	0	6.00%	0.2240%	32.0821%	1.3010	74.25	0.00	-25.19	49.06	8
43	6.60%	0	4.00%	0.2530%	30.7209%	1.0469	85.39	0.00	-25.63	59.76	9
44	6.55%	0	4.00%	0.2800%	29.4095%	1.0719	96.57	0.00	-25.59	70.98	10
45	6.50%	0	4.00%	0.3080%	28.1462%	1.0846	108.14	0.00	-25.54	82.60	11
46	6.45%	0	4.00%	0.3330%	26.9276%	1.0951	120.10	0.00	-25.47	94.63	12
47	6.40%	0	4.00%	0.3860%	25.7507%	1.1037	132.42	0.00	-25.40	107.02	13
48	6.35%	0	4.00%	0.4320%	24.6139%	1.1041	145.04	0.00	-25.31	119.73	14
49	6.30%	0	4.00%	0.4820%	23.5155%	1.0984	157.96	0.00	-25.22	132.74	15
50	6.25%	0	4.00%	0.4450%	22.4744%	1.0088	171.15	0.00	-25.11	146.04	16
51	6.20%	0	4.00%	0.4920%	21.4693%	0.9930	185.41	0.00	-24.98	160.43	17
52	6.15%	0	4.00%	0.5440%	20.4984%	0.9746	200.08	0.00	-24.82	175.25	18
53	6.10%	0	4.00%	0.6000%	19.5604%	0.9530	215.15	0.00	-24.66	190.49	19
54	6.05%	0	4.00%	0.6610%	18.6538%	0.9292	230.62	0.00	-24.47	206.14	20
55	6.00%	0	4.00%	0.7270%	17.7775%	0.9034	246.48	0.00	-24.27	222.21	21
56	5.95%	0	4.00%	0.8010%	16.9297%	0.8773	262.75	0.00	-24.05	238.70	22
57	5.90%	0	4.00%	0.8820%	16.1092%	0.8503	279.39	0.00	-23.81	255.58	23
58	5.85%	0	4.00%	0.9730%	15.3143%	0.8235	296.39	0.00	-23.56	272.83	24
59	5.80%	0	4.00%	1.0750%	14.5437%	0.7970	313.72	0.00	-23.28	290.44	25
60	5.75%	0	4.00%	1.1890%	13.7959%	0.7707	331.35	0.00	-22.99	308.35	26
61	5.70%	0	4.00%	1.3170%	13.0697%	0.7448	349.22	0.00	-22.68	326.54	27
62	5.65%	0	4.00%	1.4570%	12.3641%	0.7185	367.29	0.00	-22.35	344.94	28
63	5.60%	0	4.00%	1.6070%	11.6788%	0.6911	385.53	0.00	-22.01	363.52	29
64	5.55%	0	4.00%	1.7710%	11.0131%	0.6636	403.91	0.00	-21.64	382.27	30
65	5.50%	0	4.00%	1.9500%	10.3664%	0.6360	422.42	0.00	-21.26	401.16	31

Attained Age BOY	Interest Rt	Deferrable Expense Rt	Lapse Rate	Mort Rate	Persistency	PV of Benefits in year	Benefit Reserve BOY	PV of Deferrable Expenses	Expense Reserve BOY	Total GAAP Reserve BOY	Policy Year
67	5.40%	0	4.00%	2.3650%	9.1275%	0.5816	459.64	0.00	-20.45	439.19	33
68	5.35%	0	4.00%	2.6050%	8.5341%	0.5549	478.26	0.00	-20.02	458.23	34
69	5.30%	0	4.00%	2.8690%	7.9577%	0.5285	496.79	0.00	-19.58	477.21	35
70	5.25%	0	4.00%	3.1570%	7.3982%	0.5021	515.18	0.00	-19.12	496.06	36
71	5.20%	0	4.00%	3.4680%	6.8560%	0.4755	533.37	0.00	-18.65	514.72	37
72	5.15%	0	4.00%	3.8000%	6.3316%	0.4485	551.32	0.00	-18.17	533.15	38
73	5.10%	0	4.00%	4.1600%	5.8255%	0.4216	569.00	0.00	-17.67	551.32	39
74	5.05%	0	4.00%	4.5540%	5.3378%	0.3951	586.36	0.00	-17.17	569.19	40
75	5.00%	0	4.00%	4.9900%	4.8686%	0.3692	603.35	0.00	-16.65	586.70	41
76	5.00%	0	4.00%	5.4710%	4.4181%	0.3439	619.87	0.00	-16.12	603.76	42
77	5.00%	0	4.00%	6.0030%	3.9868%	0.3189	636.16	0.00	-15.59	620.58	43
78	5.00%	0	4.00%	6.5850%	3.5753%	0.2943	652.16	0.00	-15.06	637.10	44
79	5.00%	0	4.00%	7.2180%	3.1845%	0.2700	667.81	0.00	-14.53	653.28	45
80	5.00%	0	4.00%	7.9020%	2.8156%	0.2459	683.09	0.00	-14.01	669.08	46
81	5.00%	0	4.00%	8.6360%	2.4695%	0.2222	697.96	0.00	-13.49	684.47	47
82	5.00%	0	4.00%	9.4120%	2.1476%	0.1989	712.42	0.00	-12.99	699.43	48
83	5.00%	0	4.00%	10.2350%	1.8507%	0.1763	726.50	0.00	-12.48	714.01	49
84	5.00%	0	4.00%	11.1410%	1.5787%	0.1551	740.24	0.00	-11.99	728.25	50
85	5.00%	0	4.00%	12.1310%	1.3317%	0.1351	753.60	0.00	-11.50	742.10	51
86	5.00%	0	4.00%	13.2050%	1.1096%	0.1165	766.54	0.00	-11.02	755.52	52
87	5.00%	0	4.00%	14.3630%	0.9122%	0.0992	779.04	0.00	-10.55	768.49	53
88	5.00%	0	4.00%	15.6050%	0.7391%	0.0833	791.09	0.00	-10.09	781.00	54
89	5.00%	0	4.00%	16.9120%	0.5895%	0.0688	802.68	0.00	-9.65	793.03	55
90	5.00%	0	4.00%	18.2610%	0.4626%	0.0559	813.86	0.00	-9.21	804.64	56
91	5.00%	0	4.00%	19.6520%	0.3568%	0.0445	824.75	0.00	-8.79	815.96	57
92	5.00%	0	4.00%	21.0850%	0.2703%	0.0348	835.51	0.00	-8.36	827.15	58
93	5.00%	0	4.00%	22.5600%	0.2010%	0.0266	846.35	0.00	-7.92	838.43	59
94	5.00%	0	4.00%	24.0770%	0.1465%	0.0200	857.58	0.00	-7.45	850.13	60
95	5.00%	0	4.00%	25.6360%	0.1046%	0.0147	869.68	0.00	-6.92	862.76	61
96	5.00%	0	4.00%	27.2370%	0.0730%	0.0105	883.41	0.00	-6.28	877.13	62
97	5.00%	0	4.00%	28.8800%	0.0499%	0.0074	900.09	0.00	-5.46	894.63	63
98	5.00%	0	4.00%	30.5650%	0.0332%	0.0051	921.97	0.00	-4.33	917.64	64
99	5.00%	0	100.00%	32.2920%	0.0000%	0.0095	953.08	0.00	-2.65	950.44	65
100							0.00		0.00	0.00	

Table 11.4
GAAP Profits

Profit Margin Year	Premium Collected	GAAP Reserve BOY	Profit Retained Inv Income	Dividend Pd	CV Paid	Death Bft Pd	Expenses Pd	Income	Disburse-ments	GAAP Basis Increase in Reserve	Profit before FIT	FIT	Profit after FIT	Accummu-lated Profit	Att Age BOY
1	13500	0	-440	0	0	570	19500	13060	20070	-6698	-311	-2383	2072	2072	35
2	10794	-6698	335	957	0	565	1103	11129	2625	6996	1507	502	1004	3076	36
3	8845	298	769	854	815	628	914	9614	3210	5108	1296	492	804	3880	37
4	7422	5407	1094	825	1488	621	776	8516	3710	3709	1097	375	722	4602	38
5	6376	9116	1338	823	1771	609	674	7714	3877	2893	944	291	652	5254	39
6	5604	12009	1538	840	1805	597	600	7142	3842	2474	825	230	595	5849	40
7	5036	14484	1717	870	1673	600	546	6753	3688	2327	737	184	553	6402	41
8	4626	16811	1892	909	1418	608	508	6518	3443	2403	672	149	523	6925	42
9	4340	19213	2077	959	1057	638	483	6418	3137	2653	628	120	508	7434	43
10	4159	21866	2286	1010	1181	670	469	6444	3330	2508	607	130	477	7911	44
11	3984	24374	2482	1064	1295	699	456	6466	3514	2369	583	140	443	8354	45
12	3815	26743	2667	1101	1402	738	443	6482	3684	2217	581	150	431	8785	46
13	3653	28960	2840	1124	1501	787	431	6493	3843	2052	598	162	436	9221	47
14	3497	31012	3003	1143	1592	835	419	6499	3989	1889	621	173	448	9669	48
15	3346	32901	3155	1163	1676	882	408	6501	4128	1724	648	186	462	10131	49
16	3201	34625	3302	1320	1753	771	397	6503	4241	1772	490	195	295	10426	50
17	3063	36397	3437	1349	1823	808	387	6499	4367	1636	497	208	288	10714	51
18	2930	38033	3561	1378	1886	846	376	6491	4486	1498	507	222	285	10999	52
19	2802	39531	3677	1408	1941	883	367	6478	4600	1363	516	236	280	11279	53
20	2678	40894	3782	1440	1990	921	357	6460	4708	1228	524	251	274	11552	54
21	2559	42122	3878	1466	2031	958	348	6437	4803	1095	539	266	273	11825	55
22	2444	43217	3965	1486	2065	998	340	6410	4888	960	561	283	279	12104	56
23	2334	44177	4043	1496	2092	1039	331	6377	4958	825	594	299	295	12399	57
24	2227	45002	4113	1499	2113	1083	323	6340	5017	686	637	316	320	12719	58
25	2124	45688	4176	1494	2128	1129	315	6299	5066	544	689	334	355	13074	59
26	2024	46231	4230	1486	2137	1179	307	6254	5109	398	747	353	394	13468	60
27	1928	46630	4278	1476	2140	1231	299	6206	5146	250	810	373	438	13905	61
28	1835	46879	4318	1467	2136	1283	292	6153	5178	101	873	393	480	14386	62
29	1745	46981	4351	1462	2126	1332	284	6096	5204	-42	933	414	519	14905	63
30	1658	46939	4377	1455	2110	1381	277	6035	5223	-183	995	436	559	15464	64
31	1573	46756	4397	1445	2088	1429	270	5970	5231	-322	1061	459	602	16066	65
32	1492	46434	4409	1427	2060	1477	263	5901	5226	-459	1134	482	653	16719	66
33	1413	45974	4416	1401	2026	1526	256	5829	5209	-596	1217	506	711	17430	67

Profit Margin Year	Premium Collected	GAAP Reserve BOY	Profit Retained Inv Income	Dividend Pd	CV Paid	Death Bft Pd	Expenses Pd	Income	Disbursements	GAAP Basis Increase in Reserve	Profit before FIT	FIT	Profit after FIT	Accummulated Profit	Att Age BOY
34	1337	45378	4418	1368	1988	1574	249	5755	5179	-732	1308	530	778	18208	68
35	1263	44646	4415	1331	1945	1621	241	5678	5139	-865	1404	555	849	19057	69
36	1191	43781	4407	1295	1898	1666	234	5599	5093	-993	1500	581	919	19976	70
37	1122	42788	4396	1262	1845	1707	227	5519	5041	-1114	1592	607	985	20961	71
38	1055	41673	4382	1234	1788	1741	220	5437	4983	-1225	1678	634	1044	22005	72
39	990	40449	4364	1210	1727	1771	213	5355	4921	-1327	1761	662	1098	23103	73
40	928	39122	4343	1183	1662	1798	206	5271	4848	-1422	1845	691	1154	24257	74
41	867	37700	4320	1149	1593	1823	199	5187	4763	-1513	1937	721	1216	25473	75
42	809	36187	4295	1106	1520	1846	191	5104	4663	-1580	2020	752	1268	26741	76
43	753	34608	4269	1053	1446	1866	184	5022	4548	-1641	2114	783	1331	28073	77
44	699	32967	4244	993	1369	1880	176	4942	4418	-1694	2218	814	1404	29476	78
45	646	31273	4220	929	1291	1887	169	4866	4276	-1737	2328	847	1481	30957	79
46	596	29536	4199	866	1212	1886	161	4795	4125	-1769	2439	880	1559	32516	80
47	548	27767	4182	806	1133	1876	153	4729	3967	-1787	2549	913	1636	34152	81
48	501	25980	4169	752	1053	1853	145	4671	3803	-1789	2657	949	1708	35860	82
49	457	24190	4162	701	974	1819	137	4620	3633	-1777	2764	985	1779	37639	83
50	416	22414	4161	650	896	1781	129	4577	3457	-1756	2876	1023	1854	39493	84
51	376	20658	4168	597	820	1737	121	4543	3274	-1727	2996	1062	1934	41427	85
52	338	18930	4182	541	745	1684	113	4520	3084	-1688	3124	1102	2022	43449	86
53	303	17243	4205	485	673	1624	105	4508	2888	-1638	3259	1144	2115	45564	87
54	270	15604	4239	430	604	1556	97	4509	2686	-1578	3400	1187	2213	47777	88
55	239	14027	4285	376	538	1478	90	4524	2481	-1505	3548	1232	2315	50092	89
56	210	12521	4343	326	477	1390	82	4553	2274	-1420	3699	1279	2420	52513	90
57	184	11101	4415	281	420	1294	74	4599	2069	-1326	3856	1328	2528	55041	91
58	160	9775	4502	240	367	1194	67	4661	1869	-1224	4017	1379	2638	57679	92
59	138	8551	4603	204	320	1092	60	4741	1675	-1118	4184	1432	2752	60431	93
60	118	7432	4720	173	277	989	54	4838	1493	-1010	4356	1489	2867	63298	94
61	100	6422	4853	149	238	887	48	4954	1323	-901	4532	1549	2983	66281	95
62	85	5520	5001	131	204	789	42	5086	1166	-793	4713	1613	3100	69381	96
63	71	4727	5166	115	174	696	37	5237	1022	-685	4901	1683	3218	72599	97
64	59	4042	5346	100	147	608	32	5405	887	-577	5096	1758	3338	75937	98
65	49	3465	5541	0	3120	526	28	5590	3673	-3465	5382	1849	3533	79470	99

Table 11.5
Profits Released with Hurdle Rate
Hurdle Rate 12.5%

Profit Margin Year	Premium Collected	Statutory Basis Reserve BoY	Profit Released Inv Income	Dividend Pd	CV Pd	Death Bft Pd	Expenses Pd	Income	Disbursements	Statutory Basis Increase in Reserve	Profit before FIT	FIT	Profit after FIT	Accummulated Profit	Att Age BOY
1	13500	0	-440	0	0	570	19500	13060	20070	0	-7009	-2383	-4626	-4626	35
2	10794	0	659	957	0	565	1103	11452	2625	7026	1801	502	1299	-3906	36
3	8845	7026	1025	854	815	628	914	9870	3210	4957	1702	492	1211	-3183	37
4	7422	11983	1282	825	1488	621	776	8705	3710	3704	1291	375	916	-2665	38
5	6376	15686	1476	823	1771	609	674	7852	3877	2980	995	291	703	-2295	39
6	5604	18667	1636	840	1805	597	600	7240	3842	2622	776	230	545	-2036	40
7	5036	21289	1784	870	1673	600	546	6820	3688	2522	609	184	425	-1866	41
8	4626	23811	1934	909	1418	608	508	6559	3443	2637	479	149	330	-1769	42
9	4340	26448	2099	959	1057	638	483	6440	3137	2928	374	120	254	-1735	43
10	4159	29376	2291	1010	1181	670	469	6450	3330	2733	387	130	257	-1695	44
11	3984	32110	2470	1064	1295	699	456	6454	3514	2540	399	140	259	-1648	45
12	3815	34650	2636	1101	1402	738	443	6451	3684	2356	411	150	261	-1593	46
13	3653	37006	2788	1124	1501	787	431	6441	3843	2175	424	162	262	-1530	47
14	3497	39181	2929	1143	1592	835	419	6426	3989	2000	436	173	263	-1459	48
15	3346	41181	3057	1163	1676	882	408	6403	4128	1826	449	186	263	-1378	49
16	3201	43008	3180	1320	1753	771	397	6381	4241	1688	452	195	257	-1294	50
17	3063	44695	3288	1349	1823	808	387	6350	4367	1520	463	208	255	-1200	51
18	2930	46215	3384	1378	1886	846	376	6314	4486	1353	475	222	253	-1097	52
19	2802	47568	3469	1408	1941	883	367	6271	4600	1184	487	236	251	-983	53
20	2678	48752	3543	1440	1990	921	357	6221	4708	1014	499	251	248	-858	54
21	2559	49767	3605	1466	2031	958	348	6164	4803	851	510	266	244	-722	55
22	2444	50617	3656	1486	2065	998	340	6100	4888	690	521	283	239	-574	56
23	2334	51307	3695	1496	2092	1039	331	6029	4958	539	532	299	233	-413	57
24	2227	51846	3725	1499	2113	1083	323	5951	5017	392	542	316	225	-239	58
25	2124	52238	3744	1494	2128	1129	315	5867	5066	250	551	334	217	-52	59
26	2024	52488	3753	1486	2137	1179	307	5777	5109	107	561	353	208	150	60
27	1928	52595	3753	1476	2140	1231	299	5680	5146	-36	571	373	198	367	61
28	1835	52559	3742	1467	2136	1283	292	5577	5178	-181	580	393	187	600	62
29	1745	52378	3722	1462	2126	1332	284	5467	5204	-327	589	414	175	849	63
30	1658	52051	3692	1455	2110	1381	277	5350	5223	-470	597	436	161	1117	64
31	1573	51581	3652	1445	2088	1429	270	5225	5231	-610	604	459	146	1402	65
32	1492	50970	3602	1427	2060	1477	263	5094	5226	-742	610	482	128	1705	66

Profit Margin Year	Premium Collected	Statutory Basis Reserve BoY	Profit Released Inv Income	Dividend Pd	CV Pd	Death Bft Pd	Expenses Pd	Income	Disburse-ments	Statutory Basis Increase in Reserve	Profit before FIT	FIT	Profit after FIT	Accummu-lated Profit	Att Age BoY
33	1413	50228	3544	1401	2026	1526	256	4957	5209	-866	614	506	109	2027	67
34	1337	49362	3476	1368	1988	1574	249	4813	5179	-983	617	530	87	2368	68
35	1263	48379	3401	1331	1945	1621	241	4664	5139	-1093	619	555	64	2727	69
36	1191	47286	3319	1295	1898	1666	234	4510	5093	-1201	619	581	38	3107	70
37	1122	46085	3229	1262	1845	1707	227	4351	5041	-1308	618	607	11	3506	71
38	1055	44778	3132	1234	1788	1741	220	4187	4983	-1412	615	634	-19	3925	72
39	990	43366	3028	1210	1727	1771	213	4019	4921	-1514	612	662	-50	4366	73
40	928	41852	2917	1183	1662	1798	206	3845	4848	-1611	608	691	-84	4827	74
41	867	40241	2800	1149	1593	1823	199	3667	4763	-1697	601	721	-120	5311	75
42	809	38544	2677	1106	1520	1846	191	3486	4663	-1771	593	752	-159	5816	76
43	753	36773	2549	1053	1446	1866	184	3301	4548	-1829	582	783	-201	6343	77
44	699	34944	2417	993	1369	1880	176	3115	4418	-1871	569	814	-246	6890	78
45	646	33073	2282	929	1291	1887	169	2929	4276	-1900	553	847	-294	7457	79
46	596	31173	2147	866	1212	1886	161	2742	4125	-1917	535	880	-345	8044	80
47	548	29256	2010	806	1133	1876	153	2558	3967	-1925	515	913	-399	8651	81
48	501	27331	1873	752	1053	1853	145	2375	3803	-1922	494	949	-455	9278	82
49	457	25409	1737	701	974	1819	137	2195	3633	-1909	472	985	-513	9924	83
50	416	23499	1603	650	896	1781	129	2018	3457	-1888	449	1023	-574	10591	84
51	376	21612	1470	597	820	1737	121	1846	3274	-1854	425	1062	-637	11278	85
52	338	19758	1340	541	745	1684	113	1678	3084	-1806	400	1102	-702	11986	86
53	303	17952	1214	485	673	1624	105	1517	2888	-1744	373	1144	-771	12713	87
54	270	16207	1092	430	604	1556	97	1362	2686	-1669	345	1187	-842	13460	88
55	239	14538	976	376	538	1478	90	1215	2481	-1582	316	1232	-917	14225	89
56	210	12956	867	326	477	1390	82	1077	2274	-1483	285	1279	-993	15010	90
57	184	11474	765	281	420	1294	74	949	2069	-1375	255	1328	-1073	15814	91
58	160	10099	672	240	367	1194	67	831	1869	-1262	225	1379	-1154	16636	92
59	138	8837	586	204	320	1092	60	723	1675	-1147	195	1432	-1237	17479	93
60	118	7690	508	173	277	989	54	626	1493	-1033	167	1489	-1322	18341	94
61	100	6657	439	149	238	887	48	539	1323	-925	141	1549	-1408	19226	95
62	85	5732	377	131	204	789	42	462	1166	-825	120	1613	-1493	20136	96
63	71	4907	322	115	174	696	37	393	1022	-734	105	1683	-1578	21076	97
64	59	4173	273	100	147	608	32	332	887	-652	98	1758	-1660	22050	98
65	49	3521	230	0	3120	526	28	279	3673	-3521	127	1849	-1722	23084	99

Table 11.5A
Profits Released with Hurdle Rate
Hurdle Rate 13.0%

Profit Margin Year	Premium Collected	Statutory Basis Reserve BoY	Profit Released Inv Income	Dividend Pd	CV Pd	Death Bft Pd	Expenses Pd	Income	Disbursements	Statutory Basis Increase in Reserve	Profit before FIT	FIT	Profit after FIT	Accummulated Profit	Att Age BoY
1	13500	0	-440	0	0	570	19500	13060	20070	0	-7009	-2383	-4626	-4626	35
2	10794	0	659	957	0	565	1103	11452	2625	7026	1801	502	1299	-3929	36
3	8845	7026	1025	854	815	628	914	9870	3210	4957	1702	492	1211	-3229	37
4	7422	11983	1282	825	1488	621	776	8705	3710	3704	1291	375	916	-2732	38
5	6376	15886	1476	823	1771	609	674	7852	3877	2980	995	291	703	-2384	39
6	5604	18667	1636	840	1805	597	600	7240	3842	2622	776	230	545	-2149	40
7	5036	21289	1784	870	1673	600	546	6820	3688	2522	609	184	425	-2003	41
8	4626	23811	1934	909	1418	608	508	6559	3443	2637	479	149	330	-1934	42
9	4340	26448	2099	959	1057	638	483	6440	3137	2928	374	120	254	-1930	43
10	4159	29376	2291	1010	1181	670	469	6450	3330	2733	387	130	257	-1924	44
11	3984	32110	2470	1064	1295	699	456	6454	3514	2540	399	140	259	-1915	45
12	3815	34650	2636	1101	1402	738	443	6451	3684	2356	411	150	261	-1904	46
13	3653	37006	2788	1124	1501	787	431	6441	3843	2175	424	162	262	-1889	47
14	3497	39181	2929	1143	1592	835	419	6426	3989	2000	436	173	263	-1872	48
15	3346	41181	3057	1163	1676	882	408	6403	4128	1826	449	186	263	-1852	49
16	3201	43008	3180	1320	1753	771	397	6381	4241	1688	452	195	257	-1836	50
17	3063	44695	3288	1349	1823	808	387	6350	4367	1520	463	208	255	-1820	51
18	2930	46215	3384	1378	1886	846	376	6314	4486	1353	475	222	253	-1803	52
19	2802	47568	3469	1408	1941	883	367	6271	4600	1184	487	236	251	-1786	53
20	2678	48752	3543	1440	1990	921	357	6221	4708	1014	499	251	248	-1771	54
21	2559	49767	3605	1466	2031	958	348	6164	4803	851	510	266	244	-1758	55
22	2444	50617	3656	1486	2065	998	340	6100	4888	690	521	283	239	-1747	56
23	2334	51307	3695	1496	2092	1039	331	6029	4958	539	532	299	233	-1742	57
24	2227	51846	3725	1499	2113	1083	323	5951	5017	392	542	316	225	-1743	58
25	2124	52238	3744	1494	2128	1129	315	5867	5066	250	551	334	217	-1753	59
26	2024	52488	3753	1486	2137	1179	307	5777	5109	107	561	353	208	-1772	60
27	1928	52595	3753	1476	2140	1231	299	5680	5146	-36	571	373	198	-1805	61
28	1835	52559	3742	1467	2136	1283	292	5577	5178	-181	580	393	187	-1852	62
29	1745	52378	3722	1462	2126	1332	284	5467	5204	-327	589	414	175	-1918	63
30	1658	52051	3692	1455	2110	1381	277	5350	5223	-470	597	436	161	-2006	64
31	1573	51581	3652	1445	2088	1429	270	5225	5231	-610	604	459	146	-2121	65
32	1492	50970	3602	1427	2060	1477	263	5094	5226	-742	610	482	128	-2269	66
33	1413	50228	3544	1401	2026	1526	256	4957	5209	-866	614	506	109	-2455	67

Profit Margin Year	Premium Collected	Statutory Basis Reserve BoY	Profit Released Inv Income	Dividend Pd	CV Pd	Death Bft Pd	Expenses Pd	Income	Disbursements	Statutory Basis Increase in Reserve	Profit before FIT	FIT	Profit after FIT	Accumulated Profit	Att Age BoY
34	1337	49362	3476	1368	1988	1574	249	4813	5179	-983	617	530	87	-2687	68
35	1263	48379	3401	1331	1945	1621	241	4664	5139	-1093	619	555	64	-2973	69
36	1191	47286	3319	1295	1898	1666	234	4510	5093	-1201	619	581	38	-3321	70
37	1122	46085	3229	1262	1845	1707	227	4351	5041	-1308	618	607	11	-3742	71
38	1055	44778	3132	1234	1788	1741	220	4187	4983	-1412	615	634	-19	-4247	72
39	990	43366	3028	1210	1727	1771	213	4019	4921	-1514	612	662	-50	-4849	73
40	928	41852	2917	1183	1662	1798	206	3845	4848	-1611	608	691	-84	-5564	74
41	867	40241	2800	1149	1593	1823	199	3667	4763	-1697	601	721	-120	-6407	75
42	809	38544	2677	1106	1520	1846	191	3486	4663	-1771	593	752	-159	-7398	76
43	753	36773	2549	1053	1446	1866	184	3301	4548	-1829	582	783	-201	-8561	77
44	699	34944	2417	993	1369	1880	176	3115	4418	-1871	569	814	-246	-9919	78
45	646	33073	2282	929	1291	1887	169	2929	4276	-1900	553	847	-294	-11502	79
46	596	31173	2147	866	1212	1886	161	2742	4125	-1917	535	880	-345	-13343	80
47	548	29256	2010	806	1133	1876	153	2558	3967	-1925	515	913	-399	-15476	81
48	501	27331	1873	752	1053	1853	145	2375	3803	-1922	494	949	-455	-17943	82
49	457	25409	1737	701	974	1819	137	2195	3633	-1909	472	985	-513	-20788	83
50	416	23499	1603	650	896	1781	129	2018	3457	-1888	449	1023	-574	-24064	84
51	376	21612	1470	597	820	1737	121	1846	3274	-1854	425	1062	-637	-27829	85
52	338	19758	1340	541	745	1684	113	1678	3084	-1806	400	1102	-702	-32150	86
53	303	17952	1214	485	673	1624	105	1517	2888	-1744	373	1144	-771	-37100	87
54	270	16207	1092	430	604	1556	97	1362	2686	-1669	345	1187	-842	-42766	88
55	239	14538	976	376	538	1478	90	1215	2481	-1582	316	1232	-917	-49242	89
56	210	12956	867	326	477	1390	82	1077	2274	-1483	285	1279	-993	-56637	90
57	184	11474	765	281	420	1294	74	949	2069	-1375	255	1328	-1073	-65072	91
58	160	10099	672	240	367	1194	67	831	1869	-1262	225	1379	-1154	-74685	92
59	138	8837	586	204	320	1092	60	723	1675	-1147	195	1432	-1237	-85632	93
60	118	7690	508	173	277	989	54	626	1493	-1033	167	1489	-1322	-98086	94
61	100	6657	439	149	238	887	48	539	1323	-925	141	1549	-1408	-112245	95
62	85	5732	377	131	204	789	42	462	1166	-825	120	1613	-1493	-128330	96
63	71	4907	322	115	174	696	37	393	1022	-734	105	1683	-1578	-146591	97
64	59	4173	273	100	147	608	32	332	887	-652	98	1758	-1660	-167308	98
65	49	3521	230	0	3120	526	28	279	3673	-3521	127	1849	-1722	-190780	99

SECTION V

REGULATORY ISSUES AND ACTUARIAL STANDARDS OF PRACTICE

CHAPTER 12
REGULATORY RESERVE
REQUIREMENTS

12.1   BACKGROUND

The valuation requirements that all states have adopted in their laws and regulations reflect the concern that in the absence of such requirements, insurance companies might not set aside sufficient funds (reserves) to mature the guarantees that have been made in the insurance and annuity contracts that have been sold.

In this chapter we are going to look at the form that most of these requirements take and discuss some of the variations and interpretations imposed by certain states.

The laws and regulations that most states adopt for valuation requirements are derived from model laws and regulations promulgated by the National Association of Insurance Commissioners (NAIC). These model laws and regulations are generally developed by a subcommittee of the NAIC called the Life and Health Actuarial Task Force which consists of regulatory actuaries and which meets on a quarterly basis to address valuation issues and to propose changes to existing models or to start development of new model laws and regulations.

12.2   VALUATION

Many states make modifications to the models laws and regulations when they adopt the NAIC models. The reasons for these modifications can be to reflect previous long-standing practices of the state or can be the result of lobbying by an interest group. For example, we have seen recently modifications to some state adoptions of NAIC models which are intended to increase the legal liability of the actuary. The effect of such modifications is to expose the actuary to potential litigation over the reserves established.

Shown below is a list of some of the NAIC model laws and regulations that impact life and health valuation.

Table 12.1

NAIC Model Laws Impacting Life and Annuity Valuation

Standard Valuation Law
Actuarial Opinion and Memorandum Regulation (Model Reg.)
Universal Life Insurance Model Regulation
Variable Life Insurance Model Regulation
Modified Guaranteed Annuity Regulation
Modified Life Insurance Regulation
Life and Health Reinsurance Agreements Model Regulation Interest
Indexed Annuity Contracts Model Regulation
Accelerated Benefits Model Regulation

The most important NAIC model relating to valuation, the Standard Valuation Law (SVL), has been adopted by all states over the years. A number of changes have been made to this SVL over time and, in addition, a number of supporting model laws and regulations have been developed.

12.2.1 STANDARD VALUATION LAW (SVL)

The SVL that will be discussed in this section will be the current NAIC model at the time that this section was written. Important state variations and interpretations will also be discussed as they existed at that time.

The SVL applies to individual life insurance forms of coverage including supplemental forms of coverage such as accidental death benefit riders and waiver of premium disability income riders which can be sold in conjunction with individual life products. The SVL also applies to individual and group annuities including those in the accumulation mode as well as those in the payout stage. The annuity requirements also apply to "guaranteed interest contracts" (GIC's).

The SVL sets forth the mortality tables, interest rates and methodology to be used in calculating statutory reserves. These requirements have changed over time and since they generally apply to insurance policies based on the issue date of those policies the actuary will need to be aware of the past history of reserve requirements.

Tables 12.2 and 12.3, on the following pages, show a sample of the historic reserve requirements for the state of Illinois.

Table 12.2
State of Illinois
Life Insurance Reserve Requirements

Effective Date	Method	Table	Interest
Prior to 1-1-08[1]	FPT	Actuaries or Combined Experience Table of Mortality	4.0%
1-1-08 to 12-31-47[2]	MPT	American Experience Table of Mortality with either Craig's or Buttolph's Extension ages 10 and under	3.5%
1-1-48 to 12-31-65	CRVM	Commissioners 1941 Standard Ordinary Mortality Table	3.5%
1-1-66 to 9-7-77[3]	CRVM	Commissioners 1958 Standard Ordinary Mortality Table with not more than 3 year female age setback	3.5%
9-8-77 to 12-31-88	CRVM	Commissioners 1958 Standard Ordinary Mortality Table with not more than 6 year female age setback	4.5% 5.5%*
1-1-89 to present[3]	CRVM	Commissioners 1980 Standard Ordinary Mortality Table, or at the election of the company for any of one or more specified plans of life insurance, the Commissioners 1980 Standard Ordinary Mortality Table with Ten-Year Select Mortality Factors, or any mortality table, adopted after 1980 by the NAIC, that is approved by regulation promulgated by the director for use in determining the minimum standard of valuation for such policies [4]	Dynamic

* Single Premium Life Insurance
[1] For group insurance under which premiums are not guaranteed for five years use the valuation standard American Men 3.5%.
[2] On or after 1-1-38 American Men 3.5% may be used and the method can be the select-and-ultimate method using 50%, 65%, 75%, 85%, 95%, 100% in years one through six and later.
[3] An earlier effective date could be elected in writing.
[4] There is a 1-1-87 effective date for the section of the law that applies to life insurance with a first-year premium greater than the second-year

premium with no comparable additional benefit in the first year.

Table 12.3
State of Illinois
Individual Annuity and Pure Endowment Reserve Requirements

Effective Date	Method	Table	Interest
Prior to 1-1-38		Basis used for 1937 Annual Statement	
1-1-38 to 12-31-47	MPT	American Annuitant's Table	3.75%
1-1-48 to 9-7-77	CRVM	1937 Standard Annuity Mortality Table, or, at the option of the company, the Annuity Mortality Table for 1949, Ultimate, or any modification of either of these tables approved by the director	3.5%
9-8-77 to 12-30-83[1]	CARVM	1971 Individual Annuity Mortality Table or any individual annuity mortality table adopted after 1980 by the NAIC that is approved by regulation promulgated by the director for use in determining the minimum standard of valuation for such contracts, or any modification of these tables approved by the director	4.5% 5.5% ** 7.5% *
12-31-83 to 12-30-85	CARVM	No Change	Dynamic
12-31-85 to present[2]	CARVM	1983 Table "A" Regulation 935	Dynamic

*   Single Premium Immediate Annuities
**   Single Premium Deferred Annuity or Pure Endowment contracts
[1]   The range of dates shown assume that an election was made on 9-8-77 to use the 1971 annuity tables. This election could have been made between 9-8-77 to 1-1-79.
[2]   Could be used for business issued on or after 9-8-77.

12.2.2 VARIATIONS BY STATE IN VALUATION REQUIREMENTS

The 1990 SVL requires that the actuary opine that the reserves meet the requirements of the state in which the statement and opinion are being filed, not just the state of domicile. This leads to some interesting complications since states have adopted NAIC Model laws and regulations at different times. In addition, some states may not have adopted an updated model or may have modified the NAIC version.

These complications make it imperative that in order to render the required opinion and also to comply with the applicable Standards that the actuary be aware of variations in valuation requirements by state. Some of the areas which the actuary may wish to address in making this comparison of valuation laws including some state specific variations as of the date of publication of this text are shown below.

- The dates on which different eras of mortality tables and interest rates were adopted.
- Whether or not the state in which an opinion is filed has adopted the Smoker/Non-Smoker version of 58 CSO and 80 CSO mortality tables.
- What are a state's valuation requirements that impact accident and health insurance? A review of these will indicate a wide range of requirements. Some states require only gross unearned premium reserves while some have adopted the most recent version of the NAIC model. There are, however, many states that have adopted the prior NAIC model. This topic is not addressed in the text.
- Credit life and accident and health requirements will also vary from state to state with many states having no specific valuation requirements outside of the valuation law.
- Few states have specific reserve requirements for group life insurance and reserving for products such as group permanent and similar coverages will require actuarial judgement.
- A number of states have special interpretations of the Commissioners' Annuity Reserve Valuation Method (CARVM). These states include the states of California, Colorado, Illinois, New York, Oregon, Pennsylvania, Texas, Virginia and Washington. The states of Texas and New York have regulations which require modified CARVM calculations while California and Washington have Bulletins. The state of

Illinois sent out a letter to companies several years ago requiring "continuous" CARVM on CD annuities. (CD annuities are annuities that were designed to compete with Certificates of Deposit (CDs) and typically have high surrender charges until the end of a defined term of one to ten years at which time they automatically renew unless the contract holder withdraws the funds.) The Colorado and Oregon requirements are not in writing. The list below describes the CARVM variations.

(a) California requires continuous CARVM and Bulletin 85-3 states that reserves may not be reduced for contingent surrender charges.

(b) Colorado requires continuous CARVM and does not allow the reduction of reserves for contingent surrender charges.

(c) Illinois Bulletin 89-57 requires continuous CARVM for CD type annuities.

(d) New York Reg. 126 § 95.11(c)(5) requires continuous CARVM and restricts the use of surrender charges subject to bailouts in reserve calculations (similar to Actuarial Guideline XIII).

(e) Oregon does not allow reduction of reserves for contingent surrender charges.

(f) Pennsylvania does not permit annuity reserves to be reduced by contingent surrender charges.

(g) Texas Rule 3.1202 (Rev. 1994) prohibits the use of contingent surrender charges in reserve calculations except where the contingency is based on disability or confinement in a nursing home.

(h) Virginia Administrative Letter 1979-20 adopts the Actuarial Guidelines (Guideline XIII addresses contingent surrender charges). Virginia also follows Illinois's position on continuous CARVM for CD type annuities.

(i) Washington Bulletin 84-2 does not allow the use of contingent surrender charges in the calculation of reserves.

It will be necessary to refer to the cited source or to contact the respective insurance department regarding the exact definition of "contingent" surrender charges.

12.3   ASSET ADEQUACY ANALYSIS

As was discussed previously, changes were made to the standard valuation law in 1991 requiring that actuaries consider the underlying assets when rendering an opinion.

Those companies that have operated in New York have been subject to Regulation 126 on certain lines of business. The rest of the insurance companies operating in the U.S. have been gradually brought under the 1990 SVL as states have adopted it. State adoptions of the 1990 SVL which includes the Valuation Actuary amendment and accompanying opinion and memorandum regulation are shown in Table 12.4 on pages 190-195.

Asset adequacy analysis is described in some detail in the SVL and the accompanying Model Regulation. The process is one of modeling assets and liabilities and comparing the cash flows generated by the assets backing the company's reserves, including interest, principal payments, maturities, sales (or borrowing) and calls, to the cash flows required by the liabilities, including premium income, claim payments, surrenders and expenses.

Actuarial Standards of Practice's 7, 14 and 22 along with Compliance Guideline # 3 provide guidance to the actuary in the completion of the required asset adequacy analysis.

The assumptions used are predicated on a going-concern basis, i.e., since this is a projection of the existing business only, expenses related to continuing production should be allocated to unprojected future business. The Valuation Actuary amendments to the Standard Valuation Law were initially drafted by the Tweedie committee. This committee was given the assignment to develop the amendments to the standard valuation law, along with the supporting regulations. The Life Committee of the Actuarial Standards Board has also been involved in this process since it has supported the work done by the Tweedie committee by developing actuarial standards of practice.

The Tweedie committee and its successor organization, the Joint Committee on the Valuation Actuary, worked with the Life and Health Actuarial Task Force of the NAIC to produce the Valuation Actuary amendments which were exposed in June, 1990, at the NAIC meeting and were finalized at the December, 1990, meeting.

Table 12.4

Adoptions of Valuation Actuary Requirement
and Opinion & Memorandum Regulation

State	Valuation Actuary Requirement	Opinion & Memorandum Regulation	Comments
Alabama	Yes	Yes	
Alaska	Yes	Yes	Alaska has adopted the Actuarial Opinion and Memorandum regulation effective with the 1996 annual statement opinion. Companies do not need to file the memorandums unless specifically requested by the director.
Arizona	Yes	Yes	
Arkansas	Yes	Yes	Adds a Disciplinary section. A confidentiality provision has been added for the actuarial opinion.
California	Yes	Yes	California has applied the opinion regulation since 1/1/92; the liability provision reads "shall be liable for his or her negligence or other tortious conduct." Does not allow three year phase-in. See also Bulletin 96-7 (updated each year).
Colorado	Yes	Yes	
Connecticut	Yes	Yes	Opinion language similar to model regulation with adjustment (See CT note on prior consultation)

State	Valuation Actuary Requirement	Opinion & Memorandum Regulation	Comments
Delaware	Yes	Yes	
District of Columbia	Yes	Rule Ch. 29	
Florida	Yes	Yes	SVL does not include liability provision.
Georgia	Yes	Yes	
Hawaii	Yes	Proposed	
Idaho	Yes	Yes	
Illinois	Yes	Yes	Actuarial memorandum must also disclose methodology for allocating assets, the specific blocks of business, and the AVR.
Indiana	Yes	Yes	
Iowa	Yes	Yes	
Kansas	Yes	Yes	
Kentucky	Yes	Yes	Emergency Reg 806 KAR 6:100E
Louisiana	Yes	Yes	
Maine	Yes	Yes	

State	Valuation Actuary Requirement	Opinion & Memorandum Regulation	Comments
Maryland	Yes	Yes	SVL liability exemption for actuary does not apply in case of gross negligence, cases of fraud, or willful misconduct.
Massachusetts	Yes	Yes	
Michigan	Yes	Yes	
Minnesota	Yes	Yes	Actuary must be appointed by company board of directors, not their representative.
Mississippi	Yes	Yes	Exemption Eligibility Test for Category B has been changed to eliminate reference to second priority company. The Aggregation Rule has been changed to eliminate the ability to aggregate across lines of business.
Missouri	Yes	Yes	
Montana	Yes	Yes	
Nebraska	Yes	Yes	
Nevada	Yes	Yes	
New Hampshire	Yes	Proposed	
New Jersey	Yes	Yes	

State	Valuation Actuary Requirement	Opinion & Memorandum Regulation	Comments
New Mexico	Yes	Yes	
New York	Yes	Yes	SVL liability exemption for actuary does not apply in case of gross negligence, cases of fraud, or willful misconduct. New York Law (Section 4217) now requires asset adequacy analysis for all assets covered by the NAIC SVL. Regulation 126 was revised with an effective date of 12/31/94 and is New York's version of the NAIC Model Opinion and Memorandum Regulation. Regulation 126 differs from the NAIC Model Regulation concerning aggregation (Section 95.10(a)), market value of projected results (Section 95.10(i)), and the analysis of projected negative surplus (Section 95.10(d) (4) and (5)).
North Carolina	Yes	Yes	
North Dakota	Yes	Yes	
Ohio	Yes	Yes	Definition of Appointed Actuary is expanded to give greater instructions when Appointed Actuary is replaced. Does not allow three year phase-in.
Oklahoma	Yes	Proposed	
Oregon	Yes	Yes	

State	Valuation Actuary Requirement	Opinion & Memorandum Regulation	Comments
Pennsylvania	Yes	Yes	Actuary who ceases to be appointed actuary must notify the state and the company of material reserve issues.
Puerto Rico	No	No	
Rhode Island	Yes	Yes	
South Carolina	Yes	Yes	
South Dakota	Yes	Yes	
Tennessee	Yes	Yes	
Texas	Yes	Yes	Confidentiality provision of SVL not included. Actuarial memorandum is also required for Section 7 opinions. Confidentiality provisions relating to actuarial memorandum not included. Actuarial opinion must contain a brief explanation of amounts not included in the asset adequacy analysis.
Utah	Yes	Yes	
Vermont	Yes	Yes	SVL liability provision not included.
Virginia	Yes	Yes	

State	Valuation Actuary Requirement	Opinion & Memorandum Regulation	Comments
Washington	Yes	Yes	Additional required reserves must be phased in over two years, instead of three. Additional documentation required in the actuarial memorandum.
West Virginia	Yes	Yes	
Wisconsin	Yes	Yes	
Wyoming	Yes	Yes	SVL liability exemption for actuary does not apply in case of gross negligence, cases of fraud, or willful misconduct. Does not include exemption of actuarial memorandum from subpoena.

These amendments require that the qualified actuary (under these amendments a qualified actuary is defined as a member in good standing of the American Academy of Actuaries) will attest to the adequacy of reserves in light of the assets backing the reserves, the investment earnings on these assets, and any considerations anticipated to be received and retained on the policies and contracts to cover benefits under and expenses associated with these policies and contracts.

This opinion is to be based on standards of practice issued by the Actuarial Standards Board. The actuary is supposed to be legally liable only to the state and the company. A provision in the model states that, but it will be up to the courts to verify that this provision works in those cases where it hasn't already been modified by the adopting state. The purpose of this provision is to minimize any attempts at litigation, frivolous or otherwise, against the actuary based on the opinions that the actuary has provided. There is also the possibility of disciplinary action against the actuary by the commissioner of the state.

The valuation actuary regulation, which goes hand-in-hand with the amendments to the Standard Valuation Law, will also require that the annual statement of opinion attest to the adequacy of the reserves in light of the assets backing these reserves.

However, the qualified actuary under this regulation is defined a little bit differently. Under the regulation, the actuary must be qualified to sign the life and health statement in accordance with the American Academy of Actuaries qualification standards. To meet this standard, actuaries not only must be members of the Academy, but also have to keep up their continuing education requirements. Also, in this case, the actuary will be disqualified if they have gotten into any trouble with the state or with any other body of law.

This qualified actuary also has to be an appointed actuary, i.e., the actuary has to be appointed by the board of directors of the company or their representative. If the appointed actuary is changed by the board, the board has to let the state know that the actuary was changed and why the actuary was changed. There are, however, small company exemptions from asset adequacy analysis in this regulation.

The regulation splits up companies into four categories:

(A)   Companies with less than $20 million of assets
(B)   Companies with $20 to $100 million of assets
(C)   Companies with $100 to $500 million of assets
(D)   Companies with more than $500 million of assets

The regulation then sets forth certain ratios that members of the groups of smaller companies must meet in order to be exempted from asset adequacy analysis. These ratios include ratios of:

(i)   capital and surplus to cash and invested assets,
(ii)   annuities and other deposits to total assets, and
(iii)   the book value of non-investment grade assets to capital and surplus.

If a company's ratios fall within certain limits the actuary may not have to provide a cash flow testing type opinion or may have to provide one only once every three years. This is displayed below in Table 12.5, which shows the three-ratio requirements for the four asset categories:

Table 12.5
Company Asset Classes

(A) Under $20 Million	(B) $20 Million to $100 Million	(C) $100 Million to $500* Million	(D) >$500 Million
(i) ≥ .10	≥ .07	≥ .05	Non-Exempt
(ii) < .30	< .40	< .50	Non-Exempt
(iii) < .50	< .50	< .50	Non-Exempt

* Cash flow testing opinion required at least once every three years if ratios are met.

However, even if the ratio tests are met, a company will not be exempted from asset adequacy analysis if the company was on the NAIC's "priority one" list in either of the two preceding years, or on the NAIC's "priority two" list in both of the two prior years. (Note that a company may be excused from this requirement if the company can demonstrate to the Insurance Regulator of its State of domicile that the reasons for being placed on the NAIC priority list have been remedied.)

The actuary for an exempted company will still have to provide a statutory opinion on reserves and will also have to show what the above ratios were. The actuary must then state that the cash flow testing type opinion was not requested and also state that the company has not been requested by any state to provide such opinion. (Note that it may be difficult for the actuary, especially a consulting actuary, to ascertain that the company was not on the NAIC priority list and has not been requested to perform an asset adequacy analysis by any state.)

The actuary completing asset adequacy analysis is required to indicate the method of analysis that was used in analyzing the reserves and the underlying assets. This is typically done through the use of a table which displays the reserves and other liabilities included in the asset adequacy analysis and indicates the method used for the analysis.

Any increase in reserves that is required to be set up may be graded in over three years (except in California where additional reserves must be established immediately). However, the testing that is required to be done is not necessarily limited to cash flow testing. Referring to the ASOP's on cash flow testing, there are lines of business where cash flow testing is not the most appropriate method for testing a block of business. For example, a gross premium valuation may be an appropriate method of analysis for health insurance lines of business.

The regulation requires that a memorandum be produced to support the work that is done. The memorandum is to include the detail for the liabilities that were reviewed including product descriptions that show a risk profile of the product, the source of the in force, the reserve method and basis, any investment reserves that were included in the analysis, i.e., the Asset Valuation Reserve (AVR) and Interest Maintenance Reserve (IMR) as well as the effects of any reinsurance agreements. For the assets, the actuary has to describe the portfolio including a risk profile of the assets, the investment and disinvestment assumptions used in the modeling process, the source of the asset data, and the asset valuation bases.

The qualified actuary must also:

- detail the analysis bases that were used, the methodology, the rationale for inclusion or exclusion of different blocks of business, and how pertinent risks were analyzed.
- give the rationale for the degree of rigor that was used in analyzing different blocks of business.
- show the criteria that were used for determining asset adequacy.
- detail the effect of federal income tax, reinsurance and other relevant factors.

Aggregation of non-homogeneous lines of business is allowed in these analyses, and the actuary will be allowed to aggregate a sufficient block of business with a deficient block of business if the scenarios that are used to do the analyses are consistent and the blocks of business aggregated are subject to mutually independent risks. The qualified actuary is required to describe the method of aggregation that was used.

The qualified Actuary must analyze cash flows under at least the following interest scenarios.

- level.
- uniformly increasing over 10 years @ .5% per year and then level.
- increasing @ 1% per year for 5 years and then decreasing @ 1% per year for 5 years to original level after 10 years.
- an immediate increase of 3% and then level.
- uniformly decreasing over 10 years @ .5% per year and then level.
- decreasing @ 1% per year for 5 years and then increasing @ 1% per year for 5 years to original level after 10 years.
- an immediate decrease of 3% and then level.

The present version of the model regulation sets a minimum interest rate of 1/2 of the initial five-year treasury rate.

One question that arises in practice with respect to this area is whether these are meant to be parallel shifts in the yield curve or shifts around some pivotal year with the slope of the yield curve determined by some other means, perhaps using arbitrage free methods.

Some states may require additional scenario testing and the seven required scenarios should be a minimum number of interest scenarios. The actuary should also examine sensitivities to changes in other assumption; for example, expenses, surrenders, and mortality. The testing of variations in different assumptions can produce a large number of possible combinations of sensitivities, however, an examination of the results will allow the actuary to focus on those parameters which have the most impact on cash flows.

The qualified actuary should always retain on file sufficient documentation so that the results may be audited. An external peer review is also recommended.

12.4   ACTUARIAL GUIDELINES OF THE NAIC EXAMINER'S HANDBOOK

The appointed actuary is required by ASOP#22 and Compliance Guideline #4 to be aware of the Actuarial Guidelines of the NAIC Examiners Handbook. These guidelines are typically applied by the examination staff of an insurance department during an examination of an insurance company.

A summarization of the Actuarial Guidelines as shown in the 1994 Edition of the Life and Health Valuation Law Manual of the Academy of Actuaries is shown below. These summaries are intended to provide a quick reference for the subject matters covered by the guidelines themselves. The summaries are not necessarily complete nor have they been approved by the NAIC. The reader is advised to read the guideline itself for a complete understanding of its effect.

Note that several guidelines refer to nonforfeiture or other topics not related directly to reserves. However, since minimum reserves are related to cash values, a review of these guidelines is also recommended.

I.   *Valuation of Policies in Which the Net Premium Exceeds Gross Premium.*
       The 1976 amendments to the SVL changed the methodology of calculating deficiency reserves from an explicit extra reserve to an alternative minimum reserve calculation (using the maximum reserve interest and minimum mortality basis, and substituting gross premiums for net premiums). The guideline merely states that this change was a change in method and not a change in standards and that the minimum reserve basis is that in effect at the date of policy issue.

II.   *Valuation of Active Life Funds Held Relative to Group Annuity Contracts.*
       This guideline is only applicable where the 1980 Amendments to the SVL do not apply.

III.   *Definition of the Term "Maturity Value" in the Standard Nonforfeiture Law for Individual Deferred Annuities.*
       This affects nonforfeiture only. For contracts providing cash surrender values, the cash surrender value at maturity must equal the

minimum nonforfeiture value at maturity. For purposes of calculating cash values prior to maturity (i.e., the discounted maturity value at a discount rate 1% higher than the accumulation rate), the term "maturity value" means the cash surrender value at maturity.

IV. *Minimum Reserves for Certain Forms of Term Insurance.*
This applies only to 1958 CSO term plans without cash values. The NAIC has proposed, but not adopted, extension of this guideline to other plans. Minimum reserves, including deficiency reserves, must be calculated separately for successive periods of level premiums. This prevents large distant future premiums from depressing near-term net premiums, which would occur if the unitary method were used (i.e., if net premiums were a uniform percentage of all future gross premiums). Other points:

(1) If a reinsurer has the right to raise premiums to net valuation premiums, the reinsurer need not hold deficiency reserves, and ceding company gets no such reserve credit. If reinsurance premiums are guaranteed, deficiency reserves may be needed.

(2) The actuary should consider for term contracts of this nature the "good and sufficient" element of the reserves.

V. *Acceptable Approximations for Continuous Functions.*
The guideline shows acceptable approximations for:

$$\overline{D}_x \text{ and } \overline{C}_x$$

VI. *Interpretation Regarding Use of Single or Joint Life Mortality Tables.*
This guideline applies both to valuation and nonforfeiture. It states that for multiple life products (e.g., joint-life, last-survivor) the references in the laws to "whole life," "nineteen-year premium whole life," etc., are to be interpreted as applying to the same form of life product as the actual product, e.g., "whole life" for a last-survivor product means a last-survivor whole life plan.

VII. *Calculation of Equivalent Level Amounts.*
In calculating equivalent level amounts for valuation and nonforfeiture purposes, pure endowment benefits are to be ignored. (This is clear from the SNFL, but not so clear from the SVL.)

VIII. *The Valuation of Individual Single Premium Deferred Annuities.*
The 1976 amendments to the SVL introduced the CARVM methodology. This guideline notes that, although CARVM is required by all states that enacted the 1976 amendments, CARVM is merely a method in other states. (Note: Virtually all jurisdictions have now adopted CARVM).

IX. *Form Classification of Individual Single-Premium Annuities for Application of the Valuation and Nonforfeiture Laws.*
For purposes of the SVL and SNFL, an individual single-premium annuity is classified as immediate, as opposed to deferred, provided:
(1)   The first annuity payment is not more than thirteen months from issue date.
(2)   Succeeding payments are no less frequent than annually.
(3)   Guaranteed payments in any year are not greater than 115% of guaranteed payments in the preceding year.

IX-A.   *Use of Substandard Annuity Mortality Tables in Valuing Impaired Lives Under Structured Settlements.*
For substandard structured settlement annuities (structured settlements are defined in the guideline) where there are medical records to justify higher assumed mortality, minimum reserves are those which would be calculated by a constant addition to mortality rates such that the adjusted life expectancy is greater than or equal to the actual life expectancy and such that reserves grade to standard reserves at the end of the mortality table. This results in a decreasing extra percentage mortality.

IX-B.   *Clarification of Methods for Deferred Annuities and Structured Settlements Contracts.*
Guideline IX-B expands upon Guideline IX and provides direction on what to do if an annuity fails Guideline IX. If the first payment is deferred more than 13 months (and there are no cash settlement options) use the deferred annuity valuation interest rate based on issue-year method and a guaranteed duration equal to the years from issue to first payment. At the time payments begin, use the immediate annuity valuation rate for year of issue, year of premium received, or year payments begin (but apply consistently).

For "lumpy" payment patterns (i.e., an individual contract with a payment more than 115% of the previous year's payment, and an issue-year block with payment greater than 110% of previous year's payment) some options are defined that involve either splitting the block into smooth pieces and lumpy pieces, or calculating graded interest rate reserves.

X. *Guideline for Interpretation of NAIC Standard Nonforfeiture Law for Individual Deferred Annuities.*
This affects nonforfeiture only. Excess interest credited to individual deferred annuity contracts may be subject to a surrender charge (subject, of course, to the entire cash surrender value meeting the "discounted maturity value at a discount rate 1% higher than the accumulation rate" test). Dividends on deferred annuity contracts have treatment depending on circumstances, dividends left on deposit may not be subject to surrender charges, and dividends that increase the policy account value may be subject to charges.

XI. *Effect of an Early Election by an Insurance Company of an Operative Date under Section 5-C of the Standard Nonforfeiture Law for Life Insurance.*
This affects nonforfeiture only and is no longer relevant, since "1980 CSO" requirements are now mandatory.

XII. *Interpretation Regarding Valuation and Nonforfeiture Interest Rates.*
For policies covered by the 1976 amendments to the SNFL and SVL, this guideline points out that, although paid-up nonforfeiture benefits and paid-up additions may be calculated using interest rates higher than for the basic policy cash values, the valuation rate must be the rate used in determining the minimum standard for the basic life policy.

XIII. *Guideline Concerning the Commissioners' Annuity Reserve Valuation Method.*
The value of future guaranteed benefits under CARVM may not be reduced by contingent surrender charges. Surrender charges are considered "not available" when there is a "bail-out" provision unless the bail-out rate is low enough. "Low enough" is defined in the guideline. The guideline also addresses the meaning of "low enough"

for bail-out rates that are a function of an external index and how to treat policies that have multiple investment options if one of the options has a bail-out provision.

XIV. *Surveillance Procedure Regarding the Actuarial Opinion for Life and Health Insurers.*
This is largely superseded by the 1990 SVL and model regulation. It may still be relevant for Section 7 (non-asset adequacy) opinions. The surveillance procedures are as follows:
(1)   The regulator should accept opinions only from qualified actuaries.
(2)   The regulator should determine if an opinion is qualified or has an omission and, if so, follow up.
(3)   The regulator should examine situations where there has been a change in opining actuary.
(4)   The regulator may require an Actuarial Report, including the following:
    i.   An explanation of unusual IRIS ratios.
    ii.   What was covered by the "good and sufficient" analysis.
    iii.   The extent to which the opinion is influenced by the continuing business assumption.
(5)   The review of the Actuarial Report and documentation should be done by a qualified reviewer.

XV. *Illustration Guideline for Variable Life Insurance Model Regulation.*
This guideline addresses sales illustrations; there are no valuation implications.

XVI. *Guideline for Calculation of Commissioners' Reserve Valuation Method on Select Mortality and/or Split Interest.*
When calculating the "net level annual premium on the nineteen-year premium whole life plan," you should use:

$$19P_{[x]+1} \quad \text{instead of} \quad 19P_{[x+1]}$$

XVII.   *Guideline for Calculation of Commissioners' Reserve Valuation Method When Death Benefits are Not Level.*
        For policies issued after the operative date of Section 5-C of the SVL (i.e., 1980 CSO), when calculating the "net level annual premium on the nineteen-year premium whole life plan," you should use the nine-year arithmetic average of the death benefit at the beginning of each of policy years two through ten as the amount.

XVIII. *Guideline for Calculation of Commissioners' Reserve Valuation Method on Semi-Continuous, Fully Continuous, or Discounted Continuous Basis.*
        When calculating "the excess of (a) over (b)" in the definition of modified net premiums, you may use the same basis (e.g., continuous) as for reserves. This would produce a zero first-year terminal reserve for whole life.

XIX.   *Guideline Concerning 1980 Commissioners' Standard Ordinary Mortality Table With 10-Year Select Mortality Factors.*
        This guideline specifies how unisex versions of the 10-year select mortality factors for 1980 CSO should be determined; use formula on page 457 of NAIC Proceedings, 1984 Vol. 1.

XX.   *Guideline Concerning Joint Life Functions for 1980 Commissioners' Standard Ordinary Mortality Table.*
        Acceptable tables of uniform seniority and values are given. It is noted that "exact" calculations of joint-life functions are also accepted. Other methods "may also be acceptable."

XXI.   *Guideline for Calculation of CRVM Reserves When (b) is Greater Than (a).*
        The "excess of (a) over (b)" is used in the definition of modified net premiums in Section 4 of the SVL.
        (1)   For policies issued on or after January 1, 1987, when (b) is greater than (a), set the excess to zero.
        (2)   (a) is defined as the net level premium payable on the first anniversary. Note that this could produce a positive first-year terminal reserve if the first-year premium exceeds the second-year premium. The guideline affirms that CRVM reserves as defined may not be the same as full preliminary term.

XXII.   *Interpretation Regarding Nonforfeiture Values for Policies With Indeterminate Premiums.*
This affects nonforfeiture only. Minimum nonforfeiture values for an indeterminate premium policy are the greater of those calculated using i) the guaranteed maximum premiums or ii) the current illustrated premiums.

XXIII.   *Guideline Concerning Variable Life Insurance Separate Account Investments.*
The Variable Life Model Regulation states that the separate account shall have sufficient net investment income and readily marketable assets to meet anticipated withdrawals. This guideline defines "sufficient" over a one-year time horizon, and requires "sufficient" to be 115% of anticipated withdrawals over the next year, but not less than 11.5% of the market value of account assets.

XXIV.   *Guideline for Variable Life Nonforfeiture Values.*
This affects nonforfeiture values only. Three options are allowed for minimum cash surrender values:
Option B: Retrospective method; accumulation using whole-life initial expense allowances
Option C: Prospective method; present value of future benefits less present value of future adjusted premiums
Option D: Maximum charge method; limits on all expense charges.
The guideline provides considerable details on the methods summarized above.

XXV.   *Guideline for Calculation of Minimum Reserves and Minimum Nonforfeiture Values for Policies with Guaranteed Increasing Death Benefits Based on an Index.*
This guideline has separate sections for valuation and nonforfeiture. It applies only to policies issued on or after January 1, 1991. Regarding valuation, for policies indexed to the CPI or other cost-of-living index, the guideline specifies that future death benefits shall be assumed to increase at a rate equal to the maximum valuation rate less a spread. The spread ranges from 1.0% to 2.0%, depending on the limitations on the death benefit increases.

XXVI. *Guideline for Election of Operative Dates under Standard Valuation Law and Standard Nonforfeiture Law.*
Insurance companies could not elect an operative date for the 1980 amendments for a calendar year prior to the calendar year in which the company provided written notice of early election.

XXVII. *Actuarial Guideline for Accelerated Benefits.*
This guideline covers several topics, including policy form language. Regarding valuation, the guideline addresses the following methods of accelerating benefits:
(1) Non-Discounted Acceleration of Benefits Approach: basic CRVM methodology is acceptable, as is any other methodology allowable for life insurance. The reserve formula should consider all relevant factors.
(2) Actuarially Discounted Acceleration of Benefit: no additional reserves are needed if the actuary is convinced that the discounting reflects sound actuarial principles.
(3) Interest Accrual Approach to Financing Acceleration of Benefits: prior to occurrence, no extra reserves are needed, provided that interest rate to be charged is at least equal to the valuation rate. Following occurrence, accrued interest is an asset and the actuary should make certain that reserves are adequate.
(4) Benefit Payment Liens: the guideline does not address reserves for this.

XXVIII. *Statutory Reserves for Group Long-Term Disability Contracts Within A Survivor Income Benefit Provision.*
Claim reserves for survivor income benefits contained in group long-term disability contracts should not be ignored. A suitable approximation would be to reduce the valuation interest rate on the basic disability benefit, but testing of this approximation must be performed. A sample suitable approximation is described.

XXIX. *Guideline Concerning Reserves of Companies in Rehabilitation.*
The guideline defines reserves for life insurance contracts and annuity contracts that have been modified by a court having jurisdiction.

XXX.   *Guideline for the Application of Plan Type to Guaranteed Interest Contracts (GICs) with Benefit Responsive Payment Provisions Used to Fund Employee Benefit Plans.*
The guideline clarifies the method for determining the proper plan type for certain guaranteed interest contracts.

XXXI. *Valuation Issues vs. Policy Form Approval.*
The guideline clarifies that establishment and/or acceptance of a method for computing minimum reserves for a type of benefit should not be construed to mean that a state is required to approve a form containing that kind of benefit.

XXXII. *Reserve for Immediate Payment of Claims.*
The guideline requires an adjustment to reserves for life insurance when the method of claim payment differs from that assumed in the base reserve calculation.
   (1)   When a company practices immediate payment of claims and carries curtate reserves, the death portion of the curtate reserves should be increased by 1/3 of one year's valuation rate of interest.
   (2)   Where the contract provides for the payment of interest on the proceeds from the date of death to the date of payment, the death portion of curtate reserves shall be increased by 1/2 of one year's valuation rate of interest.
Company practices, although not contractually required, should be considered. Where the base reserves are more conservative than the minimum requirement, that redundancy can be considered in meeting this guidelines
The guideline allows a grade in period of five years starting with the effective year of 1994.

XXXIII. *Determining Minimum CARVM Reserves for Individual Annuity Contracts.*
This guideline clarifies the application of CARVM to individual annuities with multiple benefit streams, where these benefit streams can include whole or partial withdrawals, annuitizations, death benefits, or other benefits such as nursing home related withdrawals without the application of a surrender charge.
The CARVM reserve should be the largest of the present values of all possible benefit streams. The valuation rate for each benefit

stream is determined from the Plan Type and guarantee duration applicable to each benefit stream. In the case of the annuitization benefit stream, since there will probably be no cash surrender options, the Plan Type is "A" and the guarantee duration is determined as the time from the original issue date to the date that annuitization is assumed to occur.

A company may still make an election at the time of issue to value annuities with cash settlement options on a change in fund basis. However, annuity benefit streams with no cash settlement option must be valued on an issue-year basis.

If preferential annuitizations (annuitizations at a current settlement rate) are guaranteed, the reserve may not be less than 93% of the current accumulation fund.

This revised version of the Guideline is effective on December 31, 1998 for all contracts issued on or after January 1, 1981. The prior version was effective on December 31, 1995. Both versions included the option for a three-year grade in of any additional reserve requirements at the discretion of the state of domicile.

XXXIV. *Variable Annuity Minimum Guaranteed Death Benefit Reserves.*
This Guideline interprets the standards for applying CARVM to Minimum Guaranteed Death Benefits (MGDBs) in variable annuity contracts, clarifies standards for integrating of MGDBs with other benefits including surrenders and annuitizations and clarifies the level of reserves to be held in a company's General Account.

This Guideline requires that MGDBs be projected assuming an immediate drop in the value of assets followed by a recovery at some assumed rate of return until the contract matures. The level of the drop and the rate of return for the recovery are defined for five different asset classes.

This Guideline requires the use of 110% of the 1994 Group Annuity Mortality Table without projection and requests that the Society of Actuaries review the adequacy of this basis. This Guideline also addresses reserve methods for reinsurance involving MGDBs.

Companies that carry a net liability equal to the account value, assuming that the spread between the surrender value and the account value covers the liability for the MGDB will have to validate that assumption while companies that carry a net liability equal to the surrender value will have to establish additional MGDB liabilities.

REVIEW QUESTIONS

1.   What is the SVL?

2.   Do all states have the same SVL? If not, why not and what are the implications?

3.   What is asset adequacy analysis?

4.   Is it sufficient to run only the seven required scenarios? Please explain.

5.   What are Actuarial Guidelines and why should the actuary care about them?

CHAPTER 13
ACTUARIAL STANDARDS OF PRACTICE

13.1 ACTUARIAL STANDARDS BOARD

13.1.1 AN EXPERIMENT

We all apply standards in our everyday activities. These may be standards we learned in our childhood from our parents, standards we have learned through religious teachings or standards imposed upon us by the laws of our governmental bodies. These standards apply to how we treat other people and property, how we dress, or our general work habits.

As actuaries we have also developed our own practice standards. These standards have evolved from our interpretation of our actuarial teachings either in the classroom, on the job or through the examination process combined with our other personal standards.

Why do we need codified standards of practice? For a number of reasons:

- Our personal actuarial standards vary and may not get modified as the environment changes.
- Codified standards can present a distillation of the methods in general use for specific types of work.
- In our increasingly litigious society, we need standards both for a safe harbor in certain situations and as a method of defense in case of litigation.
- Standards allow the actuarial organizations to discipline those actuaries using unprofessional methods.
- Standards provide us with a checklist to make certain that we have addressed all of the issues that relate to a certain type of actuarial work.

- Standards allow us to deal with areas of concern to the insurance public either before regulatory action or in conjunction with regulatory action.

You can probably think of several more reasons justifying the need for standards of practice.

There are those actuaries that may have ignored standards of practice and others that have spoken out against the development of standards. However, we are moving toward an increasingly complex and structured society and actuarial standards are here to stay.

The **Interim Actuarial Standards Board (IASB)** was established in 1985 as an experiment in the development of standards of practice. This organization did not have the powers of the present **Actuarial Standards Board (ASB)**. The documents issued by the IASB were called Recommendations and Interpretations instead of Standards and they had to be approved by the Academy Board of Directors. However with the formalization of the ASB these interpretations gained the weight of standards of practice and have since been rewritten as standards of practice. The IASB experiment ran for two and one-half years and in 1988 the academy membership approved the present ASB by a 3 to 1 margin.

13.1.2 STRUCTURE OF THE ACTUARIAL STANDARDS BOARD

The ASB is structured in the following manner:

- The ASB is a separate entity affiliated with the American Academy of Actuaries.
- It is financed by Academy membership and is supported by the Academy staff.
- It is composed of nine members each with a three-year term. These terms are staggered so that 1/3 of the board is appointed each year and a board member cannot serve more than two consecutive terms.
- New members are appointed by a committee composed of the president and presidents-elect of the Academy, the Society of Actuaries, the Casualty Actuarial Society and the Conference of Actuaries in Public Practice. The president of the Academy serves as the chairperson of the selection committee.
- The chairperson of the ASB is also appointed by this committee.

Some of the duties of the ASB are to:

- Manage the development of Actuarial Standards of Practice (ASOP).
- Identify the need for new ASOP's.
- Review existing ASOP's for amendment or elimination.
- Cooperate with the **Actuarial Board for Counseling and Discipline (ABCD)**.
- Promote the value and the adherence to ASOP's.

The ASB functions in more of a management role to the different subcommittees that are ultimately responsible for the production of ASOP's. The ASB functions separately from the academy although it receives administrative support from the Academy staff.

The pronouncements of the ASB can take several forms. They can be Standards of Practice, they can be Actuarial Guidelines or they can be bulletins or warnings to the membership.

Standards of Practice offer guidance to and restrictions on actuaries performing certain professional duties. However, intentional non-compliance with ASOP's may constitute violation of the Code of Professional Conduct of the American Academy of Actuaries and can lead to disciplinary proceedings in front of the ABCD and even to expulsion from our professional organizations.

Compliance Guidelines offer guidance to the actuary in complying with the standards or regulations of some other body including FASB, the Federal Government and the NAIC. Compliance Guidelines are also considered Standards and intentional non-compliance with them has exactly the same implications as non-compliance with Standards of Practice.

The ASB relies on a number of subcommittees to assist in the development of ASOP's. The operating committees of the ASB include:

- Life
- Health
- Casualty
- Pension
- Retiree Health
- Specialty Committee

The specialty committee has been responsible for ASOP's such as the **Continuing Care Retirement Community (CCRC)** standard under the IASB and Risk Classification under the ASB.

Occasionally a task force will be assembled to deal with current issues, e.g., The Long-Term Care task force that was established to develop the ASOP for that topic.

13.1.3 LIFE COMMITTEE OF THE ACTUARIAL STANDARDS BOARD

The subcommittee that is of the most importance to the readers of this text is probably the **Life Committee of the Actuarial Standards Board (LASB)**. The members of this committee are representative of various interests including consulting firms, stock insurance companies, mutual insurance companies and regulators.

The number of members of the LASB is determined by the ASB. The chairperson of this subcommittee is nominated by the Chairperson of the ASB and is approved by the members of the ASB. The Chairperson of the LASB is responsible for assembling the membership roster of the LASB and presenting a roster to the ASB for their approval.

13.1.4 DEVELOPMENT OF A STANDARD OF PRACTICE

The indication of a need for a Standard of Practice can come from a number of areas including a perceived need by the members of the ASB, a regulatory request, external pressure from other actuaries or to update existing standards. Compliance Guidelines are developed in response to standards or regulations of other organizations, e.g., the FASB, the federal government or the NAIC.

Once a need has been established for the development of a Standard the actual development may be done by:

- Another Committee of the Academy: The drafts of life standards have often come from the Committee on Life Insurance Financial Reporting of the American Academy of Actuaries.
- A knowledgeable individual or group: The once proposed ASOP for HIV risks was drafted by individuals knowledgeable in that topic.
- A task force established by the LASB: The ASOP for appraisals of insurance companies was such a Standard.
- The LASB itself.

Once the initial draft has been developed, the LASB will meet to review what has been done and will make modifications. These modifications will be more to the form of the document than to the substance. All ASOP's must follow a standard structure which is addressed in a Procedures Manual and is modified from time to time by the ASB. The required structure is outlined below.

Section 1. Purpose, Scope, and Effective Date
Section 2. Definitions
Section 3. Background and Historical Issues
Section 4. Current Practices and Alternatives
Section 5. Recommended Practices
Section 6. Communication and Disclosure

The LASB will try to get the proposed draft Standard of Practice into a form that can be forwarded to the ASB for their review and potential release as an Exposure Draft. The Academy staff will assist at this point to make certain that the standard is structured appropriately and that all wording and definitions are consistent with prior Standards and established protocols. The proposed exposure draft will also be reviewed at this time by the legal staff of the Academy for problems such as anti-trust or increased litigation risk for the membership.

Finally the Exposure Draft will go to the ASB where it may be modified before being approved or it may be sent back to the LASB for more work. If the Exposure Draft is approved, it then goes to the Academy membership for a set exposure period. During that period, interested academy members are requested to comment on the exposure draft. Comments from interested parties were light for some of the earlier standards but over time have increased in volume.

All of the comments that are received are forwarded to the members of the LASB and are given serious consideration in the fine-tuning of the Exposure Draft to create a final Standard. In fact, the more frequent or more substantial comments will be summarized in the preface of the final ASOP. It is possible that the comments received may result in substantive changes to the Exposure Draft and the LASB may recommend to the ASB that the Standard be re-exposed or the ASB may make that determination themselves when the Standard is submitted to the ASB for final approval as a Standard. If no substantive changes are made, the LASB will forward the modified Standard to the ASB for their approval and if approved it will become a new Standard.

Standards can apply to all members of the Academy. An actuary should refer to the scope of any standards that may apply to a task being undertaken to determine whether or not the standard applies. The standards are not intended to be used as cookbooks to complete applicable tasks but rather as guidelines or checklists.

What if an actuary fails to realize that a Standard applies to work being done or chooses to ignore or deviate from a Standard? The ABCD is responsible for enforcing the Standards. In addition, the actuary can anticipate that if anything goes wrong, litigation will follow. In any litigation the actuary that follows to the letter any applicable Standards will fare better than the actuary that forgot to review the ASOP or deviated from recommendations included in the ASOP. However, if the actuary sincerely feels that it is appropriate to deviate from a Standard, then the actuary should document that deviation including the rationale for the deviation.

13.2   LIFE: ACTUARIAL STANDARDS OF PRACTICE

The following are summaries of selected **Actuarial Standards of Practice** (**ASOP**'s) which may apply to actuaries working in the life and annuity area. The actuary should always refer to the entire ASOP for guidance and may wish to use the ASOP's as a checklist in completing certain types of actuarial tasks.

13.2.1 ASOP #1: THE REDETERMINATION (OR DETERMINATION) OF NON-GUARANTEED CHARGES AND/OR BENEFITS FOR LIFE INSURANCE AND ANNUITY CONTRACTS

This ASOP was initially adopted by the IASB in 1986 and was reformatted as a Standard and re-adopted by the ASB. It applies to the non-guaranteed elements of Universal Life, Indeterminate Premium Life, Annuities, etc. It does not apply to dividend calculations, which are addressed by ASOP #15.

This ASOP provides some guidance to the practicing actuary on non-guaranteed elements. Specifically in Section 5 of the Standard the following recommendations are made:

- The actuary should consider the company's policy in determining non-guaranteed elements. This policy includes the company's solvency, marketing and profit objectives.
- The actuary should consider the extent to which previous gains or losses affect redetermination. In doing so, the actuary should also consider the extent to which regulatory restrictions affect the redetermination.
- The actuary should consider the company's underwriting, claims, investment, sales and administrative practices in any determination or redetermination.
- The actuary should be aware of the classes of contracts being reviewed.
- The redetermination will usually involve two types of factors.
  (a) Contract factors; face amount, cash value, contract guarantees, etc.
  (b) Anticipated Experience Factors; mortality, investment, lapse, expense, etc.
- The actuary may wish to use modeling in the redetermination process.
- The actuary should consider likely deviations from anticipated experience.
- The actuary should run sensitivity tests.
- The actuary must take into account regulatory restrictions on redetermination.

A report should be prepared detailing how the actuary addressed the above issues and describing the calculations and results. This report might be provided in its entirety to the appropriate individual at the company or it might be summarized with a notation that a more detailed report is available on request. The actuary should be aware, however, that there may be other users of this type of report including regulators, courts of law, other actuaries succeeding the actuary in that position or parties buying or selling a block of business. Therefore the actuary should make certain that an appropriately detailed report is prepared and retained.

13.2.2 ASOP #7: PERFORMING CASH FLOW TESTING FOR INSURERS

The present version of this standard replaced a version which was adopted under the IASB. The previous version was drafted during the early days of cash flow testing shortly after the Baldwin-United debacle and concentrated on the interest risk to the exclusion of the consideration of other risks including the default risk. The focus at that time was the possibility of rapid and extreme movements in the level of interest rates. Even though the levels of interest rates have recently been more stable, the actuary shouldn't downplay such a risk. However, at the same time it would be inappropriate to encourage the concentration of the actuary's attention on the interest rate risk to the exclusion of other risks such as the default risk, the non-performing asset (real estate) risk or the operations and benefit risks (expenses and AIDS). The current version was initially drafted by a joint-life and casualty committee and takes an overall approach to cash flow testing.

Cash flow testing is just that; "cash flow testing." This is something that we do in our daily lives when we check to see whether we have enough cash on us to buy lunch. Cash flow testing is considerably more complex from the perspective of an insurance company, however, since all of the company's asset and liability cash flows have to be projected. This requires specialized software, much effort and much thought in developing assumptions.

Cash flow testing for a life insurance company is the comparison of the projection of the cash flows of the assets and the obligations of an insurer. The goal is to make certain that the positive cash flows (premiums and investment proceeds) more than offset the negative cash flows (obligations).

This standard introduced for the first time to many life actuaries the term "obligations." Obligations cover more than just a company's benefits and expenses. Obligations include all of a company's obligations, including taxes and dividends.

Once the base cash flow projection is operational, sensitivities can be tested. One of the most common sensitivities, if not the only sensitivity that is analyzed, is the sensitivity to interest rate scenarios. The new valuation law with its accompanying model regulation and New York under its Regulation 126 require that you project at least seven of these sensitivities. This, however, is a rote or required set of projections and may not help the valuation actuary get a real feel for the cash flows.

A preferred approach would be to run a number of the actuary's own interest rate sensitivities through the projection process in order to understand better the sensitivities of the cash flows.

Expenses and surrenders are some of the sensitivities on the liability side that might be analyzed. Some of the sensitivities on the asset side that should be analyzed in addition to interest rate levels are the default rate, the levels of cash flows on real estate (developed and undeveloped) and cash flows on mortgages and on CMO's and other derivatives.

If an actuary multiplies out all of the combinations and permutations of the different sensitivities that might be analyzed, the result would be an extremely large number of scenarios. The number of scenarios doesn't have to be that large, however, since many of these sensitivities are mutually independent. The valuation actuary should be able to determine the changes in cash flows for different sensitivities and then possibly combine some of the more probable sensitivities to produce probable scenarios of interest rates, default rates, expense levels, claims, and so on.

Some of the advice in performing **cash flow testing (CFT)** offered by this Standard includes:

- When allocating assets between blocks of business subject to CFT the actuary should make certain that assets are not used twice and also that any assets not modeled are capable of supporting blocks of business not modeled. (Thus for example, it would not be appropriate to allocate all of the real estate to the group A&H lines.)

- The number and level of assumptions in the scenarios modeled should be appropriate for the purpose of the CFT. The actuary should be aware of any limitations of the scenarios being tested.

- When modeling the asset cash flows the actuary should consider the asset characteristics including; variability by scenario, quality, associated expenses, and experience studies (e.g., defaults). The actuary should also model the appropriate investment and reinvestment strategies.

- When modeling obligation cash flows the actuary should consider the obligation characteristics including; variability by scenario, experience information and possible non-performance of reinsurers.

- The actuary should also understand management policies with respect to expenses and their control and claim-paying practices. The actuary may also wish to consider changes in management practices as a result of CFT outcomes.

- When determining assumptions the actuary should be aware of the sensitivity of assumptions to the scenario being modeled, the internal consistency of assumptions and any external requirements that impact assumptions (e.g., laws and regulations).
- When developing conclusions the actuary may wish to analyze discounted cash flows, year-by-year cash flows or accumulate surplus at the end of some period of time. The actuary should also consider the cash flows beyond the study period, the reasonableness of results and any limitations of the model that is used.

The actuary may have to rely on others to complete the CFT process, often investment experts. Such reliance should be disclosed and documented in any report. A report detailing the purpose, process, results and assumptions should be prepared.

13.2.3 ASOP #10: METHODS AND ASSUMPTIONS FOR USE IN STOCK LIFE INSURANCE COMPANY FINANCIAL STATEMENTS PREPARED IN ACCORDANCE WITH GAAP

This Standard provides the actuary with guidance in determining actuarial assets and liabilities for GAAP financial statements prepared for stock life insurance companies. The standard provides assistance to the actuary in complying with SFAS 60 (relating to most traditional life products) and SFAS 97 (relating to investment-type contracts, e.g., universal life and annuities). The standard addresses such issues as:

- The use of actuarial judgement in selecting assumptions.
- Differentiation between best-estimate assumptions (reflecting the most likely outcome) and those assumptions which provide for adverse deviation.
- Methodologies used, including simplifying assumptions, separate calculation of deferred policy acquisition cost (DPAC), lock-in and unlocking assumptions, loss recognition, method used to amortize DPAC, UL type contracts, matching of cost with premiums and recognition of premium income.
- Participating policies issued by stock life companies.
- Indeterminate premium policies.

13.2.4 ASOP #11: THE TREATMENT OF REINSURANCE TRANSACTIONS IN LIFE AND HEALTH INSURANCE COMPANY FINANCIAL STATEMENTS

As the title implies, this standard advises the practicing actuary in the area of accounting for the actuarial aspects of reinsurance transactions. The Standard applies to both statutory and GAAP accounting and addresses the following issues:

- The actuary is reminded that a ceding company is ultimately responsible to its policyholders in spite of any reinsurance agreement.
- The standard addresses the fact that the ceding and assuming companies may calculate liabilities differently (does not require mirror imaging).
- The actuary should review all material reinsurance agreements for:
    - (a) Financial features, e.g., which risks are transferred?
    - (b) Cash flows, e.g., especially when the reinsurance doesn't parallel the underlying business.
    - (c) Accounting treatment, e.g., watch for receivables and payables.
    - (d) Termination of reinsurance, e.g., what happens at termination and when?
- Consideration of additional liabilities, e.g., does the assuming company have the right to raise premiums?
- Likelihood of collection, e.g., is the reinsurer solvent?
- Regulatory requirements, e.g., is the reinsurer admitted in the company's state of domicile?
- Use of cash flow testing to confirm net statement liabilities.

13.2.5 ASOP #12: CONCERNING RISK CLASSIFICATION

This standard addresses risk classification as it applies to life insurance as well as other types of insurance. The issues that the actuary should consider with respect to risk classification include:

- Fairness.
- Soundness of the insurance company.

- Experience of differing risk classes.
- Objectivity, consistency and practicality.
- Effect of anti-selection.
- Acceptability of genetic data.
- Regulations and prior court decisions relating to risk classification.
- Industry practices.
- Limitations on the right to reclassify risks.
- Changes in the environment, e.g., new diseases.
- Relevant data.
- Applicability of risk classes to the benefit in question.

13.2.6 ASOP #14: WHEN TO DO CASH FLOW TESTING FOR LIFE AND HEALTH INSURANCE COMPANIES

This Standard was developed prior to the adoption by the NAIC of the current valuation law and caused some concern since it seemed to require more cash flow testing than the valuation law in conjunction with the model regulation. This was further compounded when a number of states adopted the valuation law but not the model regulation which resulted in confusion over the small company exemption which is spelled out in the model regulation.

Some of the highlights of this Standard are:

- Areas where cash flow testing might be appropriate:
  - (a) Product design and pricing studies.
  - (b) Evaluation of investment strategies.
  - (c) Testing of policyholder dividend scales and non-guaranteed elements.
  - (d) Long-term financial projections.
  - (e) Reserve testing.
  - (f) Actuarial appraisals.
- The actuary should use multiple scenario testing.
- Cash flow testing is not always necessary, e.g., gross premium valuation may be appropriate for health insurance lines.
- The use of prior studies may be appropriate.

13.2.7 ASOP #15: DIVIDEND DETERMINATION AND ILLUSTRATION FOR PARTICIPATING INDIVIDUAL LIFE INSURANCE POLICIES AND ANNUITY CONTRACTS

This is a reformatted version of the Recommendation on dividend practices which was adopted in 1980 and revised in 1985 to cover participating policies of stock life insurance companies. The Standard indicates that the Contribution principle (divisible surplus is distributed in the same proportion as the policies contributed to divisible surplus) is the generally accepted practice and the actuary should explain in the report the rationale for the use of any other method.

As with the Standard for non-guaranteed elements, policy factors (face amounts, cash values, etc.) and experience factors (mortality, investment results, etc.) are addressed. The Standard also addresses the differences in experience factors between classes and the disclosure of those differences. Some of the other areas addressed include:

- Methods of allocating investment income.
- Termination factors; policy lapses.
- Expense factors and the allocation of costs to different classes.
- Tax factors.
- Charge for stockholder retention; for stock life company dividends.
- Terminal dividends; paid on termination of the contract.
- Separation of participating and non-participating accounts.
- Dividend illustrations.
  - (a)   Conservatism.
  - (b)   Disclosure concerning supportability.
  - (c)   Disclosure of effect of investment income allocations.
- An actuarial report is recommended.

Note that this Standard requires quite a few disclosures which are detailed in the section on communications and disclosures.

13.2.8 ASOP #19: ACTUARIAL APPRAISALS

This Standard of Practice applies to actuarial appraisals of insurance companies or blocks of insurance business. Note that this standard applies to both life and casualty appraisals.

The impetus for this standard was the impression among some actuaries that some of the appraisals being prepared were biased and misleading. In practice, there are buyer's appraisals and seller's appraisals and the value of a company may lie somewhere in between.

This Standard provides a little more than basic guidelines but is not a total cookbook for appraisals. Some of the areas addressed by this Standard are:

- Definition of distributable earnings (Statutory).
- Risk-Adjusted rates of return used to discount distributable earnings.
- Components of the value of an insurance company.
  - (a) Adjusted net worth.
  - (b) Value of existing business.
  - (c) Value of future business capacity.
- Cost of capital.
- Assumptions should be disclosed and commented upon including:
  - (a) Investment income and asset allocation.
  - (b) Lapse rates.
  - (c) Claims.
  - (d) Expenses and inflation.
  - (e) Reinsurance.
  - (f) New production levels.
  - (g) Federal income tax.
- Modeling and validation.
- Sensitivity testing.
- Tax liquidations.

13.2.9 ASOP #21: THE ACTUARY'S RESPONSIBILITY TO THE AUDITOR

This is a revised and reformatted version of the old Financial Reporting Recommendations 2 and 3 and applies to the actuary in any dealings with an auditor in connection with the preparation or review of audited financial statements. This Standard does not apply to actuaries in their dealings with state regulators or the IRS.

The Standard addresses the responsibilities of the preparing actuary to disclose data and assumptions to the reviewing actuary and the responsibility of the reviewing actuary to use a written plan to communicate the actuaries responsibilities to the auditor. The Standard also addresses the confidentiality, the clarity and the security of the documents involved.

13.2.10 ASOP #22: STATUTORY STATEMENTS OF OPINION BASED ON ASSET ADEQUACY ANALYSIS BY APPOINTED ACTUARIES FOR LIFE OR HEALTH INSURERS.

This Standard was developed to dovetail with the new valuation law requiring asset adequacy analysis. The Standard addresses:

- The Standard Valuation Law and the Model Regulation.
- Various state valuation requirements: The new law is a "state of filing" law as opposed to a "state of domicile" requirement.
- The actuarial guidelines of the NAIC Examiners Handbook.
- Appointment as appointed actuary.
- Asset adequacy analysis methods.
- Assumptions.
- Modeling, use of prior studies, testing horizons, completeness and consistency.
- Reinsurance.
- Forming an opinion.
    - (a) Considering limitations of models and assumptions.
    - (b) Modeled economic and experience conditions.
    - (c) Adequacy of reserves.
- Results of prescribed interest scenarios.
- Level of aggregation.
- Trends in succeeding year's tests results.
- Anticipated management action.
- Events subsequent to the valuation date.
- Reliance on others for data.
- Opinions of other actuaries.

Note that this standard requires many disclosures which are detailed in the section on communication and disclosure.

13.2.11 ASOP #23: DATA QUALITY

This Standard applies to any actuary using data to complete a task. In practice this would apply to life actuaries using in force asset or liability information or relying on experience studies. The Standard addresses the following areas:

- Selection of data.
- Use of imperfect data.
- Reliance on data supplied by others.
- A report addressing the data, its source and any limitations is recommended.

13.2.12 ASOP #24: LIFE INSURANCE ILLUSTRATIONS

This standard was developed in conjunction with the Life Insurance Illustrations Model Regulation (Model) developed by the NAIC and applies to actuaries complying with that regulation. The standard does not address the non-guaranteed elements that may be credited (See ASOP #1).

A number of new terms are defined in this standard including:

- Currently payable scale; scale of non-guaranteed elements (nge's) currently credited or paid.
- Disciplined Current Scale (DCS); scale of nge's that meets the regulation and standard.
- Experience Factor Class; class of policies to which a scale of nge's applies.
- Illustrated Scale; a scale of nge's which is not more favorable than the lesser of the DCS and the currently payable scale.
- Illustration Actuary; the actuary appointed to be responsible for illustration compliance.
- Lapse-Supported Illustration; an illustration which looks great if the policyholder stays around forever but will cause the company losses if all of the policyholders stay around forever.
- Non-Guaranteed Element; policy elements such as dividends, excess interest, and reduction in contractual mortality and expense charges (See ASOP #1).
- Recent Historical Experience; recent credible experience studies.

- Self-Supporting Illustration; an illustration using a scale of nge's such that the policy form will at least break even after the 15th year (20th year for second or later-to-die policies) or the end of the contract period if sooner. The policy form is required to have an accumulated value of all policy cash flows greater than or equal to the policyowner's value at all illustrated points in time on or after the 15th (or 20th) anniversary. Policyowner's value includes the cash value and any other illustrated amounts available to the policyholder.

  After meeting the qualifications set forth by the American Academy of Actuaries and being appointed by the company's board of directors or their representative, the Illustration Actuary must annually certify compliance with the Model to each state which has adopted the Model and in which policies are sold which are subject to the Model. The actuary is certifying that the Illustrated Scale meets the definition above, is not Lapse-Supported, and is Self-Supporting using assumptions based on Recent Historical Experience.

13.2.13 ACG #4: STATUTORY STATEMENTS OF OPINION NOT INCLUDING AN ASSET ADEQUACY ANALYSIS BY APPOINTED ACTUARIES FOR LIFE OR HEALTH INSURERS.

This compliance guideline, which has the same force as a Standard of Practice and is considered a Standard, was developed to provide guidance to actuaries not required to perform asset adequacy analysis. The compliance guideline also provides an exemption from ASOP #14 which might require cash flow testing from an otherwise exempted small company.

The Compliance Guideline addresses many of the same issues as ASOP #22:

- The Standard Valuation Law and the Model Regulation.
- Various state valuation requirements; the new law is a state of filing law.
- The actuarial guidelines of the NAIC Examiners Handbook.
- Appointment as appointed actuary.
- Exemption from asset adequacy analysis.

- Statutory reserve requirements.
- Policy provisions affecting formula reserves:
  (a)   interest guarantees.
  (b)   immediate payment of claims, etc.
- Reinsurance.
- Items covered by the opinion.

13.3   OTHER ACTUARIAL STANDARDS OR CODES

In addition to the specific standards of practice described above, an actuary may also be restricted or guided by standards not detailed above or by standards of another actuarial organization.

Members of the American Academy of Actuaries are required to follow a code of professional conduct which requires the following:

- Professional Integrity.
- Compliance with the qualification standards of the Academy which include continuing education requirements for the signing of certain actuarial opinions.
- Adherence to Actuarial Standards of Practice.
- Disclosure in actuarial communications of sources of findings, reliances, the client's identity, and the sources of compensation to the actuary.
- Address and disclose real or perceived conflicts of interest.
- Control the use of any work product and maintain the confidentiality of proprietary information.
- The actuary is expected to perform professional services with courtesy and to cooperate with others when cooperation would normally be expected.
- The actuary is expected to be truthful and honest in the advertisement of professional services.
- The actuary should use care when making use of titles and designations.
- The actuary will be deemed to have violated the code of conduct if found guilty of a felony or a misdemeanor related to financial matters.

The qualification standards referred to above apply to actuaries making public statements of opinion. The type of opinion most familiar to the readers of this text are probably the statements of opinion required by the NAIC for life and health insurance company financial statements.

The qualification standards presently in place for life and health insurance company statements of opinions are:

1. Society of Actuaries' Examinations covering:
   (a) Policy forms and coverages.
   (b) Dividends and reinsurance.
   (c) Investments and valuation of assets including relationships between cash flows from insurance liabilities and the assets backing them.
   (d) Valuation of insurance liabilities.
   (e) Valuation and nonforfeiture laws.
2. Minimum of three (3) years of relevant experience under review of a qualified member.
3. Continuing education requirements of an average of 12 hours per year over two-year periods including primarily organized activities, e.g., Society of Actuaries' but may include other activities such as studying for exams or listening to cassettes of meetings.

13.4 ACTUARIAL BOARD FOR COUNSELING AND DISCIPLINE (ABCD)

The Actuarial Board for Counseling and Discipline has been referred to several times above as the enforcement agency of the Academy of Actuaries. The ABCD also addresses discipline for the American Society of Pension Actuaries (ASPA), the Canadian Institute of Actuaries (CIA), the Casualty Actuarial Society (CAS), the Conference of Consulting Actuaries (CCA), and the Society of Actuaries (SOA).

The ABCD's duty is to make certain that all member actuaries adhere to the standards of practice and rules of conduct established by the member organizations. In addition, the ABCD is available to answer requests for guidance on professional matters.

The ABCD will hear and investigate complaints brought to it regarding professional activities. The penalties resulting from findings against actuaries can range from reprimands to temporary or permanent suspension from the member organization.

REVIEW QUESTIONS

1.   Why do we need Standards of Practice?

2.   What are the duties of the ASB?

3.   What is a compliance guideline? Is it a standard?

4.   Briefly describe the development of a Standard of Practice.

5.   Which ASOPs address cash flow testing?

6.   What is required by the code of conduct?

7.   What must an actuary do before making a public statement of opinion?

8.   Describe the ABCD and its duties.

SECTION VI

OTHER TOPICS

CHAPTER 14
EXPENSE ACCOUNTING FOR
ACTUARIES

14.1   OVERVIEW

This chapter addresses the basics of expense accounting for insurance companies and sets forth information on methods of functional cost studies. Expenses are experience assumptions that in the past have not always attracted the full attention of actuaries. For many years expense assumptions were needed only for pricing work and even then they might have been estimated or could have been set to achieve competitive objectives.

"The purposes of cost accounting in the life insurance industry have historically been limited to planning and control, pricing, and the maintenance of equity among policyholders (particularly in the case of participating business). Inasmuch as the costing process has not entered directly into income determination, it has perhaps been subject to less discipline than cost accounting in the manufacturing industries. Consequently cost accounting systems in the life insurance industry range across the entire spectrum of quality; from excellent to good to terrible to non-existent."[1]

With the advent of cash flow testing requirements, increased merger and acquisition activity and slimmer margins on products, expenses have become more critical. In addition, the new Illustration Regulation and related ASOP require that the Illustration Actuary have a firm understanding of both the fully allocated and the marginal expenses of the company.

This chapter will provide some guidance on the terminology, definitions and methods needed to calculate and understand expenses as they relate to life insurance products.

14.2   DEFINITIONS

Functional Cost: An allocation of expense that is made based on the actual functions performed by an employee or group of employees.

Cost Study: Activity undertaken to determine cost information. This can be periodic or on-going.

Units: Basis for allocating costs. For a factory it may be widgets, for an insurance company it is typically policies, units of insurance (sometimes thousands of face amount) and dollars of premium.

Fully Allocated   Total cost for a product or line of business allocated to
or Average Cost: total units.

Fixed Cost: Cost which is incurred regardless of the level of business produced.

Marginal or   The additional cost to produce an additional unit.
Variable Cost: Note that there are categories of expenses that are not fully marginal nor fixed but instead may vary for a range of production or in force and then become fixed for a succeeding amount of production or in force.

Acquisition   The expenses incurred in placing new business that
Expense: vary directly with the sale of the business.
                      Note: Under GAAP accounting, acquisition expenses can occur in years other than the first year of a policy. For example when commissions in renewal years exceed the ultimate commission.

Maintenance   The expenses incurred in maintaining a piece of
Expense: business on the books of a company.
                      Note: First-year expenses are equal to first-year acquisition expenses plus first-year maintenance expenses.

The terms acquisition and maintenance should not be thought of as synonymous with first-year and renewal. Acquisition expenses can be incurred in any year and maintenance expenses generally apply to all years.

14.3 FUNCTIONAL COST STUDIES

The method most commonly used to determine empirical expense data in the insurance industry is the functional cost study.

There are two insurance trade organizations that assist companies in determining functional costs. These organizations also provide restricted comparisons of expense data among groups of companies on a confidential basis. There are charges associated with participation in these studies and results are typically not available to companies that have not participated.

One Organization is the **Life Office Management Association (LOMA)**. The LOMA functional cost study is directed primarily toward individual life insurance. LOMA encourages its member companies to participate in its Expense Management Program, EMaP. As participants in this program, companies submit detailed functional cost data to LOMA in a defined format. [2] The companies can, on a limited basis, compare their results to that of peer companies. The process is focused on identifying expense issues and resolving them in an increasingly competitive environment. Throughout this process it is imperative that confidentiality of data be maintained both for competitive and for anti-trust reasons.

The other organization is the **Life Insurance Marketing Research Association (LIMRA)**. LIMRA's studies may have more of a marketing focus and may describe marketing-related cost in considerable detail.

14.4 METHODOLOGY

Three possible methods of accumulating functional cost data are described below; the time study approach, the armchair approach and the time sheet approach.

Each of the three methods typically uses the salaries of the personnel in the areas studied as the base for allocating much of the expense of those areas. The reason for this is that salaries are often the major component of total expenses and they also provide a good basis for the allocation of other expenses. It may be necessary to allocate other expenses using a different base, depending on the type of expense and the data available. For example there may be some expenses that are more appropriately allocated on a per capita basis.

Method 1: The first approach is the time study approach, which is often done by an outside entity or can be done by an internal "corporate system" department. This method is exactly what it sounds like, and consists of the process of one or more individuals going from person to person doing a detailed time study and allocating those individuals' time by function and possibly by line of business and company.

Time studies are often used in an industrial environment where the processes are more mechanical and more easily defined and timed. Any of you that have been through this process in an insurance company know how difficult it is to define the many functions that are performed in an insurance company and then to set a time for those functions. This can be a very tedious task for both the timer and the timed.

Method 2: The second approach is often termed "the armchair" approach. Under the armchair approach, a survey is designed to accumulate the amount of each individual's time that is spent performing specific functions by line of business and possibly by company.

The system is referred to as the armchair approach since it is often done only once a year and the individual that is completing the designed survey form may be relying on recent memory for the allocation of time spent during the entire year. The term armchair implies that the individuals completing the survey are not even getting up out of the chair during the process. This may well be the case.

This method can be enhanced by effective design of the material that is used to communicate the process to the individuals that are providing the data and by proper design of the forms that are used to accumulate the data. This may include the design of different forms for different departments, divisions or individuals in order to accumulate specific information.

Method 3: The third approach is the time sheet approach. Under this method individuals complete periodic time sheets which allocate time and possibly describe the units, such as number of contracts or number of claims to which the time was applied.

This approach is somewhat tedious to deal with and creates an additional overhead for employees which may be deemed unnecessary. However, it can provide extremely useful information once the system is in place and the methods of accumulating and processing data are developed.

14.5   PLAN OF ACTION

14.5.1 ORGANIZATION

Companies usually seem most interested in the armchair approach since it can provide much of the data that they are looking for with a minimum disruption to their operation. They may also wish to implement something along the lines of the time study or the time sheet approach for a brief period of time in order to get more exact data to validate the armchair approach. This entire process is often handled in larger companies by a corporate systems department. In smaller companies, the actuary may be the one heading up the process due to the actuaries need for the data for pricing, profitability studies and Illustration Actuary certifications.

Let's walk through some of the tasks that need to be completed and issues that may be encountered in implementing the armchair functional cost study approach in a life insurance company. It is critical to already have in place an annual budgeting system by department, preferably a zero-based budgeting process. Zero-based budgeting is a budgeting process where those preparing the budget, typically department or division heads, estimate expenses for the next fiscal period by starting from scratch. The process considers the output that the department or division will produce for the upcoming fiscal period and assigns a cost to that output. Less efficient budgeting processes are based on percentage increases of prior-year expenses. It will be necessary to obtain salary detail for all individuals included in the allocation process. This can be a tricky issue due to the confidentiality of such data.

Often within budget processes there will be allocations to some departments for work performed by another department. This is often done when resources are limited and the management of the company wants to monitor and limit the use of those resources. An example of this would be the allocation of electronic data processing (EDP) costs. It is important that any such cross allocations between departments, divisions or companies or allocations of overhead within the budget methodology be fully understood. If these cross allocations are not adequately understood there exists the risk of double counting or of undercounting total expenses.

The first step that should be taken when starting an expense allocation process would be to see what had been done in the past or possibly was still being done. It would also be helpful to identify any current or recent accumulations of time and expense information which may be useful in the functional cost process.

This data may have been previously assembled for a study sponsored by one of the previously mentioned organizations, LOMA or LIMRA. If your company is an active participant in the LOMA EMaP program you would stop at this point and use that data. If, for some reason, only one line of business was analyzed or the functional study process was previously incomplete, then you may have a starting point as well as the task of determining why the process was stopped or didn't get completed. Once you have identified any available data, it's time to communicate the entire process to the rest of the company. To do this you will need to have the process defined in a memo or a manual, any forms designed, and political support to bring all of the appropriate people together and to convey the importance of completing information in a timely and accurate manner.

The staff performing or organizing the study should have previously visited with functional areas of the company in order to interview individuals within those areas and then to possibly design specialized survey forms for those areas based on the functions performed and the units processed. Generalized survey forms will be used for the other areas, possibly with input from the specialized areas that were interviewed.

If your company has never performed a functional cost study before, it might be advisable to try a dry run on one or more departments in order to get feedback on the simplicity and the applicability of the survey forms that are to be used before you widely distribute them.

The company should then hold at least an initial round of meetings to communicate the survey process and purpose to the individuals that will be completing the survey forms. Whether or not future meetings are needed depends on the retention of the individuals within each department that are responsible for the study as well as the quality of the results of the study. If the results don't look credible, you will need to review individual department results and identify problem areas. Incorrect, incomplete or less than credible information may require additional meetings with those individuals, redesigned forms or assistance on your part.

The manual that is assembled, along with the instructions, should describe in some detail the functional cost categories that are being allocated and what type of work is covered by the respective functions.

Data gathering techniques may change over time. However, while categories can change, great care should be taken in the design phase to keep these changes to a minimum since they will make comparisons of past results more complicated and less credible. If further detail is desired in the future, it may be difficult or impossible to return to historic values and split them into the new categories.

14.5.2 SURVEY PROCESS

The survey forms should be distributed at or shortly after the suggested meetings describing the process. The survey forms themselves should be designed giving due consideration to the data sought, the ease of completion, the practicality of processing the data, and the information to be included in the reports that will be produced.

One possible approach is to create a preprinted sheet for each employee within a department, division or section. This sheet should contain a description of the functional cost categories, which are the designated categories of functional costs which are going to be collected.

Appendix I shows sample lines of business for a company and sample functional cost categories. The lines of business and the designated functional cost categories should all have a numeric code assigned to them in order to facilitate the processing of the data. The numeric codes also facilitate the grouping of the data for defined sets of these accounts. As indicated earlier, many of the expenses will be allocated by the salaries of the individuals performing the functions. In order to do this, you will have to deal with the sensitive nature of salary data.

One approach to the salary issue is to let the computer match salaries with employees by employee number with limited checking to maintain the confidentiality of the data. Another approach is to identify individuals that have been cleared to handle salary information and to involve them in that portion of the process.

Appendix II provides sample functional cost category definitions from prior functional cost projects and a detailed listing of the functions that were used in one insurer's method of accumulating functional cost data.

14.5.3 TABULATION OF RESULTS

Once all of the data is accumulated, it will have to be processed. The approach that is recommended is the use of a personal computer database system to process the data. It is a good idea to select a system that will allow the efficient design of input forms for the clerical staff that will be entering the survey data as well as one which will allow the design of detailed reports once the data is tabulated and verified. Verification should be done both as data is entered through the design of checks and balances in the data entry screens as well as through a review of the results following the first run of the designed reports.

You should also look for and be prepared to deal with one-time expenses such as major reorganizations, early retirement programs or EDP conversions. However, you should also address a category that is called recurring non-recurring expenses. This is a category of expenses that is not anticipated but nevertheless seems to crop up every year. An example could be litigation expenses. Expenses of this nature should generally be left in the functional cost results while one-time expenses might be amortized over some period of time or left out all together.

The reports designed should range from detailed reports which will be used to audit results to summary reports which will be used once the data is accepted as accurate to provide the desired management information.

14.5.4 REPORTS AND DOCUMENTATION

Reports describing the process and summarizing the results should be prepared and submitted to those who participated in the study as well as company management. Sufficient documentation should be maintained with the Illustration Actuary Certification files to support any expense assumptions that were drawn from the study's results.

14.6 SAMPLE FUNCTIONAL COST ALLOCATION

To get a feel for how the process looks for a given department or division, let's look at the possible entries for a Marketing department.

The functions performed by the Marketing department typically fall under the Sales Support - Acquisition (1) and Sales Support - Maintenance

(2) shown in Appendix I. Production is the Marketing department's primary goal and we would expect to see most of the time allocated to the Acquisition category. But the Marketing department may also perform some maintenance-related work, possibly providing policyholders with information on in force business. The Marketing department may also participate in loan (11) and surrender (7) processing, or claim check delivery (6). Note that the numbers in parenthesis refer to the numeric code of the functional cost category assigned to the respective function.

The basis for allocating the aggregate expenses of the Marketing department will be the individual allocations of time for the employees and their respective salaries. Let's say, for example, that 80% percent of the time of an employee is related to Sales Support - Acquisition (1), and that the aggregate budget, excluding any amounts accounted for as commissions, of the department is 250% of the salaries of the department, then 80% × 250%, or 2 times that individuals salary would be thrown into the Sales Support - Acquisition (1) expense bucket. The other functions handled by that individual would be allocated in a similar manner until there has been a full accounting for all of that individual's time.

By this time, you should have already determined how you are going to deal with any inter-company allocations. The 250% of salaries referred to above may have already included the allocated cost of the EDP department to the Marketing department.

In each step of this process, check totals should be maintained to see that expenses balance back to budgeted amounts. As discussed earlier, checks and balances should be programmed into the data entry process and subtotals should be reviewed for consistency with company budgets and base salaries.

This whole process is then completed for each individual that is employed in the departments or divisions that are to be allocated. Those departments or divisions that are allocated across other departments such as the earlier EDP example will not be surveyed and tabulated since their results are already included in the tabulated department/division results.

14.7 GENERALLY RECOGNIZED EXPENSE TABLE

During the process of developing a Model Regulation for Life Insurance Illustrations which both met the concerns of the regulators and still allowed the insurance industry to efficiently function, the issue of expenses became a sticking point.

A compromise position on the expense issue was proposed at the 1996 Snowbird, Utah meeting among representatives from the NAIC, consumer organizations, the insurance industry and the Actuarial Standards Board (ASB). The proposed compromise was that the actuaries and the insurance industry would be allowed to use marginal expenses in complying with the self-supporting provision of the Model Reg to the extent that these **marginal expenses (ME)** were not less than those of the GRET. GRET expenses may be used if they are greater than the company's marginal expenses. (Note: this is not clear from the Model Reg but is spelled out in the ASOP.) The company's fully allocated expenses (FAE) may always be used regardless of their relationship to the GRET. Note that company direct sales costs are in addition to the GRET.

At the request of the National Association of Insurance Commissioners (NAIC), The Society of Actuaries' Committee on Life Insurance Research (Committee) established a Project Oversight Group (POG) to develop or identify a table of expenses that would qualify as a GRET for the life insurance industry. This GRET may be used by actuaries and insurance companies in their compliance with the NAIC Life Insurance Illustration Model Regulation (Model Reg) and the Actuarial Standard of Practice "Compliance with the NAIC Model Regulation on Life Insurance Sales Illustrations."

This table represents the industry's expenses on a fully allocated basis. The use of this table, however, does not relieve actuaries and companies from the allocation of direct expenses in complying with the Model Reg and ASOP.

The following relationships result from this compromise using the acronyms previously defined and assuming that ME < FAE.

1)   If GRET < ME < FAE, then use ME or FAE.
2)   If ME < GRET < FAE, then use GRET or FAE.
3)   If ME < FAE < GRET, then use GRET or FAE.

The NAIC annual statement fields, Table 14.1 on the following page, were accessed to develop the GRET.

A set of empirically-based functional cost expense factors were provided by the Life Office Management Association (LOMA) and were used as seed expense factors to allocate the expense information extracted from the Life Insurance Company annual statements into the standard form for Life Insurance expenses of percent of premium, per policy and per unit. These seed factors also allowed for allocations between acquisition and maintenance.

Table 14.1

NAIC Annual Statement References [1]

Item	Acquisition	Maintenance	Aggregate
Policies	Exh of Life Ins.; l 2, col 3	Exh of Life Ins.; .5*(l 1, col 3 + l 20, col 3)	N/A
Units	Exh of Life Ins.; l 2, col 4	N/A	N/A
Premiums	Exh 1 Pt 1; col 3, l 9a + l 10a [2]	N/A	N/A
Expenses	N/A	N/A	P6; col 3, l 22 + l 23 [3]

[1] Group products to which the regulation is applicable were thought to be very similar in their expense elements to ordinary life. Therefore, no attempt was made to isolate the annual statement expenses attributable to group products marketed directly to individual members of a group.

[2] Single premiums were weighted using 6% after reduction for any dividends applied.

[3] Only the estimated life insurance component of FICA and unemployment tax was included. Premium taxes and other state and municipal taxes must be considered separately.

Expenses were split into four categories of distribution systems: Branch Office, Direct Marketing, Home Service and All Other. The expense factors were developed based on a review of the application of the LOMA seed expense factors to the 1996 statutory results of the 200 largest life insurance companies as measured by life insurance expenses. In order to lessen the effect of reinsurance on the factors, companies were excluded where the life reinsurance commissions and allowances were at least 25% of the sum of life general expenses. Due to the concern about the wide range of variation of expenses within the groups and to alleviate concerns over the effect of these variations "outliers" were removed from the study. Outliers were generally determined to be those companies that had expenses that were 50% or less than or 250% or more than the expenses produced by the median factors applied to that company's units. The final sample represented approximately 80% of industry life insurance expenses. The expense factors were then derived by scaling the LOMA seed factors to cover the 50th percentile of the companies in each distribution system. This produced a set of expense factors which was generally higher than the average for the respective groups. The tables of expense factors by distribution system are shown below and on the following page.

BRANCH OFFICE		
	Acquisition	Maintenance
Per Policy	$65	$33
Per Unit	$1.15	
Percent of Premium	72%	

DIRECT MARKETING		
	Acquisition	Maintenance
Per Policy	$91	$46
Per Unit	$1.60	
Percent of Premium	50	

HOME SERVICE		
	Acquisition	Maintenance
Per Policy	$53	$27
Per Unit	$0.95	
Percent of Premium	29%	

ALL OTHER		
	Acquisition	Maintenance
Per Policy	$73	$37
Per Unit	$1.30	
Percent of Premium	40%	

Note the following in applying these expense factors:

- All of the expense factors are to be used and the results summed.
- Premiums for single premium products should be multiplied by 6% prior to the application of the percent of premium factor.
- These factors do not cover premium taxes, state and federal income taxes, or commissions. All of these items must be considered in addition to the expenses generated by the GRET.

The factors by distribution system may be used by a company or division that meets the description of that distribution system. A company may use one set of GRET factors for a specific distribution system and another set of GRET factors for a separate distribution system but cannot mix GRET factors and the company's own, e.g., if a company chooses to use the GRET factors for their Home Service Division they can not use fully allocated factors for their Direct Marketing Division.

General descriptions of the different distribution systems are shown below. It is expected that actuaries will apply professional judgement in determining distribution system categories.

Branch Office: A company or division which operates an agency building system featuring field management that are employees although their compensation may be largely based on production. The company provides significant employee benefits to field employees in addition to direct compensation.

Direct Marketing: A company or division that markets directly to the public through printed or other media. No direct field compensation is involved.

Home Service: A company or division that markets smaller insurance policies through an organization that resembles the Branch Office system in organizational and compensation structure but focuses on smaller policies and agent collections of premiums. Note that we have focused only on the ordinary life business of companies and have not considered industrial business.

Other: Companies or divisions other than those described above including those that market through Brokers and General Agents.

REFERENCES

[1] Ernst & Ernst, GAAP Stock Life Insurance Companies, 1974

[2] March/April 1989 Resource, a LOMA publication, "LOMA's Role in Expense Management."

REVIEW QUESTIONS

1. Why should actuaries care about expenses?

2. What is a functional cost study?

3. Briefly describe the three methods of performing a functional cost study.

4. Discuss appropriate methods of tabulating results.

5. What is the GRET and why was it developed?

6. When should the GRET be used?

APPENDIX I

Shown below are examples of line of business codes that could be used to tabulate expenses by line. Additional codes could be assembled for companies within a group in order to allocate expenses by company.

Line of Business Categories	
Line of Business	**Line Code**
Industrial Life	01
Ordinary Life	02
Individual Annuity	03
Supplementary Contracts	04
Credit Life	05
Group Life	06
Group Annuities	07
Group A&H	08
Credit A&H	09
Other A&H	10

Function Categories	
Function	**Function Code**
Sales Support - Acquisition	01
Sales Support - Maintenance	02
Underwriting	03
Issue	04
Policy Maintenance	05
Claims	06
Surrenders	07
Actuarial - Product Development	08
Actuarial - Research and Reporting	09
Investments (excl. Policy Loans)	10
Policy Loans	11
Overhead	12

APPENDIX II

Detailed Function Cost Category Descriptions

Sales Support - Acquisition 01

The function includes all work effort connected with the production of new business, including clerical and secretarial assistance to agents, general agents and agency managers in procuring a sale.

- New business stimulation.
- Sales promotion activities including planning of contest, campaigns, bulletins, design and preparation of promotional literature and handling of sales materials.
- Preparation of sales illustrations.
- Periodic reporting of data necessary for qualifying for contests.
- Agency officer's work relating to the supervision and development of the sales force.

Sales Support - Maintenance 02

The function includes all work effort connected with the training and maintaining of an agency force.

- Market Research.
- Design and preparation of training material.
- Training of sales force.
- Recruiting agents and field management.
- Planning and conducting training meetings.
- Preparation of in force illustrations.
- Other policy maintenance functions.

Underwriting 03

The function includes all work effort from the time the application is received from the field until its acceptance or declination.

- Underwriting new business.
- Arranging for medical exams.
- Inspection reports.
- Application work.

Issue 04

This function includes all work effort from the time the risk is approved until initial reporting is completed on the issued policy or cancellation of records for not taken policies.

- Calculation of premiums at issue.
- Preparation of policies and related records.
- Completion and filing of insurance application files.
- Delivery of policies.
- Cancellation of records for not taken policies.
- Include settlement option preparation work performed in connection with new policies.

Policy Maintenance 05

- Reinsurance work (assumed and ceded).
- Disability benefits (establishment, maintenance, and payments).
- Maintenance of records and periodic payments for paid-up annuities and supplementary contracts.
- Dividend work; maintenance of records, preparing and mailing of notices, calculations and accounting.
- Service to policyholders not included elsewhere (including quotation of policy values).
- Locating missing policyholders.
- Processing of expiries and lapses.
- Nonforfeiture benefits; calculations of extended term, reduced paid-ups, and paid-ups by dividend application, including amendment of records.
- Reinstatement of written-off policies or involving policy changes.

- Change in beneficiaries and assignees.
- Partial surrenders.
- Issuance of duplicate policies.
- Calculation of policy values for information only.
- Policy changes (including work effort on amending records, underwriting, rewriting policies, preparing endorsements and calculating change allowances).
- Term conversions (except issue portion).

Note: Exclude development of dividend scales, preparation of manuals, schedules, rate books, which are in Actuarial Research and Reporting (09).

Claims 06

This function includes all work effort from the receipt of the notification of claims until the disposition of proceeds.

- Handling of notification of claims.
- Calculation of benefits and preparation of vouchers.
- Determination of premium status at time of death.
- Determination and approval of beneficiaries.
- Handling of contestable and accidental death benefit claims.
- Control and follow-up on unpaid benefits.
- Recording of termination on basic policy records.
- Payment of and accounting for vouchers.
- Legal and tax work on claims.

Note: Exclude work effort of this type related to dividends or dividend accumulations which should be charged to Policy Maintenance (05) and work effort related to policy loans which should be charged to Policy Loans (11).

Surrenders 07

This function includes the work effort related to the basic policy (as distinct from loans, dividends, etc.) from receipt of the request until the request is withdrawn or the policy is surrendered.

- Handling of request for full surrender.
- Calculation of surrender values associated with completed transactions.
- Determination of premium status at time of surrender.
- Payment of and accounting for vouchers.
- Control and follow up on unpaid benefits.
- Noting of surrender on basic policy records.

> Note: Exclude partial surrenders, expiries and lapses and the cost of placing policies on extended term or reduced paid-up basis which should be in Policy Maintenance (05).

Actuarial Product Development 08

- Development of new policy contracts and terms, including application forms.
- Research projects to determine underwriting and selection rules.
- New insurance product development including policy form filings.

Actuarial Research and Reporting 09

- Research and statistical work regarding mortality, morbidity, disability, persistency, reserve liabilities, etc.
- Development of asset shares, premium rates, nonforfeiture values, dividend scales; including calculations and preparation of tables for rate and dividend books.
- All calculation of reserves and related valuation work.

Investments (excl. Policy Loans) 10

Bonds, mineral leases, equipment trust certificates, bank certificates of deposit, common and preferred stocks, mortgage loans and real estate, and includes work activities such as:

- Acquisitions and sales of investments.
- Collection of income and principal; maintenance of accounts and records.
- Appraising properties and making tax searches.
- Legal work on acquisitions and foreclosures.
- Work related to company occupied property.
- Cash flow studies.
- Annual statement exhibits relating only to investments.
- Administration including financial analysis, legal problems, storage of securities, exchange of securities, reports, and statistical work.

Policy Loans 11

- Calculation and payment of cash and automatic premium loans.
- Determination of loan status.
- Payoff work whether at policy termination or otherwise.
- Maintenance of accounts and records, including collection of interest (through premium notices or otherwise) and repayment of principal.
- Calculation of interest and preparation of statements.
- Correspondence and conversations with policy owners regarding policy loans.

Overhead 12

This function covers the cost of home office departments performing the activities below.

Depending on the purpose of the study, some of the following detail might be assigned to its own functional cost category.

Taxes

- Tax reporting and payment regarding corporate business taxes, income taxes, personal property taxes, premium taxes, sales and use taxes, general taxation advice.

Accounting and Reporting

- Recording of company operations in the general books, including accounts payable work, and preparation of management financial reports.
- Annual Statement; all centralized work related to interim and year-end preparation of internal annual statement, including printing expense. Exclude work in connection with supporting exhibits, e.g., reserves.
- Internal auditing relating to the examination of income and disbursement controls and verification of assets and liabilities.
- Centralized budget and functional cost programs, including projection of expenses, special studies and reports for expense control.
- Reconciliation of bank accounts.

Personnel

- Home office recruiting, hiring, and placement.
- Personnel record maintenance and statistical reports prepared in home office.
- Wage and salary studies and administration.
- Employee benefit plan work.
- Staff training and development; home office only.
- Payroll, including records and accounting.
- Home office newsletter or magazine not related to sales effort.
- Subsidies to employee's activities.
- Tuition fees for employees' education.

Public Relations

- Planning and administration of corporate advertising in newspapers, magazines and other publications.
- Reports to policy owners and/or shareholders.
- Publicity and press releases.
- Centralized activities to maintain company's goodwill among policy owners, shareholders, general public and local communities.
- Fees of public relations consultants.
- Printing costs of reports to policyholders.
- Advertising (space, TV time, etc.), direct-mail printing, and sales promotional material.
- Contributions.

Office Services

- Purchasing and supply.
- Mail and general messenger service.
- Telephone operators (costs for instruments and toll calls should be included elsewhere).
- Maintenance and repair of office equipment (excluding data processing equipment) which is not included elsewhere.
- Microfilming and duplicating work of a general nature (work should be included elsewhere whenever possible).

General Management

- Work effort of executive officers and their assistants of a general corporate nature which is company-wide and does not apply to a specific function; e.g., chairman of board, president, executive vice president, and other senior officers and their secretaries (portion which does not apply to specific functions).
- Long-range corporate planning associated with the development of corporate goals and objectives.
- Legal work of a general corporate nature. Work that can be identified with a specific line of business and/or function should not be included here.
- Work effort of planning divisions whose planning is on a company-wide basis such as methods and procedures, forms control, work measurement programs, and equipment and space control and standards.

INDEX